97v

Woman Suffrage and the New Democracy

Publisher's Note

Sara Hunter Graham completed the manuscript for this book with indomitable fortitude during a long illness. When she died in April 1996, she had just finished her final review of the manuscript and was awaiting the page proofs. The proofs were read by her husband, James Boyden, and by Lewis Gould. The index was compiled by Eliza Childs.

SARA HUNTER GRAHAM

Woman Suffrage and the New Democracy

Yale University Press
New Haven &
London

Printed in the United States of America by Vail-Ballou Press, Binghamton, New York.

Library of Congress Cataloging-in-Publication Data
Graham, Sara Hunter.
  Women suffrage and the new democracy / Sara Hunter Graham.
    p.   cm.
  Includes bibliographical references (p.   ) and index.
  ISBN 0-300-06346-6 (cloth : alk. paper)
    1. Women — Suffrage — United States — History.   2. Suffragists — United States — History.   3. National American Woman Suffrage Association — History.   I. Title.
JK1896.G693   1996
324.6'2'082 — dc20   96-18148
                                                                      CIP

A catalogue record for this book is available from the British Library.

The paper in this book meets the guidelines for permanence and durability of the Committee on Production Guidelines for Book Longevity of the Council on Library Resources.

10 9 8 7 6 5 4 3 2 1

Legislators make the laws for those who make the legislators.
René Viviani

We believe that under God the people should rule; that the voice of the people is the voice of God.
Anna Howard Shaw

Contents

Acknowledgments

This book began as a dissertation at the University of Texas at Austin. I am indebted to Robert Divine, Pat Kruppa, Jane Marcus, and Standish Meacham for aid and encouragement. Lewis L. Gould was and remains all that a mentor should be. I could not possibly have become a historian without his example and generous assistance.

I received financial assistance for this project from the University of Texas Graduate Research Fellowship, the Dora Bonham Foundation Fellowship, the Colonial Dames Research Fellowship, and a research stipend from the Virginia Historical Society. Washington correspondent Sarah McClendon invited me to stay at her home while I worked at the Library of Congress and treated me to her infinite knowledge of Capitol Hill. Other friends helped make my years in graduate school memorable: Paul Charney, Judi Doyle, Dan Greene, Paul Hiltpold, Bruce Hunt, Al Tilson, and Robert Wooster. Joan Supplee was and remains a friend in need, repeatedly and often at the expense of her own work.

I would also like to thank my colleagues at Louisiana State University, especially Bob Becker, Stan Hilton, Ann Loveland, Michelle Massé, Ed Muir, Beth Paskoff, and Paul Paskoff. Gaines Foster has been the soul of kindness, while ardently fighting off any repayment. Charles Royster read the manuscript and made many improvements. Other scholars whose expertise and insights have improved this book include Nancy Cott, Ellen DuBois, Lori Ginzberg, Jacquelyn Hall, Clarence Mohr, and Marjorie Wheeler. Filmmaker Ruth Pollak contributed an important perspective to my work. Chuck Grench, Otto Bohlmann, and Heidi Downey at Yale University Press have made the final stages of publication easy and productive. Eliza Childs's expert editing has done so much to improve the finished product. Anyone fortunate enough to publish with this press is indeed lucky.

Someone once told me that all people live two lives: one that they are given and one that they make. For helping me cope with the life that I have been given, I would like to thank Dr. Jack Moncrief, Dr. Robert Kenney, and Dr. Gerald Miletello, as well as Donna Clark, Rebecca McCormick, Abigail Nobles, and Marla Thompson. Without their skill, support, and kindness this book would not have been written. Chris Baughman is doubtless glad that I have finished this project; he has been an admirable friend.

I want to thank my parents, Sara and Hunt Graham, for their love and support. My aunt, the late Professor Grace Graham, urged me toward a life of scholarship at an early age and convinced me by her example that such a life was possible. My son, Jamie Wieferman, has literally grown up with this book; he has always been a source of encouragement, and I am very grateful to him. Lastly, the person most important to my life, and thus this book, is my husband, Jim Boyden. He has helped me in sickness and in health, has provided constant love and courage, and in every way has been a reflection of integrity and loving kindness. This book is for him.

Introduction

In the late nineteenth and early twentieth centuries, the American political universe underwent dramatic transformation marked by declining voter turnout, new regional party alignments, and the subsequent rise of pressure group politics. This book examines one of the first national organizations to experiment with pressure politics. From its creation in 1890 until the ratification of the Nineteenth Amendment in 1920, the National American Woman Suffrage Association (NAWSA) forged one of the most effective single-issue pressure groups in American history. Why and how the NAWSA suffragists accomplished this feat, and what their experiences tell us about pressure politics, women's rights, and American democracy, are the subjects of this book.

When I began this project, I had in mind what I thought would be the relatively simple task of describing how suffragists identified and developed the elements of a successful pressure group. What did they need to do to turn their small, weak organization into a full-fledged mass movement? I assumed I would be greatly assisted in answering this question by the sagging shelves of political science analyses and histories of pressure politics and the woman suffrage movement during the Progressive Era. As it transpired, I shared the naivete of a *Washington Times* correspondent who in 1914 predicted: "When little Sarah Jones, along about 1950 or thereabouts, sits down to struggle with the history of the United States, she is going to study a different sort of textbook from the one the small girl person of today is conning. When the revised edition has told all about the war, and what they killed each other for, it probably will devote a few salient chapters to the struggle for woman's emancipation, and particularly her political freedom."[1]

All too quickly I learned what other historians of women and particularly woman suffrage already knew: that the woman suffrage movement has not traditionally been studied from the vantage point of pressure politics or, indeed, political history in general. There are many excellent histories of the movement by historians of women that concentrate on the leadership, the heroic nature of the struggle, the relation between suffrage and feminism, and, to a lesser extent, the tactics of the campaign.[2] Historians who have taken up the subject of specific Progressive Era pressure groups have focused on the Anti-Saloon League (ASL), despite the fact that the league and the suffrage movement adopted pressure tactics more or less simultaneously.[3] As for broader studies of Progressive Era politics, the majority of works published before the mid-1980s limit their coverage of woman suffrage to a few lines at best, a few words at worst. Simply put, the largest democratic reform in American history has been ignored in most studies of political change and progressive reform.

As for the general works on pressure group formation and characteristics, I learned that political scientists were slightly more interested in woman suffrage than political historians. Unfortunately, until very recently their work on the subject tended to stress the relative *unimportance* of woman suffrage to the major twentieth-century political trends. Although female voting was deemed to have had some effect on the overall voter decline in the twentieth century, women voters or candidates had little importance in party conventions and electoral contests.[4] All too often, historians and political scientists found little or no significance in the campaign for the vote, with its evolution of pressure politics, or in its long-term results.[5] Such scholars as Walter Dean Burnham seemed unwilling to acknowledge the suffrage movement at all. "Full democratization of politics," wrote Burnham, "had uniquely occurred in the United States before the onset of industrialism."[6] Not only did scholars give the suffragists little credit for their achievement in winning the vote, but some blamed the suffrage movement for the so-called failure of feminism that occurred after 1920.[7]

The existing literature, then, fails to provide a fully satisfactory examination of woman suffrage as a political movement with important tactical innovations. More surprising, perhaps, is that the literature on pressure group politics is hardly more illuminating. For example, the terms *interest group, vested interest, special interest, pressure group, organized interest,* and *lobby* are used more or less interchangeably by scholars, politicians, and the public to describe everything from cigar-smoking lobbyists with fists full of cash to massive reform organizations. This conflation of terms creates ambiguity and confusion. For the purposes of this book, some discussion of contemporary usage of these terms is needed. The concept of special interests was not new to the twentieth century. Efforts to define — and to warn against — the operation of extragovernmental interests in republican politics can be traced back to James Madison's famous strictures against factions in *The Federalist*.[8] Madison cautioned against the formation of factions or interests, a warning that would be repeated by many others over the course of the nineteenth century. It was during the early part of that century that the terms *vested interests* or *special interests* appeared to describe those who represented the economic concerns of specific corporations and industrial groups. By midcentury, vested interests and the lobbyists who served them had acquired the unsavory image best described by poet Walt Whitman as that of "crawling, serpentine men, the lousy combings and born freedom-sellers of the earth."[9]

Because of the negative freight attached to lobbyists and special interests, Progressive Era reformers who experimented with new forms of political activism rarely applied these terms to themselves. By the turn of the twentieth century, however, political observers began to note a new type of interest, divorced from special economic pleadings and partisan political ties. "A large number of voluntary groups have sprung up during the past twenty years," Herbert Croly remarked, devoted not only to the propagation of special economic interests but "to special political and social ideas as well."[10] Croly's choice of the term *voluntary group* to describe advocates of a new political style is especially interesting for students of women's history. Throughout the nineteenth century, middle- and upper-class women organized voluntary or benevolent associations for a variety of charitable purposes, and they often resorted to indirect political methods when dealing with state legislatures or town fathers. Lacking the vote, women's voluntary groups used petitions, delegations, and letter-writing campaigns — tactics that would become instrumental in pressure group strategy in later years — to exert indirect influence on politicians.[11] As historians Lori Ginzberg and Barbara Epstein have demonstrated, the "work of benevolence" carried with it political experimentation within the confines of indirect influence and thus nurtured the desire among some women for a more direct role in politics.

Herbert Croly may have recognized the connection between nineteenth-century women's voluntary associations and the evolution of pressure group politics and, in doing so, called the latter creation by the name of its forerunner. But nineteenth-century efforts at political persuasion made by women's voluntary associations were not true pressure politics. Although it is true that nineteenth-century women's associations often used some of the tactics of the modern, or twentieth-century, pressure group—like letter writing or petition campaigns—there are crucial differences between the two. One way to highlight these differences is through an examination of the strategies of each. Nineteenth-century voluntary associations relied on nascent lobbying techniques: using social connections to approach politicians, persuading local dignitaries to exert pressure for a favored reform, or otherwise using not only their members' social status as a bargaining chip but also the traditional indirect influence attributed to women. These tactics, however, were but a pale reflection of the male world of lobbying. Women's societies rarely monitored government activity regarding other issues close to their own or attempted such political strategies as blocking actions counter to their interests. After bringing their issues to the attention of politicians, nineteenth-century voluntary groups did little to shepherd reforms through political channels to successful conclusions or to exert partisan pressure. Instead, these groups relied on the goodwill and gentlemanly conduct of the lawmakers for the granting of their requests. Indirect influence rather than true political power and manipulation was the hallmark of the nineteenth-century voluntary association.

With the evolution of pressure group politics after the turn of the century, the woman suffrage movement still relied to some extent on the indirect influence of the old voluntary associations, but it developed a parallel direct action strategy that differed from techniques used by the women's groups of the prior century. Some of the confusion about the definitions of pressure groups and lobbies stems from this dual system of indirect influence and direct power. For example, V. O. Key, one of the first scholars to study pressure groups, defined his subject as "private associations [that] promote their interests by attempting to influence government rather than by nominating candidates and seeking responsibility for the management of government."[12] Although this description is in some ways an accurate one, it leaves the reader with little feel for the tremendous power that can be exerted by modern pressure groups.

One of the most important aspects of a pressure group is its mixture of indirect influence and direct power. If we look at the origins of the pressure group, we see that it grows from two distinct sources. A simple analogy might be two rose bushes that, when grafted together, produce a new hybrid showing traits of both parent plants. One source can be traced to the nineteenth-century women's voluntary movement, where indirect influence, gradualism, and persuasion were the major characteristics. The temperance movement contributed the "Do Everything," concept that allowed local chapters as many or as few additional reforms as they chose. The goal of the Woman's Christian Temperance Union (WCTU) was to bring together a large constituency under a loose democratic structure bound by temperance, regardless of other issues. When NAWSA was organized in 1890, Susan B. Anthony and other leaders modeled their association after the WCTU and adopted many tactics and educational principles used by the WCTU and other nineteenth-century voluntary associations.

A second source suffragists drew from in creating their pressure group system differed from that described above in its direct engagement in power politics. Suffragists adopted trade union organizing techniques, including the use of paid national organizers and recruitment of immigrant and working-class groups previously not fully exploited by the nineteenth-century suffrage movement. Popular political demonstrations were another source of inspiration. Political parties throughout the nineteenth century had staged torchlight parades and demonstrations to publicize their candidates. By the twentieth century, suffragists along with other reform groups adopted many of these publicity stunts. Publicity and propaganda would prove to be vital elements in pressure politics. Ironically, the suffragists took from the urban political machines what became the most important feature of their eventual success: organizing on the district and precinct levels in order to exert maximum constituency pressure on politicians. With this, the suffragists added the final touch to their new creation — an organization that depended on both indirect influence and direct political power.

This system of indirect influence and direct political action gave the suffrage movement great power as well as a set of powerful contradictions. Another way to understand this peculiar mixture of influence and power is to examine the dual strategies of the modern pressure group that evolved from this tangled root system. Pressure groups employ what might be called "insider" and "outsider" strategies. Insider strategy places equal importance on access to politicians and to political information. Organizations that develop an insider strategy rely heavily on a professional lobby to gather information to trade for favors, to monitor political opinion within the legislature, and to concert political pressure on such important side issues as committee hearings and floor votes. Although the lobby is a crucial ingredient in a successful insider strategy, many associations also rely on the services of hired "Washington hands" whose previously established political connections give them access to political inner circles. The organizational goals of insider strategy stress harmonious relations with politicians that yield access to information and to decision makers. A noncombative public image, reinforced in the case of the suffrage movement by deference and gentle persuasion, meshed well with this type of system.[13]

The second, or outsider, strategy differs from the former in several crucial ways. Where the insider system focuses on the internal needs of politicians, outsider strategy emphasizes the organization's constituency, or at least the appearance of mass constituency. Often the organization must educate the public to the necessity of the desired reform and then, when a sufficient membership is attained, concentrate on generating grassroots pressure through publicity, delegations, parades, and other popular forms of political expression. Here the chief goals are to convert the public, keep interest high, and build an army of advocates who can be called upon to deluge their elected officials with support for the given reform. Clearly, cooperation with politicians is less important in outsider strategy than coordination between lobby and constituency.

As pressure groups evolved — including the woman suffrage movement — most reform groups adopted a combination of both insider and outsider strategies, whereas economic interests remained faithful to insider political management alone. Although the professional lobby might seem more important to the day-to-day workings of political reform groups, the mass constituency and the publicity provided at the grassroots level generate the power on which the reformist lobby rests. For reform groups like the woman suffrage campaign, the two strategies are interdependent and equally important. Together they generate information and persuasion, both to the public and to politicians, and facilitate access to the centers of political power. On occasion, a reform pressure group might endorse a particular candidate during a critical election or vote, or campaign against a key opponent. Usually, however, nonpartisanship is the strategy of choice. Both insider and outsider politics often rely on nonpartisan cooperation with the legislative body in question and discourage any action that might antagonize or alienate politicians or parties.

A second type of outsider strategy differs dramatically from these rather benign measures. Militancy constitutes an extreme form of outsider politics. Whereas most economic lobbies and social reform organizations strive to gain and keep access to politicians, militants dramatize their lack of access as a way to publicize perceived injustice. For this reason, militancy has been called the "weapon of the weak and excluded."[14] Shock tactics, political coercion, and "publicity at any price" fly in the face of carefully cultivated political favor. Although not necessarily partisan, militants often actively engage in electoral politics in order to defeat opponents. In the case of the suffrage movement, the militant National Woman's Party's (NWP) demonstrations, hunger strikes, and partisan attacks on the Democratic Party differed sharply from NAWSA's careful cultivation of nonpartisan political access and favor. Traditional political wisdom holds that militancy is the last resort of the powerless. Others argue that militant displays can bring new support to a faltering campaign and highlight exclusion from the circles of political power through dramatic acts of martyrdom; civil disobedience; and, occasionally, violence.[15] For our discussion here, it is important to know that there are two very different types of outsider strategy, and that both were present and often in conflict in the woman suffrage movement.

Militancy had little bearing on the suffrage movement and particularly on the evolution of pressure group politics until the second decade of the twentieth century. From the formation of NAWSA in 1890 until the appearance in 1913 of the Congressional Union (later the NWP), gaining legitimacy for the suffrage cause and building a mass constituency were the tasks at hand. State suffrage amendment drives were hard-fought and often futile; each new woman suffrage state, however, meant additional access to that state's congressmen and more influence for suffragists. Political access did not depend on suffragists' efforts alone. The Progressive Era overlaps the years of this study. As progressive reformers gained positions of power in state and federal government, suffragists found new audiences for their issue. Although Presidents Roosevelt and Taft did little to aid the cause, the election of Woodrow Wilson in 1912 gave the NAWSA its first real entrée to the White House. Timing, then, conspired to help and shape the suffrage cause.

In an age of experimentation and reform, it is not surprising that after years of struggle the suffrage crusade would seek new ways to bring political equality to women. Detecting a new set of political strategies means concentrating on the leaders who developed those strategies, more than on the rank-and-file members who carried them out. This book, therefore, places an intentional emphasis on the national and state leaders of NAWSA, and to a lesser extent on the organizers who translated the strategy into working policy at the local levels.

In addition to this focus on leadership, this book is about NAWSA and only incidentally concerns the National Woman's Party. There are several reasons for this. First, I wanted to address the question not only of how NAWSA established a pressure group system but of what that system did to a traditionally democratic association. Therefore, I felt that it was necessary to limit the scope of the book to one organization. For that reason, the National Woman's Party and other state or local groups (for example, Harriet Stanton Blatch's League of Self-Supporting Women) are either not mentioned or given minor treatment. This is not meant to imply that NAWSA "won" suffrage single-handedly; only that my treatment falls elsewhere. Second, it took NAWSA roughly twenty years (1895–1915) to evolve the pressure system. The militant wing of the suffrage movement was not in existence until 1913, and although the militants galvanized NAWSA and contributed in many ways to the success of the federal suffrage amendment, it is possible to trace the evolution of the pressure system only by following the fortunes of NAWSA. Lastly, there are already published works on the NWP's militant strategy, and while there is also an impressive list of titles that focus on NAWSA, none look at NAWSA from the standpoint of its role in the formation of what some scholars term "a new party system."[16] I am aware that the NWP played an important part in the last years of the woman suffrage campaign, and therefore I have tried to include its members' activities when relevant and some discussion of the two groups' contrasting strategies.

Many scholars today choose to refer to women in the past by their first and last names, regardless of what these women preferred to call themselves or how their names appear in historical documents. Throughout this work, however, individuals will be referred to by the name they themselves used; to do otherwise seemed unhistorical and a bit condescending. I have also retained the original titles of offices held by the suffragists, titles that today may seem outdated — for example, "chairman" rather than the more modern "chairperson."

The book's division into two parts also needs explanation. Part 1 examines the actual experimentation and formation of the NAWSA pressure group during the years 1890 through roughly 1915. With the "suffrage machine," as anti-suffragists called the pressure group, in place, part 2 examines both the machine at work and the changes that took place within NAWSA as a result. Some parts of the story of NAWSA's crusade for the vote have been told before; students of the movement will recognize many of the characters and events. To paraphrase Eleanor Flexner, I have tried to bring "new life to an old story," a story whose significance to both modern politics and modern women demands that it be told in new ways and by new generations.

PART I

A New Look for Suffrage

Woman Suffrage in 1900

"Aunt Susan" had never looked lovelier. First-time delegates to the week-long National American Woman Suffrage Association (NAWSA) convention that assembled in Washington, D.C., on February 8, 1900, were astonished to find not a bloomer-clad fanatic but rather a grandmotherly figure impeccably dressed in satin and old lace. In a severe black dress brightened by a red crepe shawl, her white hair caught back in a demure bun, Susan B. Anthony was the picture of high-Victorian respectability. "Up to that time," one convert to the cause recalled, "I had been of the opinion that it must be she who was the cause of all the newspaper jokes about the freaks in the woman suffrage movement." After one glimpse of the graceful woman who was to preside over the thirty-second annual suffrage convention, old stereotypes were laid to rest. In the young convert's opinion, Susan B. Anthony was "truly regal."[1]

One hundred seventy-three delegates representing all but four states gathered to see and hear Anthony and other suffrage pioneers like Clara Barton, Julia Ward Howe, and Anna Howard Shaw. One of the major functions of the annual convention was to rally the suffrage troops by inspirational speeches, sentimental reminiscences, and pageantry. To the beleaguered minority of American suffragists, the convention represented a chance to experience an all-too-fleeting sense of solidarity with like-minded women and to rub shoulders with the heroines of the movement.

Anthony, in her eightieth year, presided at three public sessions daily and at all executive and business meetings. In addition, she made a speaking tour in nearby Baltimore, addressed a Washington parlor meeting, attended several receptions, and called on President William McKinley in the East Room of the White House.[2] Meanwhile, other suffrage leaders conducted sessions on a variety of topics. In one afternoon session, for example, delegates were instructed in the art of holding state conventions, with special attention to preparation of programs, public speaking, and parliamentary procedure. Nighttime meetings featured speakers who extolled the suffrage pioneers, discussed needed reforms, and provided delegates with an array of prosuffrage arguments. The speakers, many of them professional women, social reformers, or civic leaders, were among the first of many women who turned to suffrage as an avenue of personal advancement and thereby served as role models for their more tradition-bound colleagues.[3]

Pageantry and sentiment were interjected in the convention program at well-spaced intervals to lighten the serious aspects of suffragism. Sentimentality held the delegates together in the months between conventions. A special feature of the 1900 convention was the fete scheduled for February 15, Susan B. Anthony's eightieth birthday. This celebration, the zenith of suffrage pageantry and emotionalism, helped to create and sustain the movement psychology that was critical to the suffrage cause. At the appropriate hour, Anthony entered the Lafayette Opera House to the strains of chamber music provided by the Ladies Mandolin Club. After a long series of toasts from women representing a variety of professions and organizations, eighty children passed across the stage in single file, each depositing a red rose in the honoree's lap. Following several inspirational speeches and a violin solo and a poem performed respectively by the sons of abolitionists Frederick Douglass and William Lloyd Garrison, NAWSA vice president and famed orator Anna Howard Shaw summarized the elderly suffragist's career and accomplishments. By the time Anthony rose to make her response, many in the audience were in tears. In her brief remarks, she touched on the progress made by women in the past fifty years and recalled those who had made lasting contributions to the woman's rights movement. Assuring her audience that she was "not through working" for the cause, she promised that "I shall work to the end of my time, and when I am called home, if there exists an immortal spirit, mine will still be with you, watching and inspiring you." According to one witness, Anthony "thrilled every heart and left the audience in a state of exaltation."[4]

The ceremony was all the more stirring because Anthony had retired from the presidency of NAWSA on the preceding day. Her retirement signaled the end of an era of suffragism that stretched back to the antebellum period, an era dominated by Anthony's leadership and that of her friend Elizabeth Cady Stanton. Both women had become advocates of women's rights through their experience in the abolition movement. Stanton and her fellow abolitionist Lucretia Mott were denied seats as delegates on the basis of their gender at an 1840 British antislavery convention; both vowed to return to the United States and hold a women's rights convention. In 1848, the two women staged the first of many such conventions at Seneca Falls, New York. The high point at Seneca Falls came when Stanton presented her Declaration of Sentiments, a document listing demands that included higher education, property rights, and suffrage for women. So radical was the concept of woman suffrage that many of the delegates to the convention refused to sign Stanton's declaration or later removed their signatures.[5]

Undaunted, Stanton and a growing number of abolitionists continued to press for women's rights, as well as for freedom and political rights for enslaved blacks. Through their work in the abolition movement, Stanton and Anthony formed a partnership that would last over fifty years.[6] The two were remarkable more for their differences than for their similarities. Stanton was a wife and mother; Anthony never married and looked upon children as impediments to female independence. Stanton's restless intellect grappled with the concept of a social revolution that would amalgamate women's rights with other causes; she wrote voluminously on subjects ranging from divorce reform to separation of church and state. Anthony was more preoccupied with the practicalities of reform. She was a powerful speaker and an indefatigable organizer, content to leave the ideology to Stanton while she concentrated on building suffrage sentiment among women.

The American woman suffrage movement was born in the radical reform milieu of abolitionism, but contradictions eventually appeared between the goals of the two groups. After the Civil War, some suffragists, including Stanton and Anthony, split with their former allies over the Radical Republican plan for Reconstruction, which made no provision for woman suffrage. Many male abolitionists and one wing of the suffrage movement agreed to postpone women's demand for the vote in order to secure immediate civil rights for black males. To Stanton and Anthony, this comprised a betrayal of the ideal of universal suffrage, and with their supporters they withdrew to form their own organization. The price of their secession was the charge of racism, a charge justified by their "tendency to envision women's emancipation in exclusively white terms." Stanton, for example, had argued that a grave injustice had been perpetrated by giving the ballot to illiterate freedmen instead of to elite white women, a statement that both shocked and alienated her one-time abolitionist allies.[7]

From the schism of 1869 emerged two associations: the American Woman Suffrage Association (AWSA), led by Lucy Stone and Henry B. Blackwell and devoted to state-by-state amendment campaigns, and Anthony's and Stanton's National Woman Suffrage Association (NWSA), favoring a federal amendment campaign as well as state action. Under pressure to find a new constituency, Anthony, Stanton, and their supporters initially tried to reach out to working-class women; this initiative soon foundered when bourgeois and professional women came to dominate its membership. The lesson that Anthony drew from this experience was to have dramatic consequences for the future of the woman suffrage movement. If working-class women proved difficult to organize, white women from the middle and upper classes seemed more amenable to the suffrage message. As a result, in the decades that followed Reconstruction, the suffrage movement was characterized by a tension between the ideological radicalism of Stanton and the increasingly conservative and pragmatic tactics of AWSA and, to a lesser degree, of Anthony herself. Although Stanton and Anthony continued to espouse a broad-based movement that, in Stanton's words, "recognise[s] the equal rights of all parties, sects and races, tribes and colors," both wings of the movement did little to recruit women who fell outside the elite white profile. Moreover, both factions, fearful that the issue would cost them the support of social conservatives, refused to address the question of black political rights. Henry Blackwell, AWSA cofounder and one-time abolitionist, for example, even suggested to southern legislators that they might support woman suffrage on the grounds that it would numerically strengthen white supremacy.[8]

By the 1890s, the suffrage movement had set its course in a narrow channel that would become even more constrictive as the twentieth century progressed. Although working women and the occasional black activist were sometimes included in suffrage affairs, there were deep divisions along class and race lines that lay beneath the surface of the crusade's democratic rhetoric. In spite of these potential problems, some progress was made. A handful of prominent women like Julia Ward Howe and Louisa May Alcott joined the cause, recruitment efforts in several states were initiated, and the rival organizations agreed to reunite in 1890. The new organization was called the National American Woman Suffrage Association, and Elizabeth Cady Stanton was elected president. In her presidential address, Stanton again urged an all-encompassing movement that would provide a platform for all women. "Colored women, Indian women, Mormon women, and women from every quarter of the globe have been heard in these Washington conventions," she proclaimed, "and I trust they always will be."[9]

To many of the pioneer suffragists, the 1890 convention symbolized a new beginning. Carrie Chapman Catt, a new recruit to the cause, also heard in Stanton's words the prospect of a revitalized, unified woman's movement. Catt had joined the woman suffrage movement in 1885. Within four years she was an officer in the Iowa suffrage association, and in 1890 she traveled to Washington, D.C., for the first suffrage convention since 1869, the year that the suffrage movement had split over strategic questions.[10] Her debut before the 1890 delegates, therefore, was well timed. Catt gave a short speech at the convention, and her enthusiasm was quickly rewarded with an invitation to accompany Anthony, Blackwell, and others on an organizing tour through South Dakota. Although the trip failed to secure the vote for South Dakota women, Susan B. Anthony saw in her young protégée great leadership potential, with the additional attraction that she entered the national movement without ties to either AWSA or NWSA. In this way, Catt could represent the new organization that would produce a new woman suffrage movement.

At the 1895 NAWSA convention Anthony's instinct proved to be correct. Catt blasted the convention delegates with a pithy summary of the movement's shortcomings. Although suffragists had been agitating for forty years, they had not turned the sentiment generated into success. Calling for sweeping tactical changes, she put before the convention a three-pronged plan: a special committee to raise money for state amendment campaigns; a new standing committee of organization to coordinate national, state, and local suffrage work; and a cadre of specially trained organizers to direct state campaigns.[11] When the convention delegates enthusiastically endorsed her plan and voted to establish an organizational committee, Catt was the obvious choice for its chairman.[12]

During a difficult first year of research, organizing, and planning, Catt's Organization Committee founded nine new state branches and over one hundred local clubs, raised and spent $5,500, and placed fourteen organizers in the field. By 1899, the committee could report a rudimentary organization in every state.[13] In Catt's home state of Iowa, for example, NAWSA organizers established two hundred fifty local clubs, opened a state headquarters in the capital, and canvassed most counties for new members.[14] While the NAWSA Executive Board urged state presidents to carry the "suffrage gospel" into every association in the United States, Anthony began the search for her replacement as leader of NAWSA. Catt was a natural choice in many ways. The younger woman's passion for the cause, her great organizational skills, and her political acumen all appealed to the elderly suffragist. Passing over Vice President Shaw, who was an ordained minister, a physician, and her close friend, Anthony picked Catt as her successor and lobbied for her election during the 1900 annual convention. In introducing her to the delegates after the votes had been tallied, Anthony hailed Catt as "my ideal leader."[15]

Anthony and Catt were convinced that by constant organization and agitation, "the opening of the twentieth century would find our entire people all aglow with woman suffrage sentiment."[16] If the populace was not "all aglow" with suffragism in 1900, the fault did not lie with Carrie Chapman Catt. At the convention that year, she reported she had given fifty-one lectures, visited twenty-one states, and traveled over 13,000 miles in the course of the previous year's work.[17] But no new states had been won for woman suffrage, the federal woman suffrage amendment lay trapped in hostile congressional committees, and a host of internal problems faced the beleaguered NAWSA leaders. In spite of strenuous efforts by Catt and her coworkers to organize suffrage associations at the state and local levels, the total number of dues-paying members stood at a fraction over 8,900.[18] Moreover, many of the newly established clubs were highly unstable, often lapsing into inactivity or quietly folding as soon as the charismatic NAWSA organizers left the area. Although eighteen states reported increases in their membership during 1899, New York, with the largest state association and the largest recruitment figures, showed a gain of only one hundred thirty-seven members.[19]

Financing the suffrage movement was a chronic problem. Dues comprised about one-fourth of the association's treasury, yet fewer than half of the forty-one dues-paying states contributed more than ten dollars apiece in yearly assessments. The Deep South was a particular burden. Three hundred sixty-three suffragists resided in the southern states, but only the border state suffragists of Kentucky contributed more than ten dollars in yearly dues. Half of all individual contributions was given in amounts of twenty-five dollars or more, but the remainder came in small amounts ranging from one dollar and up. The annual conventions played an important role in fundraising. In 1900, for example, the treasurer reported a debt of $1,900, but after an urgent appeal from Susan B. Anthony, the debt was liquidated through delegate contributions. Debt liquidation, however, had the unfortunate effect of reducing delegate pledges for the next fiscal year.[20] Without a solid financial base to support organizers and state campaigns, the movement would continue on the slow path of gradualism and frustration. As Carrie Catt once remarked, "our work . . . will only be limited by the amount we can raise."[21]

If the lack of money crippled state campaigns, the federal amendment campaign received a yearly blow when the NAWSA convention routinely appropriated no funds whatsoever for congressional work. The existence of a NAWSA Congressional Committee could be attributed solely to the traditional suffrage testimonials at annual House and Senate suffrage hearings, held on the last day of each NAWSA convention. For the rest of the year, congressional work was abandoned because Congressional Committee members were rarely residents of Washington, D.C. In 1899, for example, none of the committee members lived in the District of Columbia. Consequently, their entire efforts were concentrated on distributing prosuffrage pamphlets to congressmen via the mail and submitting petitions urging Congress to grant woman suffrage to Hawaii. During the 1900 convention, Anthony discussed the need for a "Watching Committee" in Washington, modeled along the lines of big business lobbyists, but no action was taken on the matter.[22] Even the initial appearance of a group of antisuffragists at the congressional suffrage hearings in 1900 failed to galvanize NAWSA leaders to activity, and the federal suffrage amendment was left to languish in committee.[23]

Congress was not the only stronghold of antisuffrage sentiment. The striking lack of national recognition for the movement was reflected in poor press coverage, little support from other organizations, and public apathy toward woman suffrage. A NAWSA Press Committee chairman noted that while systematic press work had been first attempted in 1899, much of the work was haphazard and amateurish. Members of the Press Committee had attempted an ambitious plan of state, county, and local press work, with a supervisor to coordinate press relations at each level. Unfortunately, few women had training for the enterprise; little progress was reported. Even in New York, a state boasting a large, stable suffrage association, it proved impossible to find press supervisors for more than sixteen of sixty counties. As one presswoman exclaimed, "like ideal organization, [press supervisors] are still found only in the realm of the ideal." Some press supervisors, unused to exacting editors and deadline demands, simply gave up after failing to place a single article. Others received the weekly articles prepared and distributed by NAWSA but made no attempt to place them with local newspapers. Despite these setbacks, the fledgling Press Committee managed to furnish regular articles to 1,360 newspapers and seven press associations.[24]

More worrisome to some NAWSA leaders was the lack of interest in suffrage demonstrated by other associations and clubs. The only national women's organizations to support woman suffrage were the Woman's Christian Temperance Union, which added a Franchise Committee to its organization in 1881, and the National Association of Colored Women (NACW), a firm advocate for woman suffrage. In spite of black women's almost universal support for the issue, NAWSA refused to acknowledge bids for membership in white clubs by blacks or requests by black organizations to affiliate with NAWSA.[25] The all-white General Federation of Women's Clubs steered clear of the issue of woman suffrage until 1913. For NAWSA, allies were hard to win. At the 1900 convention, for example, only such relatively obscure groups as the Universal Peace Union, the Baltimore Yearly Meeting of Friends, and two female journalists representing the National Press Association brought frater-nal greetings to the suffragists. And if clubwomen, noted for their activism, were apathetic toward the suffrage movement, what could be said of the general public, who regarded suffragists as man-haters, fanatics, or worse? Addressing the 1900 NAWSA convention, Anna Howard Shaw unwittingly testified to the movement's poor public image. Discussing a recent lecture tour, Shaw recalled that she deliberately avoided any overt references to suffrage, instead giving the audiences "strong doses" of the subject indirectly while calling for social reform or better government. Concluding that most of her lecture audiences "did not know what woman suffrage meant," she exclaimed in disgust, "they think it only means to berate men!"[26]

To the suffragists who assembled in Washington in 1900, there seemed little reason for optimism. Small gains in membership and in press coverage paled when compared to financial woes, public indifference, and lack of national recognition. Even more ominously, suffragists themselves seemed apathetic. Two years earlier, Catt had complained: "If I were asked to name the chief cause obstructing organization, I should not hesitate to reply. It is not to be found in the antisuffragists nor in ignorance nor in conservatism. It is to be found in the hopeless, lifeless, faithless members of our own organization. We find them in the state executive committees, where appalled by the magnitude of the undertaking they decide that organization is impossible because there is no money, and they make no effort to secure funds. They are to be found in our national body, ready to find fault with plans and results. 'It cannot be done' is their favorite motto."[27]

To Susan B. Anthony, however, the future seemed bright. Long accustomed to ridicule and hardship, she had developed the patience so often associated with old age. "Our women all over the country are sleeping, if not absolutely dying for the want of some practical thing to do," she wrote shortly before the 1900 convention, "and in some way or another we must set before them some-thing which they must do, or admit themselves indolent, ignorant and indiffer-ent."[28] As the twentieth century opened, the suffragists of NAWSA would awaken to meet the challenge.

2

Anxiously Doubting Democracy

In addition to low membership totals, poor funding, and public indifference, at the turn of the century NAWSA leaders also confronted growing numbers of antisuffragists who waged war against the suffrage campaign in national magazines, newspapers, and privately published tracts. The antisuffrage movement has received scant attention from historians, despite its prominence as a conservative force in the Progressive Era.[1] Although antisuffragism can be interpreted as a symbol of deeply ingrained sexism within American society, such vehement opposition to expansion of the franchise may also be seen as one side in an intense debate over democracy itself. The significance and depth of feeling generated by this debate have been obscured by scholarly works that focus on the end results of American democratic reform, such as implementation of the direct primary, direct election of senators, and passage of the Nineteenth Amendment, rather than on the uncertain process of their acceptance by the American public. Emphasizing the democratic achievements of the Progressive period, historians often have given the impression that the era was marked by a general consensus on democracy.

On the contrary, Americans in the Progressive decades debated the scope and implications of democracy. They did so, not smugly accepting the inevitable triumph of their nation's democratic tendencies, but revealing uncertainty and grave suspicion of the *demos*. Would the voice of the people speak prudence or pandemonium? Should the vote be extended not only to women, but to blacks and immigrants as well? Would total enfranchisement of the American people lead to cohesion or to chaos? Suffragists in the first years of the new century would become the most vocal advocates of a new democracy, blind to gender and, some said, to race and to class. After 1900, the debate over democracy catapulted into the national arena and shaped not only suffragism but the course of American politics in the years to come.

Antisuffrage opposition exerted an important influence on the terms of debate and the tactics of the woman suffrage movement. The antisuffrage campaign used two basic arguments, which can be labeled *traditionalist* and *tory*. These arguments shared the same general objective and were often employed interchangeably by the same individuals, but they rested on different premises. The traditionalist argument drew on the conception of woman's sphere and on the concomitant notion of the feminine ideal. Nineteenth-century standards for middle- and upper-class womanly decorum discouraged participation in activities outside the home, with the exception of church work and some forms of charitable endeavor. In spite of the growth by 1900 in the number of wage-earning women and the emergence of a new cohort of college-educated professional women, older cultural norms were slow to die. The woman suffrage movement proclaimed the need for better working conditions for women workers and boasted within its membership many professional women; traditionalists perceived it as a threat to the sanctity of the home, marriage, and the family. As one critic wrote, "the question of woman suffrage is more than merely political; [it] concerns the nature and structure of society."[2]

The traditionalist argument assumed that the family was the basis for and a microcosm of American society. Within this microcosm, sexual differentiation provided the natural balance and cohesion that in turn produced stability and harmony. As Lyman Abbott argued in 1903, "Woman is not man inhabiting temporarily a different kind of body. Man is not a rough-and-tumble woman. . . . The difference in the sexes is the first and fundamental fact in the family; it is therefore the first and fundamental fact in society, which is but a large family."[3] This analogy between the family and society included the concept of evolution in both. Traditionalists maintained that as the family changed over time, individuals within the family unit evolved special functions according to their gender. Specialization of function determined the "sphere of woman" and simultaneously ensured familial harmony by conforming to immutable natural law.[4] Such antisuffragists as Mrs. Schuyler Van Rensselaer often appealed to traditionalist social theory, defining woman's work as "the making and molding of human character and social characteristics," while reserving for men the obligation "to protect her as she does this."[5] Others were more specific. In a speech to the Ladies Congressional Club of Washington, D.C., a former Supreme Court justice lectured his audience on the womanly duties of child rearing, nursing the sick, and household management and complimented women on their "superior and patient endurance of suffering."[6] And lest the burdens of woman's sphere should seem too heavy, other social critics were quick to allocate the more romantic virtues of sentiment, instinct, and beauty to the female realm. To women, then, traditionalists assigned the domestic and maternal functions of the family, and to men, the duties of "the ballot-box, the jury-box, the cartridge-box, [and] the sentry-box."[7]

As for the unlucky females who worked outside the home, traditionalists agreed that working women represented only a temporary aberration from nineteenth-century societal patterns. Journalist Ida Tarbell, for example, insisted that female industrial workers were mere "transients" whose temporary work status precluded any real need for suffrage. After a brief work experience, wage-earning women would marry and return to their proper sphere or, as Tarbell put it, "graduate from shop or factory to real life."[8] Black women, who often worked at low-paying jobs in domestic service or agriculture for the entirety of their adult lives, were simply ignored in the rosy picture of the working woman painted by antisuffragists. By overlooking women's permanent entry into the work force and by obscuring the widening gap between cultural ideals and reality, traditionalists harkened back to a society governed by family units, polarized into spheres of influence, and stabilized through the bonds of tradition.

Female antisuffragists who subscribed to the traditionalist viewpoint defended older cultural standards for women. They argued that, far from occupying an inferior position to that of men, they enjoyed a separate but equal station within the family and society. Priscilla Leonard, labor law reformer and social critic, explained that "the suffragist wants equality of a like kind; the anti-suffragist an equality 'not like in like, but like in difference.'" Claiming that suffragists represented only a tiny minority of the population, Leonard maintained that the majority of American women believed themselves to be "co-equal and on some planes superior just because of [their] sex."[9] Another antisuffragist cited the laws of nature that governed woman's place in society, warning that "to set oneself across this well-marked path is like trying to turn the planets from their orbits with a parasol."[10]

The ideas of functional specialization and coequal spheres struck a responsive chord with the opponents of woman suffrage. When suffragists pointed out that disfranchised women were placed on a level with felons and illiterates, antisuffragists were quick to retort that the majority of women were perfectly content with their sphere. As one writer remarked with regard to the various disfranchised classes, "There is a real distinction between being placed among the beasts, and being placed among the 'ministering angels.' "[11] And for the women who were not content to sit among the angels, traditionalists showed little sympathy or understanding.

Citing suffrage defeats and public indifference as proof that the majority of American women were satisfied with their disenfranchised state, the antisuffragists forced their opponents into a defensive posture by portraying suffragists as termagants. In an antisuffrage pamphlet entitled "Equality of Suffrage Means the Debasement Not Only of Women but of Men," John Dos Passos complained that women were "fast becoming masculinized" in their dress, speech, and activities and railed against the unfeminine influence exerted by suffragists. "As between female suffrage and an absolute monarchy or despotism," he avowed, "I should unhesitatingly choose the latter."[12] The leaders of NAWSA were favorite targets for unflattering stereotypes. Grover Cleveland excoriated those suffragists who "with noisy discontent and possibly with not too much disinclination for notoriety, exploit in the newspapers their unpleasant temper, and their indifferent attempts to commend woman suffrage accompanied occasionally by something very like unwomanly abuse and misrepresentation."[13] Unmarried suffragists were categorized as man-hating fanatics who, if given the opportunity, would abolish the institution of marriage and destroy American family life. Their married colleagues fared no better with antisuffragist critics. When Carrie Chapman Catt resigned the presidency of NAWSA in 1904 after her husband became seriously ill, Priscilla Leonard warned of the dangers of suffrage work: "Mrs. Catt has done her duty by both home and the suffrage movement, and has broken under the strain."[14] The antisuffrage message was clear: to engage in suffrage work meant a loss of femininity, status, and influence, threatening woman's separate but equal sphere.

Leonard and other antisuffragists reiterated the perils of suffragism to those unwise enough to dabble in it. Senator Elihu Root cautioned against women's entrance into politics; once caught in the "arena of conflict," he insisted, women would become "hard, harsh, unlovable, [and] repulsive."[15] Others cited the corrupting influence of politics as detrimental to standards of female decency and urged women to eschew the quest for political power in favor of "womanly influence." After a trip to the woman suffrage state of Colorado, social theorist Elizabeth McCracken argued for a return to old-fashioned feminine influence, which she believed to be "as effective as power, and perhaps also a little less crude, and more than a little less rasping." "Women," she concluded, "don't change politics as much as politics change women."[16]

In contrast, female antisuffragists depicted themselves as feminine, quiet, modest, and thoughtful. Antisuffrage articles and tracts often carried pictures of famous opponents of the vote, dressed in confections of white lace and posed with several small children at their knee. The difference between suffragists and their opponents was underscored by antisuffrage essays in books and popular periodicals with such titles as "Feminine versus Feminist," "The Profession of Motherhood," "The Non-Militant Defenders of the Home," and "Woman Suffrage vs. Womanliness." In a pamphlet with the benign title of "Household Hints," antisuffragists laid claim to the image of the competent housewife while facetiously suggesting tips like the following: "If an Anti swallows bi-chloride, give her whites of eggs, but if it is a suff[ragist], give her a vote."[17] By pitting the nineteenth-century ideal woman against the suffragist ideal, antisuffragists cast their adversaries in the role of fanatical, masculinized extremists. Moreover, manipulation of traditional symbols of motherhood and womanly virtue tainted the suffrage movement with the stigma of a reform against nature. As one critic asserted, "with all that is, literally and metaphorically machine-made, vulgar, coarse of fibre, in this century, the Suffrage Ideal has shown itself identified."[18]

Antisuffrage advocates portrayed the suffrage movement as a threat to individuals, to the family, and to society as a whole. To individual women, the vote meant exposure to the "mire of politics," which in turn would lead "not only [to] stunting and degeneration of the feelings, but to abnormal growth of the intellect and to the inevitable exhaustion of the brain through social strife."[19] Equally dangerous was the dread "club habit," an addictive activity that Grover Cleveland believed to be prevalent among suffragists.[20] Others expressed fear that expectant mothers would become "over-excited" when exposed to suffragism and would inadvertently contribute to "the sterility of American homes."[21] In an article entitled "The Assault on Womanhood," Lyman Abbott warned that woman suffrage would bring easy divorce, daycare "asylums" for children, and an end to the institution of marriage and urged women to resist the suffrage siren's song.[22]

Traditionalists feared the social upheaval that would take place with the advent of woman suffrage. The traditionalist worldview of society composed of familial units, each with its own harmony of interests, was at stake. Believing that women constituted a class apart, some critics reasoned that women would vote as a class as well. Antisuffrage forces were quick to incorporate the concept of gender warfare into their propaganda. "America has suffered much from the voting of section against section; much from the voting of race against race," cautioned one writer, "but neither sectional nor race nor class nor religious voting could inflict on the community so disastrous results as would follow from sex voting."[23] At a New Jersey legislative hearing, an antisuffrage speaker maintained that the antisuffragists stood "for the conservation of the home, [and] the suffragists for the sex revolution that means the disruption of the home."[24] Or as an antisuffrage flier stated, "A Vote for Federal Suffrage Is a Vote for Organized Female Nagging Forever."[25] Traditionalists saw in woman suffrage the first in a series of challenges that would mark the twentieth century; preferring the past, they chose rusty tradition for their weapon and fought an endless battle against the forces of change.

The second antisuffragist argument shared the objective of refuting the suffragists' appeals for the vote, but it differed from the traditionalists' approach in its analysis of society and in its proposed solutions to societal problems. Adherents of this view espoused a tory philosophy that was similar in many respects to that of their British counterparts; it acknowledged class divisions in society and favored rule by a paternalistic elite. Tory antisuffragists held that democracy was experimental and should be limited to responsible, dutiful citizens who would exercise suffrage in the interest of society at large. Arguing that American democracy "is a government of the people, but not necessarily of all persons constituting the people," one tory maintained that the word *people* was used simply to distinguish democracy from despotism or oligarchy. "The power of actually governing," he continued, "has always rested with an exceedingly small number of men, the great body of the people being merely represented by them."[26]

The Burkean concept of virtual representation meshed well with other antisuffrage tory theories. Calling suffrage "that doubtful boon, a duty rather than a privilege," tories rejected universal suffrage because only society's elite would use the vote for the good of all. Adopting the tory argument in favor of franchise limitation, one antisuffragist wrote: "The dainty man shrinks from the task [of government], the careless man avoids it, the indifferent man neglects it."[27] Another antisuffragist, contemplating universal suffrage, foretold political disaster: "Democracy is to-day on trial in no other direction more serious than in this, its inability promptly and adequately to educate its less intelligent voters, and to hold them to any adequate sense of their electoral responsibilities."[28] Confronting mass immigration and suffragist demands, advocacy of limited democracy and elite representation became the hallmark of the tory creed.

With the tory vision of an uneducated electorate ran the recurring theme of the perils of pure democracy. In an antisuffrage pamphlet entitled "The Practical Limitations of Democracy," Mrs. William Forse Scott argued that "government by all is anarchy." Individual participation in the affairs of state would prove disastrous for the nation. "Unrestrained democracy . . . makes law subservient to the impulses of the mass," she continued, "and these impulses are as unreasoning as the impulses of the individual, and less capable of restraint."[29] Contrasting rampant individualism with guided democracy, antisuffragists pictured government by universal suffrage as a train without brakes, hurtling down the slope to chaos and destruction. Responding to a suffragist's claim that "the highest good is the good of the individual," an antisuffragist replied, "Not so fast sister . . . 'the good of all' is the watchword of today," and concluded that limited suffrage was the best way to achieve that lofty ideal.[30] And if pure democracy was anathema to many tories, some agreed with Columbia University Professor James H. Hyslop in calling for further restriction of the franchise. Hyslop proposed a tax-based suffrage to limit the number of existing voters and to deprive democracy of "its power for mischief-making."[31] Many tories said that American society needed not more democracy but less.[32]

Unlike their traditionalist allies, the tories addressed the status of women as a question of economic class rather than defining the place of "a class apart." Within this framework, working-class men and women constituted the broad base of society, an economic group that antisuffragists believed to be inarticulate, uneducated, and unrestrained. The woman suffrage movement proposed to double the vote of this class while simultaneously lessening the impact of elite votes by doing away with the concept of virtual representation. To whip up tory sentiment against suffragism, antisuffragists often maximized class and racial distinctions in order to demonstrate the irreconcilable differences that prevented political consensus. Some antisuffragists suggested that if the vote were given to the poor, class warfare would ensue. Others pointed to the growth of the Socialist Party as proof that suffrage radicalism walked hand-in-hand with other forms of extremism. "Well-known suffragists have established a sympathetic link with this revolutionary party," cautioned one critic, "and it will be impossible to separate it in the future development of the movement."[33] The fact that socialists and trade unionists often proved to be advocates of woman suffrage gave credence to antisuffrage rhetoric. As a Virginia antisuffrage flier warned, "A Vote for Woman Suffrage Will Help Socialism."[34]

More useful to the tory argument than trade unions and socialism, however, were the immigrants who streamed into the country during the late nineteenth and early twentieth centuries. Tory wisdom held that these individuals provided a fertile recruiting ground for labor organizers and anarchists. Discussing immigrant women and woman suffrage before the Joint Judiciary Committee of the New York legislature, a Commission of Immigration inspector testified: "The immigrant woman is a fickle, impulsive creature, irresponsible, very superstitious, ruled absolutely by emotion and intensely personal in her point of view. In many things much resembling a sheep. She would be as capable of understanding just about as much of political matters as a man deaf and blind would of the opera."[35] Warming to her theme, the inspector quoted a labor organizer who, when asked what effect woman suffrage would have on the immigrant woman, had replied, "Why, she would sell her vote for a pound of macaroni!"[36]

Antisuffragist Margaret Deland used class and race to qualify her objection to woman suffrage, pointing out that she was not opposed to the idea of limited suffrage for exceptional women. Instead, she protested only "against suffrage for all women, just as I would protest (if there was any use in doing so) against suffrage for all men."[37] In an address to the National League for Civic Education, Deland remarked, "We have suffered many things at the hands of Patrick; the New Woman would add Bridget also, and — graver danger — to the vote of that fierce, silly, amiable creature, the uneducated Negro, she would add (if logical) the vote of his sillier, baser female."[38]

The issue of race proved to be one area where the traditionalist and tory arguments converged; both groups considered the notion of black suffrage, whether male or female, a danger to society. Mrs. Schuyler Van Rensselaer appealed to tory and traditionalist alike in calling for franchise restriction for certain groups: "We must think of the tens of thousands of illiterate and vicious women in New York City, and just as carefully of the scores of thousands of ignorant negresses in the south."[39] Most white southerners objected to expansion of suffrage to blacks, and Dixie-based antisuffragists played on whites' racism by circulating fliers and posters denouncing suffragism. One poster asked white southerners to "remember that Woman Suffrage means a reopening of the entire Negro Suffrage Question; loss of state rights; and another period of reconstruction horrors, which will introduce a set of female carpetbaggers as bad as their male prototypes of the sixties."[40] Forecasting the day when white women would be "crowded into the polling places with *negroes of both sexes* [emphasis in original]," propaganda labeled the federal suffrage amendment a "force bill" and hammered home the fact that its passage would more than double the black vote in the South.[41] Perhaps most damaging to the cause of woman suffrage, however, was the objection bluntly expressed in a pamphlet issued by a Virginia men's antisuffrage group: "Every argument for sexual equality in politics is, and must be, an argument also for racial equality."[42] To white supremacists, woman suffrage was anathema on these grounds alone.

Virtual representation based on familial units or defined by class and racial distinctions gave women no place in the commonweal. So prevalent were these assumptions that antisuffrage societies often combined traditionalist and tory arguments in their propaganda. An antisuffrage flier called on Americans to "Remember that the average woman is no better than the average man, that every Socialist and every Feminist is a suffragist, and that the great majority of women do not want the ballot thrust upon them by a fanatical minority!"[43] Regardless of color, class, or national origin, women were deemed political exiles, to be represented by their husbands if they were fortunate, and by no one if they were not.

Traditionalists and tories shared a definition of civic virtue: the absence of power or personal interest. They often equated political power with corruption. The traditionalist notion of women as a class apart made women keepers of civic virtue for as long as they remained outside the "mire of politics." Tories, too, believed that civic virtue resided in the distaff side of society, but they qualified the belief along class lines. Implicit in tory social theory was the assumption of identity of interests between men and women, an identity based on economic station rather than on family loyalties. Emphasizing class distinctions as shaping individual behavior, the tory vision of a class-divided society contained a second cleavage that separated male and female political functions only at the top echelons of society. Ideally, the male elite would represent the inarticulate masses through the concept of virtual representation, while their female counterparts ministered to the working class through charity and personal example. Moreover, charity work would bring these twentieth-century Lady Bountifuls into personal contact with the working class and enable them to identify for the representative elite the "public interest." Unlike the traditionalist vision, which sought to hold the twentieth century at bay, this nineteenth-century paternalism recognized class stratification and endeavored to defuse social tensions through personal influence and the promise of indirect representation. The tory scheme of influence and representation was designed to return society to the pattern of life idealized by the traditionalists. Accordingly, the antisuffrage appeal stressed common ground between traditionalists and tories, despite their different visions of society.

Because the tory concept of civic virtue relied on charity and disinterested intervention by exceptional women, antisuffragists were quick to connect these activities to the perils of suffragism. In an *Atlantic Monthly* article entitled "Woman Suffrage and the Tenements," Elizabeth McCracken described her experiences as social worker among working-class women. Although an antisuffragist, McCracken interviewed her clients on their views regarding woman suffrage and at times even urged them to support the issue to test their reactions. Detecting a growing coolness in her clients whenever she pressed the issue, she concluded that her discussion of suffrage had led the tenement women to suspect that she expected political payment in return for her charity. After her "field research" was done, she reported that all "thoughtful" tenement women repudiated the idea that the vote would benefit them.[44] Farfetched as McCracken's conclusions may seem, the notion of devaluation of charity by political opportunism was quite common at the turn of the century and doubtless won many a convert to the antisuffrage cause.

More dramatic, however, was McCracken's "research" in the woman suffrage state of Colorado. There she interviewed female politicians and politically active women whom she reported to be "hysterical" over politics. After a trip to an orphanage with one female politician, McCracken despaired over what she believed to be the degradation of charity in such a state. Convinced that the young orphans were aware of the politician's profession and thus cynical toward her professed interest in their plight, McCracken wrote in disgust: "By making coin of that most lovely of all human virtues, charity; by regarding the rendering of deeds of kindness as the spending of so much coin for political support, women in Denver, prominently engaged in politics, have not only lowered their own standards; they have lowered also the standards of the less fortunate, the less protected women of the tenements who so sadly need . . . women whom they may revere."[45] McCracken's message was clear: political power meant the degradation of charity, the loss of working-class trust, and, ultimately, the erosion of civic virtue.

Another critic defined the problem as one of civic virtue versus "platform virtue." "The most subtle moral danger," she wrote, "lies in the fact that it is so easy to be noble, to be generous, to be unselfish, on the public platform — in one's typewritten Confession of Faith." Citing the "platform habit, the club habit, the President and Secretary habit" as activities that led women away from home duties and disinterested "encouragement of the wearied wageearner," the critic warned that political affiliations and aspirations would deprive upper-class women of their virtue and leave them morally bankrupt.[46] By equating political power with corruption and civic virtue with disinterestedness, the antisuffragists could appeal both to traditionalists, who favored a separate sphere of influence for women, and to tories, who required "exceptional women" to detect through private channels the public interest. Suffragism posed a threat to both groups by offering to women a public role that need not accord with their private rank in society, either as family members or as members of an economic class. Through the vote, a woman could express opinions that were her own. Expressions of such opinions, hitherto unspoken, alarmed the antisuffragists and provided yet another argument against votes for women.

The idea of female self-representation was anathema to traditionalists and tories alike. Whether one believed that woman's interests were identical with those of her family or those of her class, one could see the danger of women outside their niche expressing interests of their own. Antisuffragists combated the idea of a collective female interest in several ways. Some questioned the concept of women as a separate class and returned to the theme of familial identity of interests. Implicit in this argument was the concern that women would not vote as their husbands or fathers did, but instead would endorse their own hidden agenda.[47] Similarly, others expressly warned of breaks in class solidarity and asked for assurance that voting women would retain their class allegiance. "Give me the slightest inkling that women will fight the tyrannous hand of the Labor Unions," pleaded one antisuffragist, who also asked, "Will the woman who quails before the departing cook stand firm before the District Leader?"[48]

Through suggestions of familial and class betrayal, antisuffragists depicted women as undependable, impulsive, and easily corruptible — adjectives used by traditionalists and tories to describe the state of American democracy. By linking woman suffrage to popular fears of democracy, antisuffragists highlighted the instability of both, warning that neither was to be trusted. "The New Woman," remarked one critic, "is willing to multiply by two the present ignorant and unconscientious vote, a vote which many thoughtful persons, anxiously doubting democracy, believe is already threatening our national existence."[49] The woman suffrage movement faced two sets of opponents. Each had its own theory of society; each shaped elements of the other's argument. One resisted expansion of woman's sphere into the public arena on the grounds of traditional patriarchal values; the other used stereotypes of class and race to reject further expansion of the franchise. Antisuffragism meant more than a simple constellation of conservative, misogynist attitudes. It encompassed a tangled calculus of overt sexist sentiment, entrenched adherence to the Burkean concept of virtual representation, racial and class prejudice, and, at its core, a deeply rooted fear of democracy. Enjoying the relative luxury of fighting a campaign shaped by public indifference as much as by active recruits and with clear objectives well-grounded in tradition, the antisuffragists could be sure that the majority of social and political conservatives would understand their message and approve of their efforts.

Unlike their antisuffrage opponents, suffragists were often unsure of the implications of their cause. The suffrage movement owed its origins to female abolitionists who had employed a broadly drawn theory of natural rights in their argument for the vote. As we have seen, however, the ideals of the pioneer suffragists were gradually diluted over time by elitism, racism, and expediency.

Although a thread of their democratic idealism still remained by the early twentieth century, the pioneers themselves were passing from the scene. They were replaced by a younger cohort of women who felt few ties beyond those of sentiment to the older reformers. Faced with an increasingly vocal antisuffrage opposition, some NAWSA leaders equivocated over the organization's traditional goal of universal suffrage. During the four years of her first NAWSA presidency (1900–1904), Carrie Chapman Catt on occasion expressed reservations about unlimited franchise expansion. In her 1901 president's address to the NAWSA convention, Catt cited the "aggressive movements that with possibly ill-advised haste enfranchised the foreigner, the negro and the Indian" as detrimental to the suffrage cause.[50] Other NAWSA activists shared Catt's suspicion of these newly enfranchised groups. Even pioneer suffragist Elizabeth Cady Stanton advocated the use of literacy tests for aliens, as well as a five-year waiting period for citizenship, in order to defuse antisuffrage arguments.[51]

The idea of an educated electorate defined by literacy tests especially appealed to white southern suffragists who were eager to perpetuate white supremacy. When the 1903 NAWSA convention met in New Orleans, Louisiana, southern delegates made their presence — and their wishes — felt. In spite of a prior agreement among NAWSA officers to avoid the race question, the issue surfaced during a question-and-answer period led by Anna Howard Shaw. "If you give the ballot to women," asked one delegate, "won't you make the black and white woman equal politically and therefore lay the foundation for a future claim of social equality?" Shaw pointed out that disfranchisement had already made women of both races political equals and dodged the issue of social equality entirely.[52] Delegates directly addressed the question of limited woman suffrage at a symposium on educational qualifications later in the week. After denouncing the Fourteenth and Fifteenth Amendments, the president of the Mississippi Suffrage Association voiced an opinion shared by many southern delegates when she called for strict literacy tests as a means of limiting the electorate. Socialist and social critic Charlotte Perkins Gilman stood alone in her protest against such restrictions, and an informal vote of the delegates revealed overwhelming sentiment in favor of an educational restriction for the vote. Despite the informal vote, NAWSA leaders were able to prevent a formal motion on the subject, and consequently the association's endorsement of unlimited, or universal, suffrage remained intact.[53] But the fact remained that there was no consensus among white suffragists in any region on extending the vote to black women, regardless of NAWSA's official stand on equal suffrage for all women.

Aside from endangering NAWSA's commitment to universal suffrage, the race issue threatened the organization's internal harmony. White southern suffragists bristled at the notion of Yankee rule, whether in Congress or in their suffrage work. And although some northern suffragists shared their southern colleagues' racism, most found it hard to condone the blatant racist appeal so often prevalent in southern suffrage oratory. During the 1903 convention, for example, one Dixie orator took as her text the premise that educated woman suffrage would ensure white supremacy and nativist control of politics, an argument that proved offensive to many northern delegates. Moreover, a highly critical editorial in the *New Orleans Times-Democrat* assailed NAWSA leaders in much the same spirit that southern newspapers had attacked abolitionists in the 1850s. To defuse a possible schism, the Executive Board distributed to the press a signed statement disavowing any policy that would threaten white supremacy or states' rights. "The doctrine of State's rights is recognized in the national body," the statement read, "and each auxiliary State association arranges its own affairs in accordance with its own ideas and in harmony with the customs of its own section."[54] To ease internal tensions, Catt reaffirmed the states' rights initiative in a speech to the delegates and dismissed the obvious contradictions between NAWSA's goal of full female enfranchisement and states' rights rhetoric. By keeping the peace at the expense of rhetorical and ideological consistency, NAWSA leaders undermined the traditional ideal of unlimited suffrage for women and allowed sectional divisions to continue uncontested. In a sense, the association recognized the tory argument for a qualified electorate while simultaneously ignoring the implications of this sentiment within its theoretically democratic organization.

There was more to the states' rights compromise arrived at during the 1903 NAWSA convention than simply allowing southern organizations to perpetuate their racist policies. The NAWSA leadership found themselves faced with a dilemma. In the late 1890s, the black women's club movement had spread throughout the states, and many of the associations generated by this movement had established franchise departments. With the union of the National Federation of African American Women and the National League of Colored Women to form the National Association of Colored Women (NACW) around the turn of the century, the black women's club movement had grown to more than fifty thousand members by 1914. Led by Mary Church Terrell, the NACW became a major force for reform among the black community and eagerly sought the vote as a tool with which to gain educational, economic, and political advances.[55] But when black clubwomen turned to NAWSA, the only national suffrage association in existence until 1914, their applications for membership were more often than not politely refused.

For NAWSA leaders, the existence of black suffragists raised a series of embarrassing questions that were easier to ignore than to address. On the one hand, black men and women viewed woman suffrage much more favorably than did whites of either gender. As Adele Hunt Logan, a leader in the black club movement and ardent suffragist, explained, "If white American women with all their natural advantages need the ballot . . . how much more do black Americans, male and female, need the strong defense of the vote to help to secure their right to life, liberty and the pursuit of happiness?"[56] A cadre of capable black leaders had emerged from the NACW, including Logan, Mary Church Terrell, Josephine St. Pierre Ruffin, and Ida B. Wells, and unlike the whites-only General Federation of Women's Clubs, which did not endorse woman suffrage until 1914, the NACW membership overwhelmingly favored the reform.[57] Black Americans, then, offered a zealous constituency for NAWSA at a time when the organization was desperate for higher membership totals.

On the other hand, NAWSA leaders believed there were serious drawbacks to accepting black suffragists into the association, either as individual members of existing clubs or as segregated auxiliaries. If the national organization openly announced that it would admit blacks, many white Americans in every region of the country would strenuously object. Antisuffragists would raise the race issue to discredit the suffragists with the unconverted public. Moreover, the careful efforts to recruit prominent women and gain respectability that had begun in the late nineteenth century and would intensify in the twentieth, would prove futile. Leaders also worried that individual suffrage societies, so carefully organized and nurtured, would be torn apart over the issue of whether or not to admit blacks.

From the viewpoint of the NAWSA leadership, the inclusion of black women would cost the organization members, money, internal harmony, and a positive public image. Pragmatic considerations aside, there were many white suffragists who had little interest in defending or expanding black civil rights. Disfranchisement of southern black males had come in a wave of violence and intimidation that was barely remarked on by the nation at large; it is hardly surprising that white suffragists felt little compulsion to risk their movement's already shaky credibility by embracing black women. Whether from overt racism, fear of negative publicity, or simple indifference, the unwritten and largely unspoken NAWSA policy on black suffragists was to ignore them whenever possible or, if pressed, to refuse their advances politely but firmly when black activists offered their allegiance and aid.[58] Although a few white clubs accepted a small number of black members, and some black societies were accepted as NAWSA auxiliaries, these were the exception, not the rule. In a rare discussion of black membership, Carrie Chapman Catt responded to a Texas coworker's question about racial membership rules in 1918:

The question of auxiliaryship within the state is one for the state to decide itself. I presume that no colored women's leagues are members in southern states, although I do not know positively that this is true. There are great many clubs in different northern states and they have been members for many years. I think in some northern states, individual colored women are direct members. Of course these women in the North are women with a good deal of white blood and are educated women, otherwise they would not be asking auxiliaryship. This [black] woman may desire to enter because she wishes to help the cause and she may merely be desirous of the recognition to her race. I am sure if I were a colored woman, I would do the same thing they are doing. In some southern states it would be impossible to have a colored league without gravely upsetting the work and ruining the influences of a suffrage association."[59]

Catt advised her correspondent to write the black suffragist and "tell her that you will be able to get the vote for women more easily if they do not embarass [*sic*] you by asking for membership and that you are getting it for colored women as well as for white women."[60]

For the most part, twentieth-century NAWSA leaders broke with the tradition of the pioneer suffragists and excluded blacks from any meaningful participation in their association. The exclusion of blacks was practiced in a limited fashion as early as the 1890s. Susan B. Anthony, for example, asked her friend Frederick Douglass to stay away from the 1895 NAWSA convention, which was held in Atlanta, for fear his presence would cause dissension among white southern delegates. It should be kept in mind, however, that Anthony, Stanton, and many of their supporters' views on race were considered by many to be extremely tolerant for the times. Although it is clear that blacks were not directly recruited for membership in the white suffrage movement, neither were they as actively excluded in the nineteenth century as they would be after the turn of the century.[61]

This unwritten policy on blacks' admission to NAWSA would be the first of many such steps that would narrow the movement over time and make exclusion rather than inclusion the basis of its success. But if NAWSA leaders were willing to compromise its democratic principles on the race issue, they proved less tractable in other areas of the debate over democracy. In response to traditionalist claims that suffrage would endanger the home and family, suffragists argued that the vote was of primary importance to the security of these institutions. Addressing the antisuffrage objection to female participation in public life, Anna Howard Shaw responded: "Does an intelligent interest in the education of a child render a woman less a mother, does the housekeeping instinct of woman manifested in a desire for clean streets, pure water, and unadulterated food destroy her efficiency as a homemaker? Does a desire for an environment of moral and civic purity show neglect of the highest good of her family?"[62] While redrawing the boundaries of woman's sphere to include "public housekeeping" as well as private housework, suffragists met their opponents' attacks with propaganda of their own. One method employed by suffrage advocates was the personal testimonial, in which a suffragist would testify to the salutary effects of voting. One writer, for example, described the benefits of growing up in a "suffrage home." Far from being neglected as a result of her mother's suffrage work, the young woman averred that her mother spent less time voting than other mothers spent "reading novels and considering fashion plates."[63]

Suffragists also made use of songs and jingles to link their cause symbolically with familial interests. Especially popular was a NAWSA songbook that contained suffrage lyrics set to patriotic music. Nine songs were based on "The Battle Hymn of the Republic" alone, including the following:

> Let women weave the charm of home for city and for state,
> Where children and the poor and lost her ministry await,
> And by the magic of her love bid her inaugurate
> The new and glorious day.[64]

Equally appealing was the campaign song that advocates sang during the California suffrage fight in 1911:

> A ballot for the Lady!
> For the home and for the Baby!
> Come, vote ye for the Lady,
> The Baby, the Home![65]

Even Charlotte Perkins Gilman, who in later years would attack the domestic bonds of womanhood, tried her hand at sentimental verse in her "Song for Equal Suffrage":

> By every sweet and tender tie around our heart strings curled,
> In the cause of nobler motherhood is woman's flag unfurled,
> Till every child shall know the joy and peace of mother's world,
> As Love comes marching on![66]

By linking woman suffrage to such American icons as patriotism, motherhood, and the home, suffragists engaged the antisuffragists on their own ground. Moreover, through the skillful use of new advertising methods like testimonials, catchy jingles, and songs, the suffrage movement made its first tentative efforts at public opinion management.

Simultaneously, suffrage advocates began to cloak their cause in sweeping moral terminology. Suffrage supporters equated their cause with the forces of reform, virtue, and public good while depicting their opponents as agents of evil: white slavers, saloon-keepers, corrupt politicians, and the like. As one suffrage propagandist wrote: "if we should call the role [*sic*] of [suffrage] opponents, we should find among them about all savages, enemies of society, of the family and of good government, rum-sellers, drunkards, constitutional stand-patters and weak-minded men in general."[67] Especially prevalent in suffrage propaganda were denunciations of the liquor trust. Many suffragists were also prohibitionists, and in the first years of the new century NAWSA maintained close ties to the WCTU, thus assuring a ready audience for arguments that promised victory through cooperation between the two movements. The Ohio WCTU, for example, circulated a speech by Anna Howard Shaw entitled "Influence versus Power," which defined woman suffrage as an important weapon in the fight for prohibition. Shaw called on prohibitionists to remember that distillers, brewers, saloon keepers, and bartenders were armed with the ballot, while "the home-maker, the child-rearer, is powerless against such a foe" without the vote.[68]

Suffragists stepped up their attacks on the "vice trust" during the first decade of the twentieth century. When a referendum on school suffrage was defeated in Kentucky in 1910, angry suffragists publicly blamed the "liquor men" and corrupt officials and vowed to seek revenge.[69] Although the publicity generated by such tactics doubtless won some converts to the suffrage ranks, in other cases the taint of prohibition cost suffragists needed support. In 1900 and again in 1906, Oregon suffragists had protested in vain when NAWSA leaders pursued similar tactics during suffrage contests in their state. Fearful of a wet backlash, some local leaders had attempted to conduct the campaign on the principle of a "still hunt"—seeking no publicity and quietly pushing the suffrage amendment through without stirring up the wet opposition. Unfortunately, Anna Howard Shaw and other non-Oregonians insisted on linking the suffrage battle with the prohibition crusade, and both campaigns ended in defeat.[70] The leaders of NAWSA moved away from directly linking the two reforms in the following years, but association propaganda continued to label its opponents as an active conspiracy of evil.[71] By pitting suffragists against the vice trust, the suffrage movement forged an "alliance of virtue" that countermanded the restrictive female sphere depicted by antisuffrage traditionalists. In addition to "housekeeping on a grand scale," voting, according to suffragist propaganda, was a moral necessity to combat the forces of evil, overriding such outmoded concepts as indirect influence in favor of direct intervention for the good of society.

While expanding the boundaries of woman's sphere to include municipal housekeeping and moral reform, suffrage rhetoric also stressed the benefits of woman suffrage to individual women. "It is for the growth of woman's character that the ballot is needed primarily," wrote one suffrage advocate, "and the more adverse and indifferent women are, the more its need is evident to break up the frivolity, wastefulness of time and money, social struggles and imitation of luxury into which they are driven from lack of occupation."[72] Or as Max Eastman, president of the New York Men's League for Woman Suffrage, put it, "The great thing to my mind is not that women will improve politics but that politics will develop women."[73] Others equated societal evolution with individual growth and argued that because of educational and technological advances, women possessed the training and the leisure to participate in public life. "To set women back into the limited sphere of fifty years ago," warned Susan B. Anthony, "would be to arrest the progress of the whole race."[74]

Louisiana suffragist and social reformer Jean Gordon agreed. Gordon and her sister Kate were active in a variety of reforms through their membership in the New Orleans Equal Rights Association Club.[75] While Kate steered the club through the shoals of southern Progressivism, Jean served as factory inspector for New Orleans and reported to her club constituency on new areas for investigation and relief. To Jean Gordon, the vote was of paramount importance to civic reform, but in a speech to the NAWSA convention in 1908, she directed her remarks instead at the concept of indirect influence and the tory notion of upper-class charity. Excoriating the Lady Bountiful ideal as an ineffective anachronism, Gordon called for upper-class female participation in direct reform. "All offices such as superintendents of reformatories, matrons, and factory inspectors should be filled by women of standing, education, refinement and independent means," she maintained, pointing out that upper-class women would be immune to coercion from manufacturers and mill owners since the two groups would in fact be social equals. "American women of leisure," she concluded, "must awaken to an appreciation of the democratic idea of Noblesse Oblige."[76] To women like Gordon, suffrage meant more than a means to achieve civic reform; it encompassed a new landscape for elite women's employment, which in turn would produce an opportunity for societal regeneration and social control.

The possibilities that Gordon saw for elite women proved to be one of the chief attractions of suffragism, and it attracted a constituency that chafed under the restrictive bonds of woman's sphere. Suffrage leaders recognized and shared the desire so frequently expressed by educated women and women of leisure for "something more" out of life. Carrie Catt appealed to this sentiment when she proclaimed: "Woman's hour has struck at last, and all along the line there is a mobilization of the woman's army ready for service."[77] Even antisuffragists were aware of the new spirit that emanated from their opponents, and they scornfully referred to their adversaries as "New Women." To suffragists, the term seemed merely amusing. "What is the new woman?" queried one suffrage advocate, "are advocates of woman suffrage new? Is Mrs. [Julia Ward] Howe new at ninety? Is Anna Howard Shaw new at sixty-two, after forty years of public work?"[78] Despite the longevity of both suffrage leaders and their cause, to some advocates the label seemed to capture the essence of their movement. Julia Ward Howe sought the term's origins in scripture: "In Christ Jesus there is neither bond nor free, neither male nor female, but a new creature."[79] When Howe later called the suffrage movement "the harbinger of a new creation," she meant more than a simple expansion of the franchise to women; she envisioned an across-the-board expansion of woman's sphere that would result in new opportunities, new responsibilities, and, ultimately, new women. Kentucky suffragist and reformer Madeline Mc-Dowell Breckenridge believed that through suffrage work women would learn of their own potential and, in a sense, educate themselves to be active participants in society. "Our idea," Breckenridge argued, "the idea of even the most conservative of us — of what is womanly has changed. Even those timid souls who think it unwomanly to cast a vote for mayor no longer think it is to cast a school vote, and gradually our idea of woman's sphere is enlarging until soon we shall describe its limitlessness in the words of Dr. Newton, that 'Whatever woman can do that, by divine ordination she ought to do; by human allowance she should be privileged to do; by force of destiny in the long run she will do.' "[80]

The idea of a limitless sphere inhabited by new women included an organic view of society in which individuals, regardless of their gender, would freely participate in both marketplace and polling place. Unspoken assumptions further defined the new woman, however. In addition to her education and limitless opportunities, she was white, native-born, upper or middle class, and probably Anglo-Saxon. Even egalitarian suffragists like Anna Howard Shaw rarely acknowledged the women who had little chance of attaining the status of new women. When Shaw defined democracy as "the right to develop the whole nature through self-expression," she did not stop to ponder the racial, class, and ethnic limitations that prevented a large segment of America's women from achieving this lofty goal.[81] To women like Shaw, the suffrage movement incorporated both political and economic self-expression as its goals, and it served to articulate the growing desire for full female participation in public life. Reformers like Jane Addams and Florence Kelley, although agreeing with Shaw's egalitarian philosophy, saw the vote as a way to gain specific national reforms that would undercut the societal divisions that prevented all women from sharing Breckenridge's vision of a limitless sphere. To Kelley in particular, woman suffrage was a powerful lever with which female immigrants and factory workers could pry protection from their representatives and employers, and her suffrage work took second place to a larger reform agenda. As chairman of the NAWSA Committee on Industrial Conditions Affecting Women and Children and as NAWSA vice president in 1905, Kelley served as a constant advocate for working women's concerns as well as for universal suffrage. Suffrage was an important weapon in the fight for a broad-based program of reforms, and for many suffragists like Kelley it remained a means rather than an end unto itself.[82]

Other suffragists believed their movement was a monumental reform in itself. Historian and journalist Ida Husted Harper linked political corruption and other social ills to the lack of true democracy and suggested that only through woman suffrage would American government attain purity. In response to antisuffrage demands for franchise limitation as a solution to social problems, Harper maintained that an infusion of female votes would create a climate of egalitarianism, which would in turn produce needed reform. "A true democracy, a genuine republic, must be founded upon a representation of the whole people," she argued, and she concluded that since the "real republic" lay somewhere in the future, the "experiment is yet to be made."[83] Harper's "real republic" depended less on concrete legislation than on the idea of *vox populi vox dei*. Unlike Kelley, she believed that through the democratic process, a spontaneous equality would be generated that would correct societal ills and establish a virtuous government.

Shaw, Kelley, and Harper, however, shared a basic belief in egalitarian democracy, and in this sense they were representative of a sizable faction of progressive women who sought societal perfection through woman suffrage. Some historians have labeled these women "social feminists" and have argued that their commitment to reform overrode purely feminist considerations.[84] Similarly, other scholars have suggested that egalitarian suffrage rhetoric was more common in the period of activity ending roughly at the turn of the century. They cite the growth of politically expedient arguments for the vote as proof that the movement drifted away from a strict natural rights ideology as the century progressed.[85] Such an interpretation implies that the woman suffrage movement also moved away from a strict feminist agenda in favor of a wider social reform program while simultaneously diluting the movement's democratic ideology with the rhetoric of expediency.

The presence of suffragists like Harper, Gordon, and Kelley indicates the diverse opinions that existed within suffragism. In reality, the suffrage crusade harbored a wide variety of philosophical, class, and racial positions under the banner of votes for women. A more accurate ideological division might be made between those women who espoused egalitarian ideals and those who favored an elitist concept of society and social reform. Echoing Jean Gordon's idea of democratic noblesse oblige, some suffragists wanted the vote as a means to gain new avenues of service and employment for educated women and to achieve power for themselves and their economic class. In a sense, this concept engaged the tory argument on its own ground by restricting the expansion of woman's sphere to elite women. Antisuffrage protests against female participation in the public sphere grew increasingly hollow as they were forced to argue their case before state legislatures, at congressional hearings, and in public debates. Moreover, leading antisuffragists in reality were far from modest homebodies. Antisuffrage advocates were often active in charitable organizations and women's clubs, and some held well-paying jobs.[86] Their associations involved many of the same activities as did suffrage work, and antisuffragists were called upon to publish newsletters, solicit funds from the public, and make speeches.[87] An expanded sphere for elite women was not so far removed from the paternalistic ideal of indirect female influence through charity, and as such it found a receptive audience among a faction of conservative suffragists.

For suffrage paternalists, the appeal of the movement did not extend much past its possible utility in expanding opportunities for the upper class. Others favored restricted suffrage as a means of preserving white supremacy. The 1903 NAWSA resolution affirming states' rights allowed a separate-but-unequal ideology to remain dormant within the movement, and some white suffragists — although few in number — continued to resist the more egalitarian views held by others in the movement. The cleavage between a purely democratic ideology and one of limited suffrage did not follow strict sectional lines. Suffragists in Pennsylvania, for example, could choose between the NAWSA affiliate and the smaller, but equally persistent, Pennsylvania Limited Suffrage League, a group that espoused educational requirements for the vote. Other suffrage advocates shared with antisuffragists an antipathy for the newly naturalized immigrants and argued that women would provide a conservative counter to what one prosuffrage editorial called the "greed and radicalism" of the working class.[88]

While the conservative element within NAWSA was at no time in the majority, its presence dictated to some extent the organization's future course. Philosophically close to the tory concept of virtual representation, conservative suffragists constituted in the best of times a drag on the egalitarianism of the majority, and in the worst of times, a vocal intransigent minority opposed to universal suffrage. Suffrage leaders recognized the problem of diverse ideologies housed under one shaky roof, and they endeavored to maintain unity at the expense of principle. In a period of low membership totals and financial woes, association leaders chose a path of moderation in an effort to boost the organization's numbers without an ideological split. Elite women had the resources and prestige to rescue the movement from oblivion; if principle was to be the cost of salvation, then many suffragists were willing to pay the price.

To categorize the woman suffrage movement in the first decade of the twentieth century as wholly opportunistic would, however, be incorrect. Suffragism embodied a wide range of philosophical viewpoints and political strategies. Parallel to the conservatism of white supremacists and nativists ran a deeply embedded faith in pure democracy that found a voice in the oratory of Anna Howard Shaw. Schooled in suffrage work by Susan B. Anthony, Shaw served as the conscience for egalitarian suffragists tempted by the siren song of expediency. As president of NAWSA from 1905 to 1915, Shaw preached the doctrine of universal suffrage to growing numbers of converts. "Whatever others may say or do," she warned in 1905, "our Association must not accept compromises. We must guard against the reactionary spirit which marks our time and stand unfalteringly for the principle of perfect equality of rights and opportunities for all. We must refuse to restrict our demand for justice or bound it by any line of race, sex [or] creed. . . . We must persistently insist that in the purpose of the Infinite, self-government is the ultimate destiny of mankind. This is our Ideal."[89]

The first two decades of the twentieth century saw the emergence of a new debate regarding the nation's political future, with woman suffrage as its focal point. Embracing more than simply votes for women, the discussion encompassed a wide spectrum of political assumptions and as such revealed the uncertain course of American democracy in a period celebrated for democratic reform. As one antisuffragist put it, "Our feet are always in the water, for in a republic, men sail on a raft."[90] Who would sail, and for what distant shore, was the question of the age; by 1920, America would know the answer.

3

The Suffrage Renaissance

Suffragism in the early nineteen hundreds was burdened with an image arising from its history that was in many respects a hindrance to further progress. Advocacy of divorce reform, experimental dress, and feminist interpretations of the Bible had given nineteenth-century suffragists a reputation for radicalism that was exploited by their enemies to dissuade more conventional women from participating in the movement. Consequently, during the years 1896–1910 suffragists made little tangible progress in state referenda or federal amendment campaigns. No new states were won for suffrage, and the federal amendment lay dormant in committee, prompting one historian to label the period "the doldrums."[1] Despite the poor record generated by state campaigns, however, "the doldrums" were in reality an important period of growth and renewal for the movement. So significant were these years of regeneration that the period might more appropriately be called "the suffrage renaissance." Aware of the movement's negative image but unwilling to disavow the contributions of its pioneers, the suffragists of NAWSA sought to create a tradition that would reconcile the heroic and somewhat controversial past with their pragmatic plans for the future. With a reinterpreted, sanitized version of the past coupled with a sincere celebration of the heroism of pioneer suffragists, NAWSA leaders forged a link between the heroic age of confrontational politics and a new organizational approach to reform.

A turning point for the woman suffrage movement came on election day 1895, when the Massachusetts Assembly held a mock, or nonbinding, suffrage referendum. The state's legislature had been besieged for years by both suffragists and their opponents to act on the issue. In an effort to determine public opinion on the question, the legislature ruled that both women and men would vote in the referendum. In a singularly odd twist, both suffragists and antisuffragists opposed the contest. The former objected to the nonbinding status of the vote, while the latter expressed disgust at being forced to cast a vote in order to demonstrate their aversion to voting. Antisuffragists resolved their dilemma, however, by clever strategy, good organization, and effective propaganda.[2]

The Massachusetts Association Opposed to Further Extension of the Suffrage to Women (MAOFESW), founded in 1882 by Mrs. Henry O. Houghton and revitalized several months before the November 1895 referendum, attempted to persuade women to abstain from voting on the issue. Arguing that a low female voter turnout would indicate the wishes of Massachusetts women far more convincingly than a large "no" vote, antisuffragists solicited contributions from well-wishers and embarked on a house-to-house canvass of Boston to bring their message to the people. Aiding the MAOFESW workers were a group of prominent Boston men who formed the Man Suffrage Association (MSA). Boasting a membership that included two ex-governors, the president of Harvard University, noted religious leaders, professors, businessmen, and attorneys, the MSA raised more than $3,600 in less than two months at a time when the combined expenditures of all Massachusetts suffrage advocates was a mere $1,300.[3]

In contrast to the wealthy and prestigious individuals who opposed woman suffrage, suffragists relied on such reformers as Henry Blackwell, his daughter Alice Stone Blackwell, Julia Ward Howe, and Thomas Wentworth Higginson for leadership and support. Blackwell and Higginson had served together in the abolition movement, and along with Julia Ward Howe, they were among the pioneers of the nineteenth-century woman's rights crusade. In addition, U.S. Senator George F. Hoar agreed to preside over the Suffrage Referendum State Committee, formed in July 1895 to coordinate the suffrage forces. Unfortunately, most suffragists continued their longtime practice of suspending suffrage work during the summer months. By the time the committee reassembled in October, its members faced a well-organized and active opposition. The antisuffragists had used the summer to advantage, circularizing each ward, publicizing their position in the press, and plastering walls and fences with huge placards bearing the message, "Men and Women, Vote No!"[4]

More effective than these publicity measures, however, was the antisuffrage strategy that encouraged women to abstain from voting. On November 5, antisuffragists gleefully pointed to the low female turnout as proof that the vast majority of Massachusetts women did not want the vote. Of approximately 612,000 women eligible to register, only 42,676 did so, and of those, only 23,065 cast a vote. Although women voters supported the measure 22,204 to 861, in forty-four towns not a single female vote was cast. Of the 273,946 male votes cast, a resounding 186,976 men voted against the measure.[5] By shifting attention away from the actual female vote and emphasizing instead the percentage of the female population that stayed away from the polls, the antisuffragists managed to interpret the mock referendum as an overwhelming victory for their position.

The 1895 referendum cast a long shadow: never again would suffragists call for a test of strength if that test were to include the disfranchised members of their own sex, and never again would antisuffragists believe that the majority of women favored woman suffrage. Although suffrage leaders continued to maintain that a large latent sentiment for their reform existed, the strategic course they pursued as the new century unfolded revealed a pragmatic acceptance of the weakness of their position. There was little doubt among suffragists that the majority of Americans accepted the idea of a separate domestic sphere for women. Moreover, in taking the position of defending the status quo and opposing any change in the status of women, the antisuffragists had occupied the high ground in the coming battle for the vote. During the Massachusetts referendum campaign, MAOFESW had demonstrated its ability to mobilize an influential constituency, utilize modern advertising methods, and raise large sums of money to finance its work. The suffragists, although dedicated to their cause, were unable to compete with the superior funding and efficiency of their opponents. The antisuffragists had effectively turned the referendum into a demonstration of indifference on the part of Massachusetts women and had placed the suffrage forces in the defensive position of supporting a democratic reform that the majority of women did not desire. In the aftermath of the contest, many Massachusetts suffrage clubs lost members or disbanded completely, while MAOFESW and other organizations like it grew in size and strength. Repeatedly cited in national periodicals and in antisuffrage tracts as proof of female indifference to woman suffrage, the referendum of 1895 shaped the opposition to suffrage for years to come.

More immediately, the 1895 Massachusetts referendum forced suffragists to reassess the strengths and weaknesses of their organization. The lesson of

'95 seemed to point toward a continuation of the NAWSA policy of educating the public to the benefits of woman suffrage, but with a new emphasis on effective organization and strong financial support. In addition, suffragists began to recognize the need for a new public image. In response to antisuffrage propaganda that characterized them as fanatics and in an effort to attract a larger, more stable membership, suffragists in the first decade of the twentieth century attempted to win respect for their cause and legitimize their organization through a variety of tactics. Their efforts demonstrated a new awareness of the importance of public opinion and marked a turning point in the movement itself. Suffragism of old, shaped by the dedication of a few faithful friends, was to become the movement of the masses, and as such it had to be packaged in a form more attractive to a wider audience.

Most suffragists believed that the greatest obstacle to woman suffrage was not antisuffrage opposition or male recalcitrance, but rather the indifference of American women. Doubtless many agreed with one antisuffragist's diagnosis of the problem her opponents faced. "What [the suffrage movement] has to overcome," she explained, "is not an argument but a feeling."[6] Even when this feeling manifested itself in overt hostility to the movement, suffrage leaders remained convinced that their foremost task was to exorcise the demon of indifference by converting the apathetic masses to the idea of distaff democracy. In an age that saw the proliferation of female associations and voluntary societies, it is not surprising that suffrage advocates turned to women's clubs for their organizational model and to society women for the talisman of respectability.

The active recruitment of prominent women by NAWSA officials was not an innovation at the turn of the century; pioneer suffragists had made repeated efforts along those lines throughout the Gilded Age. One of the first successful attempts came in 1893, when Lucy Stone and Carrie Catt attempted to organize the prominent women of Denver, Colorado, according to the "society plan." Although the Colorado Equal Suffrage Association could boast a small but dedicated number of "respectable middle-class women," Stone believed there was an untapped reservoir of suffrage support among wealthy Denver clubwomen. Stone wrote to Denver civic leader Mrs. John R. Hanna, imploring her to make Catt's acquaintance and help her protégée organize the city's leading citizens for suffrage. Hanna duly asked the young suffragist to dinner, and after a long discussion, the two embarked upon an ambitious plan to recruit the city's society women for woman suffrage. Within weeks of their initial meeting, the Denver Equal Suffrage League was formed, composed almost entirely of wealthy clubwomen and socialites. One of the league's first functions, a large public meeting ostensibly in honor of Catt, featured a long list of distinguished speakers from Denver's political and financial circles and was attended by what local suffragists considered the city's "best people." "A most marked result," wrote one Denver suffragist, "was that not one paper in Denver said a word of ridicule or even mild amusement concerning suffragists"; she went on to attribute the press's favorable coverage to the presence for the first time of prominent citizens among the suffrage ranks.[7] Catt's society plan was hailed as the crucial factor in the suffrage referendum later in the year. Another star was added to the suffrage flag in 1893 when Colorado joined Wyoming as the second woman suffrage state.

With her election to the NAWSA presidency in 1900, Catt laid plans to recruit prestigious women of wealth to the suffrage fold at the national level. Initially most of the NAWSA leadership agreed with Catt's society plan. Susan B. Anthony, for example, endorsed the idea and urged NAWSA Corresponding Secretary Rachel Foster Avery to include in the annual convention program a list of all delegates and alternates, in order to display prominently the names and addresses of prestigious converts to the cause.[8] Moreover, Catt asked Business Committee members to compile lists of influential clubwomen, ministers, and politicians from which to solicit new members, and she included well-heeled men as well as society women in her recruitment scheme. Suffragists also sought to win over influential labor and agricultural leaders and drew up lists of union officials and Grangers for postal propaganda.[9] In 1904, the association acknowledged the society plan at the annual convention, when the official plan of work for the year recommended that suffragists become active in civic, charitable, or educational work in their communities.[10] Through local clubs and organizations, suffrage advocates could recruit wealthy women who had both time and money to devote to the cause. Experience gained in club work could be turned to account in suffrage societies, enabling suffrage leaders to draw on a ready-made constituency already trained in parliamentary procedure, public speaking, and fund raising. Notably missing in the list of organizations to recruit, however, was the burgeoning black women's club movement. The unspoken assumption of NAWSA leaders was that the society plan was for whites only.[11]

In addition to recruiting from white civic or charitable organizations, suffragists sought new members through parlor meetings, the traditional form of middle-class female assembly. Held in the privacy of the home, parlor meetings were deemed respectable by even the most modest Victorian women and served to attract a conservative set that would have blanched at attending a public lecture or rally. One suffrage advocate described her role as a parlor meeting speaker: "You had these little afternoon gatherings of women, maybe six or eight women. You had a cup of tea. A little social gathering. While we were drinking tea, I gave them a little talk and they asked questions about what was going on. It was alot [*sic*] better, I thought at the time, than to have a lecture. Because a lot of them wouldn't go to a lecture. And it was what I could do."[12] Occasionally, professional suffrage speakers would address parlor gatherings in the afternoon before a major nighttime suffrage rally. In this way advocates could reach both the timid and the bold; suffragists believed that through gradual education, encouragement, and attention to individual sensibilities, even the most timid souls could be transformed into "new women."

Although the days of ridicule experienced by nineteenth-century female reformers had passed, speaking in a public forum remained unthinkable for many women. Through the parlor meeting, elite women could gather in a nonthreatening environment to discuss a wide range of topics. Woman suffrage, birth control, municipal reform, and labor conditions found their way into parlor conversations, along with the more traditional subjects of literature, history, and religion. Some women, like those who attended the Monday Club of Richburg, New York, combined the new with the old: on alternating weeks, club members turned their attention from New York history and birdwatching to the history of women and prosuffrage arguments.[13] The growing interest in nontraditional subjects was reflected in other conservative women's groups like the General Federation of Women's Clubs. Evidence of this trend was demonstrated by the newly elected president of the GFWC, when she informed the biennial convention that "Dante is dead, [he] has been dead for several centuries, and I think it is time that we dropped the study of his *Inferno* and turned our attention to our own."[14] By concentrating their efforts on prosperous though conservative women, suffragists sought to take advantage of the awakened interest in public affairs manifested by the GFWC and other women's organizations. The results of this strategy, however, intensified the serious ideological divisions that would trouble the NAWSA forces in the years to come.

Initially, the society plan drew applause from many suffragists who had labored unsuccessfully to recruit new members in the past. Active recruitment in the woman suffrage state of Colorado drew influential women into the crusade and provided workers in nonsuffrage states with ammunition to refute the negative stereotypes that had plagued the movement. One suffragist told congressmen at the 1904 Judiciary Committee Hearing on Woman Suffrage that a leading antisuffragist, when introduced to several prominent Colorado women, expressed admiration of their ability and dedication. "As social leaders, as philanthropists, as clubwomen and church women, she had swallowed them whole and found them delicious"; the suffragist testified, "they only disagreed with her after she knew them also to be suffragists."[15] Although many society women limited their involvement in the suffrage crusade to timely financial support, others played a more important part in the movement. Wealthy New York socialite Mrs. Clarence McKay, for example, organized her own suffrage league, contributed large sums to the cause, and recruited many of that state's most influential women into the suffrage camp.[16] Virginia's Equal Suffrage League included prominent Virginia writers Ellen Glasgow and Mary Johnston, as well as the great-granddaughters of Thomas Jefferson and George Mason.[17] Name recognition, handsome contributions, and social prestige were welcome boons to an organization that had borne the stigma of fanaticism for decades.

Though few NAWSA members questioned the strategy that brought such bounty, the society plan led a minority to protest. To some suffragists the society plan smacked of impropriety and elitism. "I could not help wondering what Lucy Stone would have thought to have seen the Special representative of the cause she gave her life to, promenading in low neck and arms bare to the shoulders at the Governor's reception," one elderly suffragist wrote in despair. "Mrs. [Evelyn H.] Belden worked bravely . . . according to her ideas of the right way — the *Society Way* — but there are some old workers who do not think that some of the methods tended to elevate the cause."[18] Others, like Harriet Stanton Blatch, chafed under the yoke of gradualism. Blatch characterized the suffrage movement at the turn of the century as "a rut worn deep and ever deeper," and in 1907 she founded the League of Self-Supporting Women in an effort to escape the tedium and elitism embodied in NAWSA's society plan.[19] New York socialists like Ida Crouch Hazlett viewed with apprehension the new emphasis on upper-class status and spoke out against mainstream suffragists' "snobbish truckling to the women of influence and social position."[20] So pronounced was the effort to woo socialites that one popular periodical labeled the suffrage crusade a "gilt-chair movement" in reference to suffragists' swank gatherings.[21]

Although the gilt-chair movement offended some, most suffragists believed that their newly won sense of respectability more than compensated for what little criticism the society plan generated. And in keeping with the new emphasis on image at the expense of ideological unity, NAWSA leaders took steps to legitimize their organization through the creation of a formal suffrage historical tradition. On a simple level, tradition may be used to legitimize events, groups, or causes by associating them with the rhetoric, rituals, or personalities of a historic past. A political party, for example, may employ tradition to establish a link between its heroic past and its present platform, as in the recurrent allusions to "the Great Emancipator" made by Republicans trolling for black votes. Used in this way, tradition may represent a series of unspoken assumptions and loyalties and serve as a symbol of organizational unity.

At a deeper level, however, tradition may mask the varied ideological perspectives of a diverse constituency with what one historian has called its "undefined universality."[22] The trappings of tradition allow leaders to deemphasize conflicting opinions and ideals by focusing attention on noncontroversial rituals and rhetoric. Moreover, the creation or reinterpretation of traditions may help to steer a group or movement away from an unsavory past or a discarded ideology without the discussion or disagreement engendered by the democratic process. A salient characteristic of tradition is that, for all its presumed foundation in the past, it can be manipulated with singular ease to suit the purposes of the present.

The "new" suffrage tradition was a mixture of established or genuine rituals and reinterpreted symbols, rhetoric, and practices that had been customized over time to suit the changing nature of the movement. One of the oldest and most important elements of suffrage tradition was an authorized history of women, with suffrage activism as its focal point. Suffragists had long insisted on the place of women in history. In this regard, nineteenth-century suffrage associations may be considered to have been the first American organizations to promote actively women's history as a discipline. The monumental *History of Woman Suffrage,* begun by Elizabeth Cady Stanton, Susan B. Anthony, and Matilda Joslyn Gage in 1881, was more than propaganda for the cause; to suffrage advocates it filled the void in history textbooks left by the omission of American women. The multivolume history was continued until the passage of the Nineteenth Amendment in 1920, and it remains a testimony to the suffragists' conviction that the women's rights movement deserved a permanent place in history. One of Susan B. Anthony's last acts was to arrange for shipment of the unsold volumes, totaling over ten tons in weight, to NAWSA headquarters, whence the books were distributed to every major library in the country.[23]

The national association showed a commitment to women's history by its efforts to disseminate works on the subject. Beginning in 1902, provisions were made to establish circulating suffrage libraries. These libraries gave women access to the major works on feminist theory and literature, as well as to biographies of famous women and histories of the woman's rights movement. The 1903 NAWSA plan of work included the compilation of a catalog of woman suffrage literature, to be donated to libraries to encourage the use of such materials.[24] Five years later, journalist Ida Porter Boyer expanded the original catalog to include all works on the women's rights movement. Carrie Catt showed great enthusiasm for both the catalog and suffrage libraries, and she urged each NAWSA suffrage league to appoint a committee on libraries to keep women's history before the public. "Perhaps someday we shall have in the Congressional Library in Washington a story of the work of women," Catt mused to her friend Alice Stone Blackwell, "We must keep a careful record of our progress for the story is an important one."[25]

Many suffragists shared Catt's vision of the long-term significance of their cause, and they despaired over the omission of women from traditional American histories of the period. "There never was another nation with as many parents as we have had," one suffragist wrote in disgust, "but they have all been fathers—Pilgrim Fathers, Plymouth Fathers, Forefathers, Revolutionary Fathers, City Fathers, Church Fathers—fathers of every description but no mothers!"[26] In response to such discontent, Pauline Steinem, chairman of NAWSA's Committee of Education, conducted a rudimentary investigation in 1909 of history and civics textbooks used in the public schools. Steinem wrote to four hundred school superintendents and twenty-six textbook publishing companies in an attempt to survey educators and publishers on the extent of female representation in history books. Although some responses pointed to a handful of famous women like Martha Washington and Betsy Ross who had found their way into the schoolbooks, most replied that they had never considered the problem at all. Steinem attributed this lack of recognition to the "masculine point of view which has dominated civilization," and vehemently protested against the impression conveyed by textbooks "that this world has been made by men and for men."[27]

Steinem's findings, coupled with a growing frustration with "the masculine point of view" as it related to suffragism, led NAWSA officials to take their message directly into the schools in 1910. One plan of attack was to hold suffrage debates in classrooms across America. The association initially furnished a packet of debate material at a modest price, including citations for both pro- and antisuffrage works, but by 1912 debaters could turn to the latest volume in the Debaters Handbook Series, *Selected Articles on Woman Suffrage.*[28] School debates offered an opportunity to educate the young on the role of women in history, as well as attracting free publicity for the movement. As one suffragist pointed out, "get the young people involved and you [also] catch mothers!"[29] The injection of women's history or woman suffrage into the schools, while applauded by suffrage advocates, outraged antisuffragists. "The woman suffrage question has no place in the schools," one antisuffrage press release maintained, and it went on to insist that as long as parents were divided on the issue, school boards should refrain from tampering with textbooks.[30]

Suffragists' efforts to place women's history, and particularly suffrage history, in classrooms and public libraries reflect NAWSA's belief in the importance of suffrage recruitment. On the one hand, suffragists' enthusiasm for women's history could be interpreted as the natural desire for the self-gratification and glory that a heroic history can bestow upon its participants. Legendary feats and heroine worship can help to sustain an organization in the face of adversity, and so it was with the suffrage movement. But beyond its capacity to distract and stabilize a troubled membership, suffragists used the idea of women's history to provide justification for their cause while simultaneously shaping that history to fit the needs of their movement. In a sense, the suffragists created a "great woman" history to parallel the contemporary historical works that excluded them. And throughout that history runs the recurrent theme of the steady evolution of women toward an egalitarian, if distant, utopia.

Advocates of suffrage did not question the belief that women were subject to the forces of evolution and were making progress throughout the ages. This sense of progress marked the rhetoric of suffrage orators like Anna Howard Shaw, who made repeated references in her speeches to the gains women had won through decades of sacrifice. "The real reformer," Shaw told one audience, "does not judge of the reform from the day or of an hour, but traces its progress from the beginning, and no human being with the eye of faith can fail to see traversing the whole progress of our movement a divinity shaping our ends . . . and that divinity is the gospel of democracy."[31]

Others, like writer Ida Husted Harper, drew on the theory of female evolution in widely circulated articles and pamphlets. In a *North American Review* article, Harper traced the history of the franchise in America and pointed out that religious, property, educational, and racial qualifications had all been abandoned for male Americans. She then cited the changing status of women from colonial times to the twentieth century that had resulted from hard-won legal reforms and educational advancements. Harper found the most conclusive evidence of progress in the area of education: in 1902, for example, there were more girls than boys enrolled in high, normal, and manual-training schools, and over a third of all college students were female. Moreover, of the total number of college degrees conferred in 1902, almost half went to female graduates. Coupled with statistics on the dramatic rise in the number of women entering the professions, Harper's findings documented the evolution of American women to an audience eager to believe in progress.[32]

From an unenlightened past into a clear, well-lighted future, the women of an unwritten history were made to march, and their suffragist creators made the most of their progress. "Women [of the past] lived in a twilight life, a half-life apart, and looked out and saw men as shadows walking," wrote M. Carey Thomas, president of Bryn Mawr College and an ardent suffragist. "Now women have won the right to higher education and to economic independence. The right to become citizens of the State is the next and inevitable consequence of education and work outside the home. We have gone so far; we must go farther. We cannot go back."[33] If evolution of women and the inevitability of their progress provided the philosophical foundation of early women's history, accounts of educational, legal, and professional advances served as testimonials to the doctrine of female progress. Women's history as seen by suffragists was comprised of a factual body shaped by an ideologically informed philosophy or, in other words, a content and meaning that were intricately entwined and mutually supportive.

History of this sort was important to the suffrage movement in several ways. First, NAWSA leaders drew from women's, particularly suffrage, history a tradition of leadership handed down from pioneer suffragists and women's rights activists, canonized in *The History of Woman Suffrage* and hagiographic accounts of the movement's early workers, and imbued with the legacy of a century of heroic struggle. As the lineal successors of Anthony, Stanton, and Stone, twentieth-century leaders found legitimation for their position through the celebration of and association with what might be called the "founding mothers" of their organization. Their interpretation of the suffrage pioneers, however, was strangely reticent about some of their predecessors' more controversial actions.

Retaining the philosophy of female progress and the legend of heroism and self-sacrifice, NAWSA leaders presented to their constituents a sanitized version of the past that robbed the pioneers of much of their color, complexity, and principles. Such issues as divorce reform, racial equality, and feminist religious reinterpretations were quietly dropped from the suffrage liturgy in an effort to pasteurize the pioneer experience. Most notable in this reinterpreted history was the disappearance from the suffrage canon of none other than Elizabeth Cady Stanton, one of the founders of the Seneca Falls Convention and, with Anthony, a dynamic force in the nineteenth-century suffrage crusade. Although both women worked together for decades and shared many of the same ideas and goals for the movement, Anthony's vision of the cause was more pragmatic and in some ways more limited than that of Stanton. For Anthony, the primary goal of the suffrage crusade was unity with other women's groups to form a broad-based constituency for the vote for women. As time passed, Anthony became convinced that rather than addressing working women's issues in order to bring them into the suffrage fold, it was easier to recruit elite women to the cause. Moreover, elite advocacy of suffrage would provoke less hostility among the public and the press.

Stanton shared Anthony's vision of unity but envisioned the movement as an open platform for any issue that concerned women. Rather than narrowing the focus of the movement to elites, Stanton urged suffragists to "stir up a whole group of new victims from time to time, by turning our guns on new strongholds."[34] True to her word, she had over the years endorsed a variety of reforms considered radical for the time. Divorce reform, dress reform, separation of church and state, all were subjects for her pen; her writings and speeches constantly put forward the notion that once women had the vote, they would use their ballots to enact an explicit political agenda including these and other reforms. Stanton's radicalism can best be seen in her belief that all movements for freedom were linked inextricably, and that suffrage was part and parcel of that radical tradition. In her concluding remarks to the 1890 NAWSA convention, she characteristically linked a wide variety of movements for liberation worldwide: "It is justice, and that alone that can end the impossible conflict between freedom and slavery going on in every nation on the globe. That is all the Nihilists, the socialists, the Communists ask, and that is all Ireland asks, and the Freedmen and women of this Republic ask no more."[35]

Stanton's radicalism, however, was on a collision course with NAWSA's growing conservatism. After completing her term as the president of NAWSA in 1892, she published *The Woman's Bible* (1895), a feminist interpretation of the Old Testament. Most suffragists wanted no part of the controversy that swirled around its publication. In defense of her lifelong friend, Anthony warned the convention that "you would better not begin resolving against individual action or you will find no limit. This year it is Mrs. Stanton; next year it may be I or one of yourselves who will be the victim. If we do not inspire in women a broad and catholic spirit, they will fail, when enfranchised, to constitute that power for better government which we have always claimed for them."[36] After a lengthy debate, the 1896 NAWSA convention resolved to disavow *The Woman's Bible,* despite Anthony's objections. This rankling rejection began the process of erasing Stanton from the official historical memory of NAWSA. By the time of her death in 1902, she was largely eclipsed in suffrage hagiography by the less-threatening image of her old friend Anthony. More important, NAWSA's disavowal of Stanton signaled the narrowing of the movement's goals and constituency that was to be a crucial component of the twentieth-century campaign for the vote.[37]

For the NAWSA rank and file, however, the reinterpreted suffrage tradition bridged the gap between the content and meaning of their history. The membership rolls contained the names of radical feminists, timid society women, socialists, moderates, and states' rights southerners; the old adage "politics makes strange bedfellows" was especially true of the suffrage movement at the turn of the century. Suffragist leaders used both genuine and reinterpreted traditions to bind this diverse constituency together and to create what may be called a movement psychology. Through ritual and pageantry, selected events and individuals were molded into a form of popular history that encapsulated both the pasteurized version of the past and a diluted dose of suffrage ideology.

Perhaps the most revered of all NAWSA traditions centered on the veneration of selected suffrage pioneers. Since the amalgamation of the two suffrage associations in 1890, a generous part of every convention was dedicated to the movement's early adherents. This celebration took several forms, including memorials for deceased workers, greetings from those too old or infirm to attend, and tributes from younger members who recognized the contributions of their predecessors. During her years as president, Susan B. Anthony often spoke of the pioneers' achievements, using the time between speakers to informally recognize members of the audience who had served the cause for years. Moreover, her stories of what one suffragist called "the cabbage and rotten-egg days" served to immerse converts in a kind of "living suffrage history," providing both role models and a heroic legacy to inspire the new recruits.[38] Formal recognition for the movement's early advocates was also included in convention programs in the form of "Evenings with the Pioneers," and in 1910, a "Decoration Day for Our Heroines" became a permanent suffrage tradition.[39]

A second and equally important suffrage tradition, although similar in some respects to that of the pioneers, was in fact the creation of twentieth-century suffragists. Beginning in 1906, NAWSA conventions regularly featured "College Evenings," events designed to appeal to the young, well-educated recruits who increasingly flocked to suffrage functions. Active recruitment of college women was the brainchild of Boston suffragists Maud Wood Park and Inez Haynes Gilmore. While students at Radcliffe College, Park and Gilmore had been initiated into the suffrage ranks by Alice Stone Blackwell, president of the Massachusetts Woman Suffrage Association (MWSA), and with Blackwell's encouragement, the two founded the Massachusetts College Equal Suffrage League in 1900.[40] Their efforts were so successful that at the NAWSA annual convention in 1906, delegates overwhelmingly voted to establish a national College Equal Suffrage League (CESL).

The delegates' enthusiasm for the new organization was in part a result of the first of many NAWSA College Evenings, held at the Lyric Theatre in Baltimore on February 8, 1906. Susan B. Anthony, M. Carey Thomas, and Mary E. Garrett had conceived the idea of such an evening in fall 1905 when Anthony, worried that the suffrage convention would not be well received in conservative Baltimore, urged her two coworkers to do what they could "to make [the convention] respectable."[41] The three women planned the event both to involve new workers in the convention program and to "illustrate distinctly the new type of womanhood — the College Woman" as an integral part of their movement. Together they incorporated the disparate yet vital elements of heroism, respectability, and progress into a suffrage tradition that symbolized the new membership, methods, and image of twentieth-century suffragism.

The president of the Johns Hopkins University presided over the 1906 College Evening, and area college women clad in cap and gown served as ushers for the event. With pioneer suffragists Clara Barton and Julia Ward Howe seated on the podium, an array of college presidents, professors, and deans spoke on the topic, "What has been accomplished for the higher education of women by Susan B. Anthony and other woman suffragists." One by one, the distinguished guests reminded the audience of the pioneers' achievements and lauded their efforts to open the doors of higher education for women. "We are indebted to [the pioneer women]," Vassar College historian Lucy M. Salmon told the audience, "for making it possible for us to spend our lives in fruitful work rather than in idle tears." Others singled out Susan B. Anthony for special praise. "The women of today," one speaker maintained, "may well feel that it is Miss Anthony who has made life possible for them."[42] By linking the advancement of women's education to the pioneers and, in particular, to pioneer suffragists, College Evening dignitaries firmly bound a new generation of women to the historical continuum of the movement. By presenting carefully selected early suffragists in a light that was clearly attractive to a college audience, the speakers attributed to them an inflated influence on developments in women's education, which were both respectable and popular with young college women.

In the years that followed the first College Evening, NAWSA leaders increasingly exploited this pioneer-college connection and in doing so further steered clear of the radicalism of the movement's origins. According to Maud Wood Park, the purpose of the College Equal Suffrage League was to help college women "realize their debt to the women who worked so hard for them, and to make them understand that one way to pay that debt is to fight the battle in the quarter of the field in which it is still to be won, to make them realize the obligation of opportunity."[43] The "debt to the pioneers" became a kind of suffrage slogan; it was even adopted as the title of a 1907 Boston program to honor longtime suffrage workers. In her concluding remarks at that event, Park listed the names of women's rights activists like Frances Wright, Margaret Fuller, Ernestine Rose, and the Grimké sisters and the dates they began their agitation, pointing out that many women's colleges were founded at the same time. "It seems to me," Park concluded, "that the so-called higher education, along with many other improvements in the standing of women, owes a heavy debt to the movement which advocated equal rights."[44] The debt to the pioneers resurfaced yearly at NAWSA conventions, as the College Evening took its place beside such regular traditions as pioneer memorials and the president's address.

A third and final suffrage tradition grew out of both College Evening and pioneer memorials and served as the touchstone of twentieth-century suffrage ideology, rhetoric, and ritual. The creation of this potent symbol occurred over a number of years, but it reached fruition in March 1906 with the death of Susan B. Anthony. As past president of NAWSA and a representative of pioneer activism, Anthony had attained celebrity status within the movement long before her death. The conventions were carefully scheduled to coincide with her birthday, and convention-goers could count on lavish celebrations, emotional speeches, and a personal word or two from the celebrity herself. In addition to her appearances at the annual conventions, Anthony had traveled extensively for years and was well known to suffragists throughout America, who increasingly viewed her as the living embodiment of their cause. Local fund-raisers often took the form of "Susan B. Anthony Day," and state suffrage convention badges and programs routinely bore her picture.[45] Such was her stature in the movement that during her later years she often witnessed her own apotheosis. In 1903, for example, while dining on bluefish and "diplomate pudding" with a Brooklyn, New York, suffrage league, she heard a series of speeches presented on the topic "Susan B. Anthony: Lessons and Inspirations from Her Life."[46]

Ida Husted Harper was in part responsible for Anthony's transformation from reviled fanatic to adored leader. Her two-volume biography of the reformer was published in 1898, and it provided readers with the day-to-day occurrences of her subject's life in almost Boswellian detail. A third volume, added after Anthony's death, extended the work to more than 1,600 pages and included excerpts from over a hundred highly favorable editorials on Anthony that appeared after her death. In addition to her work as a hagiographer, Harper proved to be unsurpassed as a nascent press agent. In keeping with NAWSA's new emphasis on respectability, she composed an article in 1903 for *Pearson's Magazine* entitled "Miss Anthony at Home" that portrayed the aging suffragist as "domestic in every fiber of her body."[47] With an eye to her prospective audience, Harper cloaked her subject in the rhetoric of domesticity with such feminine attributes as neatness, hospitality, self-sacrifice, patience, and loyalty. According to the article, Anthony sat down at the breakfast table looking "like a lovely grandmother," to a meal "strictly of the feminine order." Later she embarked upon a day of womanly pursuits that included cooking, cleaning, and sewing. "Miss Anthony," concluded the article, "never has suggested ways for repairing the damages of society with one-half the skill she employed in teaching her nieces her wonderful method of darning rents in garments and household linens."[48] Through her literary efforts, Harper helped to replace the stereotypical image of masculinized fanatic with a nonthreatening feminine heroine imbued with domestic virtues.

The sanctification of Susan B. Anthony was not completed until her death in 1906. At that year's convention, the aging reformer appeared before her devoted disciples for the last time. Her health gone, she exhorted the delegates in a faltering voice to continue in the great work begun at Seneca Falls and closed her remarks with the words, "Failure is impossible!" After the convention, she traveled to Washington to attend the annual congressional hearings but was too ill to leave her bed. Returning to her home in Rochester, New York, Anthony was attended by her niece and sister and, in her final hours, by Anna Howard Shaw. Profoundly shaken by the loss of her closest friend, Shaw would help to create the most enduring and vital of suffrage traditions: the suffrage saint.[49]

Like Harper, Anna Howard Shaw was uniquely fitted to the role of hagiographer. She met Anthony at a suffrage meeting in 1888, and a lifelong friendship had ensued. Shaw clearly worshipped the older woman. One of her favorite stories featured the seventy-year old Anthony, wrapped in a dressing gown and talking until dawn, "foreseeing everything, forgetting nothing, and sweeping me with her in her flight toward our common goal until I . . . experienced an almost dizzy sense of exhilaration."[50] Such was Shaw's devotion that in her 1915 autobiography, Anthony figures almost as prominently as does the author herself. As both president of NAWSA and an Anthony disciple, Shaw hurried to Rochester when word came that the end was near.[51] What followed would provide an important source of inspiration for the cult of personality that adopted Anthony as its patron saint.

Deathbed scenes were a popular literary device for turn-of-the-century novelists, and it is therefore not surprising that Shaw chose to record the scene she witnessed in both the periodical press and in her autobiography. Indeed, her vivid description of Anthony's pale visage and prophetic words lend credence to the expression "life imitates art." Two passages in particular express the motif Shaw sought to capture. On the last afternoon of her life, Anthony suddenly began to recite the names of the women who had worked for women's rights over the years. The women of this "final roll-call . . . seemed to file past her dying eyes that day in an endless, shadowy review," Shaw wrote. She quoted Anthony as saying "I know the sacrifices they have made, but it has all been worth while!" With this benediction, Anthony lapsed into silence for a time, but she rallied once more to assure Shaw that, after death, she would continue to be an active force in the woman suffrage movement. "Who knows?" she speculated, "Perhaps I may be able to do more for the Cause after I am gone than while I am here."[52]

In a sense she was right. Anthony's vision (or Shaw's invention?) of "the shadowy review," coupled with her prophecy of a kind of mystic activism beyond the grave, suggests a type of secular sanctification well known to readers of sentimental fiction of the period. The theme of suffrage saint was also conspicuous in a selection of poems written about Anthony and published after her death in volume 3 of Harper's biography. "She is not dead but more alive / than in her fairest earthly days," one poet proclaimed, while another pictured her "with eyes that looked beyond the gates of death" and crowned by a "halo of her venerable age."[53] Perhaps the most explicit example of sanctification was by John Russell Hayes, who poetically recorded Anthony's entry into a supernatural suffrage procession:

> And then my vision faded,
> And a lordly melody rolled
> As down celestial vistas
> The saintly company strolled.
> But the face of that latest comer
> I longest kept in sight —
> So ardent with consecration,
> So lit with angelic light
>
> .   .   .   .
>
> Crowned is she and sainted
> In heavenly halls above
> Who freely gave for her sisters
> A life of boundless love.[54]

On March 15, 1906, the suffrage saint was buried in Rochester, New York. The mayor of Rochester, the president of Rochester University, and other local dignitaries were present, in addition to suffrage and temperance leaders, aging abolitionists, college women, friends, and family members. Despite a heavy snowfall, an estimated crowd of ten thousand assembled outside the church, pressing against the doors and windows to hear Anna Howard Shaw's eulogy. Touching briefly on Anthony's "womanly attributes," she then described her subject's heroism and devotion to the cause. "There is no death for such as she," Shaw concluded, and she predicted that "the ages will come to revere her name."[55] When the church doors were opened at the close of the service, crowds of mourners streamed past the body. One mourner in particular caught the attention of some reporters: an elderly black woman, covered with snow and leaning heavily on a crutch, paused by the coffin and sobbed aloud into a frost-covered handkerchief. Other journalists chose to feature an aged black man, also limping, who took as a memento mori a single leaf from the funeral wreath. The heroic eulogies, patriotic rhetoric, and weeping black spectators reminded some witnesses of another fallen emancipator. Describing the long line of mourners who filed past the body, one observer called them "the plain people, the people Susan B. Anthony and Abraham Lincoln loved." After the long procession had passed, a female honor guard from the university escorted the coffin past houses draped in black to the grave site where Shaw delivered the final words.[56]

In the days that followed, friends worked to ensure a lasting memory for their patron saint. Rochester educators named an elementary school after her, a local church commissioned a stained glass window bearing her likeness, and women's clubs, temperance groups, and civic organizations honored her with memorials. Ida Husted Harper collected more than a thousand editorials that eulogized Anthony, including one from the antisuffrage *New York Times* lauding "the tender, womanly loveliness of the great reformer."[57] Suffragists across the nation held memorial services like the one that was conducted by the Kentucky Equal Rights Association (KERA) a week after Anthony's death. Mary Clay, a longtime suffragist and descendant of the Great Compromiser, presided over the service that took place in the Clay family home. In the center of the parlor draped in yellow satin and black crepe stood a large picture of Susan B. Anthony, flanked by a small candle in a pink candlestick, a souvenir from the suffrage leader's eightieth birthday celebration. On a nearby table was a smaller portrait of the reformer, surrounded by photographs of other pioneers like Lucy Stone and Isabelle Beecher Hooker. After a roll call of pioneer suffragists and a sketch of the reformer's work for women's rights, the assembly heard a series of elegies and a dramatic reading based on Anthony's final days. Following a rosary and benediction, the women sang "Nearer, My God, to Thee" and adjourned for refreshments.[58]

The nature of the Kentucky memorial service closely follows the form routinely employed by literary, church, or civic gatherings of women, but with a suffrage theme. Within this structure, songs, poems, and dramatic readings provided a thread of continuity between old forms and new meanings. The intimate atmosphere of the parlor meeting encouraged participation by women who would have shied away from speaking to a large, mixed audience. Overtones of religious ritual endowed the service with both familiarity and stately respectability in accord with the tastes of the times. The parlor decor approached ecclesiastical parody with its makeshift altar and display of icons. In addition, the service followed a quasiliturgical pattern, employing both poetic and prose readings and ending with the litany of the rosary and the benediction.

Kentucky suffragists also shaped the memorial service to suit the private agenda of their movement. Tradition played an important role: the veneration of the pioneers, the idea of a parallel women's history, and the philosophy of female progress were all incorporated into the ceremony. In her posthumous role, Susan B. Anthony became what no living woman could be: a universally shared symbol of the cause whose very name could conjure a constellation of images and sentiment. Across the nation clubwomen and suffragists met for similar services.[59] Within a decade Anthony had become, like Lincoln and Altgeld before her, part of the common mental property of Progressive Era Americans. Her picture was hung beside those of the Founding Fathers in schoolrooms across America, her memory achieving a measure of the vague immortality accorded to the heroes of American democracy.[60] In 1917, for example, Eugene V. Debs characterized her as "synonymous with the cause of human freedom and equal rights, . . . a moral heroine, an apostle of progress, a herald of the coming day."[61]

Mary Clay's memorial service, with its quaint sentimentality and solemn naivete summons up a lost world of women, conceived within the pages of popular fiction of the period, adorned with the trappings of Victorian respectability, and bound by parlor walls. Although trivial when compared to the larger course of world affairs, it reminds us that political participation for women at the turn of the century was not accomplished merely by the conversion of Congress or the ratification of an amendment. Instead, women entered the political arena through a lengthy process that included such seemingly apolitical institutions as historical biography, sentimental fiction, and parlor meetings, as well as the more familiar processes of state referenda campaigns, lobbyist activity, and direct political coercion. It would be unjust to downplay the early efforts at women's political organization. Given the high degree of female participation in Progressive Era movements like temperance, child labor reform, and civic betterment crusades, the timid parlor meetings of the first decade of the twentieth century should be seen as the training ground for many progressive activists.

Thus by 1910 the visionary cause of the pioneers had been transformed into an eminently safe program for middle-class club meetings. This stage of development, which first brought a wealthy and respectable class of women into comfortable participation in suffrage, was seen by NAWSA leaders as a necessary precondition of the movement that would eventually win the vote. For better or worse, these middle-class leaders could not conceive of conducting a successful campaign without the approval and the financial support of the social elite. As tangible proof of the wisdom of their strategy, leaders of NAWSA could point to a dramatic increase in support for their reform. Membership rolls soared from about 12,000 in 1906, the year of Anthony's death, to more than 117,000 in 1910. After 1910, a wide-scale organizational scheme was put into effect, and a corps of dedicated organizers largely drawn from the ranks of college-educated women was active throughout the country. Moreover, by 1914 a professional lobby was at work to push the federal amendment through Congress. This expanded effort was fueled by an ample treasury; in 1916, NAWSA's operational budget stood at $100,000 annually. The suffrage political strategy, based on the precondition of a respectable image, had paid high dividends and was the foundation of their victory in 1920.

In a few years' time, NAWSA leaders had built a solid political base for suffrage by attracting into the movement large numbers of women who previously were uninvolved in politics. They had accomplished this by giving a political meaning to traditional forms of female assembly, organization, and entertainment. For the women involved, the familiar surroundings and rituals legitimized and demystified the alien world of political action. Antisuffrage propaganda and the unflattering stereotype of nineteenth-century suffragists had hammered home the proposition that femininity and politics could never mix. In the first decade of the new century, however, a generation of women drew a different message from what they soon would call the "suffrage ideal." Women who had always been excluded from political participation were drawn, not to party affiliations, bosses, and smoke-filled rooms, but rather to a new kind of political activity: active membership in a reform or single-interest pressure group. Scholars who lament the decline of popular political participation in the Progressive Era fail to take into account this shift from party affiliation to interest group loyalty. In fact, movements like suffrage, temperance, civic reform, and other progressive causes involved and included vast numbers of people who had had no part in the political process during the heyday of the parties yet were involved in a popular politics of their own making.

In the first decade of the twentieth century, suffrage leaders set out to create a new image for their movement. Their basic goal was to forge a notion of women's history and female progress that could be accepted as consonant with the wider aspirations of mainstream society. In a sense they banished the radical past, turned their back on nonconformity, and in the process captured the support of quietly influential groups of women. Gone was the taint of extremism that had haunted the movement for decades; the parlor meeting had adopted "Aunt Susan" as its patron saint, and suffragism had come of age.

4

Building a Constituency

"Ye might as well face it," Mr. Dooley remarked to Mr. Hennessey in a 1909 *American Magazine* article. "It's sure to come now that I see be th' papers that female suffrage has been took up be the ladies in our best s'ciety." Building on his theme, F. P. Dunne's comic creation continued: "The first iv them lady suffragists had a hard time iv it, . . . an' they were took up in th' streets be polismen f'r pretindin' to look like gintlemen. Now, by hivens, tis' diff'rent. I pick up th' pa-apers an' read: 'Great sufferage revival. Society queens take up th' cause. In th' magnificent L. Quince dhrawin' rooms iv Mrs. Percy Lumley's mansion in Mitchigan avnoo yesterdah afternoon wan iv th' most successful sufferage teas iv th' season was held.' "[1] Mr. Dooley was not the only observer to note the change that had taken place in the woman suffrage movement during the first decade of the new century. The *New York Tribune,* describing a suffrage delegation to the New York State Assembly, reported that "it was no deputation of short-haired, short-skirted, masculine femininity — there were wives of men of large importance in the community, bankers, merchants, and lawyers, . . . there were women of the best lineage whose influence is in most circumstances exerted only for the good."[2] Even the confirmed antisuffragist Lyman Abbott admitted that "the old resistance to the [suffrage] movement has disappeared; the old arguments against it are forgotten, or like some ancient hieroglyphs, are regarded only as curiosities in literature."[3]

Suffragists themselves noticed the change. "Four years ago the public did not concern itself about woman suffrage," wrote Anna Howard Shaw. "Today . . . we overhear it in railway trains above the din of driving wheels; it is pounded in to your ears in street cars and jolting omnibuses; it is presented in the drama, and, as if that were not sufficient, it is discussed between the acts."[4] Writing to her friend Maud Wood Park, College Equal Suffrage League co-founder Inez Haynes Gilmore Irwin also tried to depict the new spirit that had invigorated the movement: "[The suffrage movement] is actually fashionable now. The lectures on suffrage, the benefits for suffrage, the articles about suffrage, . . . are actually uncountable. It's lovely! . . . Altogether, dear Maud, the movement which when we got into it had about as much energy as a dying kitten, is now a big, virile, threatening, wonderful thing. Oh, God, it's so good."[5] Park had been touring in Europe for two years and was unaware of the change that had taken place during her absence. Another friend wrote to urge her to return to the States and rejoin the campaign: "Your letter shows me that you do not realize the change in public sentiment here. . . . We are in a current that is a great deal bigger than we are."[6]

The current that had swept up the suffragists and their cause was to some extent a part of the Progressive tide that had caught America in its swell. But the suffragists' efforts to win respect for their reform was the ultimate reason for the movement's new look. So diligent had the activists been in their endeavors that some advocates began to chafe under the new, more feminine image. "I had to laugh at your 'Mother, Home and Heaven' remark," one suffragist responded to another's complaint about the movement's emphasis on respectability, "but if that's what some people need, of course we'll have to work it."[7] But while most suffrage clubs continued to follow the society plan, a few innovative workers turned to a new field of endeavor, pioneered by NAWSA past-president Carrie Catt.

Catt had been responsible for the implementation of the society plan, but she had considered it to be the first stage of a three-pronged strategy. After respectability brought both prominent members and financial backing to the cause, the crusade would enter a second and crucial stage, dependent on a sound political strategy. So while the society plan was left to do its work, Catt tackled the problem of tactics. Drawing on her experience as a suffrage organizer, she recalled the precinct organization that she and coworker Mary Garrett Hay had put into effect in California and Idaho in the 1890s.[8] Precinct organization had also been used by the New Orleans ERA Club at the turn of the century, when its members took up municipal reform work. Although precinct organization had been temporarily effective, no permanent structure remained from these earlier efforts. Catt also remembered the bitterly contested suffrage referendum held in New Hampshire in March 1903. Suffrage went down in defeat, and Catt and other suffragists were told by party politicians that elections in that state "had to be paid for." The politicians' words left their mark; as one of her close friends later recalled, Catt then realized that "you could not beat machines which had money to spend except by building a better machine."[9]

Catt's idea of a better machine was closely modeled on the urban political machines that were under constant attack by Progressive reformers. In 1908, after careful study of New York's powerful Tammany Hall, Catt, Hay, and several coworkers made plans for an ambitious new scheme for the suffrage movement in New York City, a system that was later expanded to include the entire state. First, the women appointed a chairman for each of the state's twenty-two senatorial districts, who in turn selected a chairman for each assembly district. These senatorial and assembly district chairmen would conduct personal interviews with each senator and assemblyman in their district, both before and after elections. The following year, each assembly district chairman would hold a districtwide convention, elect a permanent chairman, and appoint delegates to a city suffrage convention. According to plan, on October 29, 1909, 804 delegates and 200 alternates representing every assembly district in Greater New York gathered in Carnegie Hall. The delegates demanded the submission to a popular vote of a woman suffrage amendment to the New York State Constitution and endorsed the federal suffrage amendment.[10] In addition, the convention overwhelmingly supported the creation of a new, permanent local association built on district and precinct organization.[11]

All but one of the suffrage associations in New York had taken part in the Carnegie Hall convention, and after that gathering had adjourned, the associations assembled to select a name for their new organization. Because the structure was closely modeled on the political parties, and because the work was to be conducted along political lines, the suffragists chose the name Woman Suffrage Party (WSP).[12] The WSP leaders embarked on a large-scale program of organization in early January 1910. At the top of the complex WSP hierarchy stood the City Committee, made up of elected chairmen from each of the city's five boroughs. Next, each assembly district was headed by a leader, who in turn appointed an election district captain for each precinct. District WSP clubs were also created, with the captains and district leaders in charge.[13] Altogether, the plan called for sixty-three district leaders and two thousand election captains. "This plan of work is that which men have evolved after a century of political experience," Catt explained, "It is a vain hope that an idea so radical as woman suffrage can be adopted . . . by any plan less thoroughgoing."[14]

Catt's dream of a Woman Suffrage Party first came to fruition in New York City. By fall 1910, workers had opened a four-room headquarters, held four hundred public meetings, and enrolled almost twenty thousand members. In addition, the WSP had distributed more than one hundred and fifty thousand leaflets in English, as well as circularizing the Yiddish, Italian, and Bohemian quarters of the city with translated suffrage propaganda. The suffragists also circularized the delegates of 269 local political conventions and sent suffrage delegations to Albany from each assembly district in the city.[15] After a year of precinct organization and canvassing, the Woman Suffrage Party of New York City was incorporated in December 1910. "It requires much labor and pain to bring forth a *party,*" Catt exclaimed to Mary Gray Peck, "but *she* has come, been christened, wrapped in her 'swaddling clothes' and is getting an endowment for her education and training. . . . I think she may live and make trouble for the anti-suffrage sinners!"[16]

Despite such reassuring sentiments, many suffrage advocates were alarmed by what they believed to be a break with the nonpartisan position the national organization had traditionally embraced. In particular, Anna Howard Shaw, president of NAWSA, protested against the new organization's name and the titles given to precinct and district leaders.[17] Shaw probably viewed the new party as a rival to NAWSA, and with some justification. Yet in spite of her friends' urgings to go national with the newly formed party, Catt steadfastly resisted the temptation to compete openly with the national association.[18] Instead, she preferred to publicize the WSP as a *method* of organization rather than an organization in its own right.

Catt and other WSP supporters continued to show allegiance to NAWSA, although they clearly believed that the time was ripe for tactical innovation. How far to carry that innovation was a constant worry. Even Carrie Catt wondered whether it were "possible for a 'machine' to remain operative which has no 'bosses,' no graft, no personal rewards to offer, and whose sole motor power is self-sacrificing, conscientious service to a noble cause?"[19] To downplay the partisan overtones of precinct organization and to lessen the rivalry between the fledgling WSP and the parent organization, the Woman Suffrage Party incorporated a second innovative idea, the brainchild of Chicago suffragist Frances Squires Potter. Professor Potter described her idea, called the *political settlement,* at the NAWSA convention in 1909: "This settlement shall be a centre whose workers are directly interested in non-partisan local politics. It shall be a center of education for those who have been to college and those who have not. Together the workers shall know every voter and his wife, mapping out the wards of the city among them. . . . If we have influence we should be making it felt in an organized manner; and as soon as we get the vote . . . we will be in a position to make it count."[20]

Potter thus managed to confirm the nonpartisan policy of the national association through the vehicle of the political settlement while holding out the promise of future partisan activity once the vote was won. In this sense the Woman Suffrage Party in 1910 was symptomatic of several unresolved contradictions within the suffrage movement. On the one hand, its leaders were building a suffrage machine modeled on political party organization, but on the other, the membership resisted using the machine to enter the arena of partisan combat. Eventually the very existence of the machine would dictate that it be used, when events ran ahead of the scruples of members. As the movement entered the second decade of the twentieth century, a gradual transition from traditional educational efforts toward greater political activism was underway.[21]

Potter's idea of a political settlement was an adaptation of two Progressive Era institutions: the social settlement work of Jane Addams and others, and the so-called department principle evolved by the WCTU and the General Federation of Women's Clubs. Woman Suffrage Party workers planned to found political settlements in each precinct, from which the political activities of the community would radiate. The settlement would be established in a storefront or office, and activists operating from this headquarters would attempt to "awaken, educate, and mobilize workers" through a suffrage school, complete with classes, study groups and "laboratory training" run by NAWSA organizers. Suffrage schools served a dual purpose: to educate the public on the issue of woman suffrage and to train suffrage organizers in public speaking, organizational procedures, and rhetorical style.[22] In addition to the suffrage schools, the political settlement would work to establish and coordinate a series of suffrage departments, to be formed in political, industrial, and social reform organizations. As one activist put it, "The political settlement has a hospitable roof, and invites suffragists of all beliefs to form suffrage groups and become members of the suffrage family."[23]

In point of fact, "suffragists of all beliefs" were hardly welcomed into the "suffrage family." At the very time Catt was establishing the Woman Suffrage Party political settlements, Socialists were gaining strength nationwide and particularly in New York City. As nearly all Socialists were in favor of woman suffrage, they might have formed a natural constituency for suffrage recruitment. Instead, the organization paid little attention to Socialist women, despite their obvious interest in the issue. The national association housed a diverse collection of women of varying political persuasions and, at least in theory, from different classes. Its strategy, however, was to downplay these divisions whenever possible. With heavy recruitment within the wealthy class during the first decade of the twentieth century, this became more and more difficult. The gilt-chair movement, for example, was suspicious of the Socialists' concern for the immigrants and working class, while Socialists found the elitism of NAWSA's society plan repellent. A few Socialist women were members of NAWSA, but little effort was made by either the national organization or the New York City Woman Suffrage Party to tap this strong source of support.[24]

Antisuffragists quickly realized the suffragists' dilemma, and they exploited any suffrage-Socialist connection, not only to damage the suffragists' credibility in the eyes of the elite, but also to widen the existing class tensions between radical and working women and the suffrage movement. For example, the New York State Association Opposed to Woman Suffrage (NYSAOWS) issued two fliers entitled "Woman's Suffrage the Vanguard of Socialism," and "The Red Behind the Yellow: Socialists Working for Suffrage." Although produced in New York where the Socialist movement was perhaps strongest, these fliers were distributed nationwide. This suggests that the merest hint of a suffrage-Socialist alliance had the power to excite opposition to woman suffrage, even in such states as Virginia where little possibility of such a fusion existed. Within the suffrage camp, the fear of bad publicity through association with Socialism often led NAWSA leaders to steer clear of what they deemed to be the radical fringe.[25]

The Woman Suffrage Party of New York City was also increasingly indifferent toward the immigrant and working women of the city. Although it founded an Industrial Section, technically to recruit these groups, the party relied heavily on the Women's Trade Union League (WTUL) to carry the suffrage message to the working class. Run by a coalition of working women and women of wealth called "Allies," the WTUL took up the task of organizing for suffrage among the immigrant, the poor, and the laboring women of New York City. Although originally the WTUL's main goal had been unionization of women workers, by the early teens suffrage grew to be a prominent issue for the group, and in the 1915 New York referendum campaign, it was given total responsibility for the WSP's Industrial Section.[26]

Thus the majority of women in the city remained outside the suffrage family envisioned by Frances Potter when she conceived of the WSP political settlement idea. Although paying lip service to the need for working-class participation, the WSP was in fact eager to divest itself of the chore of organizing women outside the social and economic elite. In a pamphlet entitled "Organizing to Win by the Political District Plan," WSP leader Harriet Laidlaw addressed the labor issue indirectly. After stating that the WSP "will naturally be in close sympathy with the Woman's Trade Union League," she suggested that suffragists show their support for working women by participating in the Labor Day parade and once-a-year mass labor meeting. Laidlaw then cautioned suffragists not to become distracted from suffrage by the urge to reform conditions they might witness while canvassing the political districts. "No single-minded suffragists," Laidlaw warned, "will be diverted by the individual instance, by even the most crying social defect."[27] These class assumptions, attitudes, and divisions seen in the New York City's WSP were duplicated in other states as the WSP method of organization, as well as Laidlaw's pamphlet, were adopted by NAWSA affiliates nationwide.

The Woman Suffrage Party symbolized the suffrage crusade at the crossroads. In its first years of existence, the organizational plan claimed to be mobilizing all women for suffrage while simultaneously holding Socialist, immigrant, and working women at arm's length. Moreover, its emphasis on nonpartisanship continued to coexist with the unspoken promise of future political action when the suffrage machine was put to use. The WSP of New York City, for instance, embraced both perspectives in a series of talks presented at its 1911 "School for Suffrage Workers." On the agenda were such educational and nonthreatening subjects as "Women's Place in American Education" and "Women Social Workers," side by side with lectures on the history and ideals of the Democratic, Republican, Progressive, and Prohibition parties. (Significantly, the Socialist Party was not included.)[28] Together with courses on fund-raising, press work, and organizational strategy, the political education activists received was tantamount to a crash course in practical politics, despite the WSP leaders' protestations to the contrary.

Longtime activists were gratified by the publicity the suffrage school attracted, as well as by the growing numbers of trained organizers who emerged from the New York classes and others like them in Massachusetts, Illinois, Ohio, Wisconsin, and Pennsylvania.[29] Organizers typically enrolled for the entire course of study for a nominal fee, although some suffragists attended single sessions at a reduced price.[30] The majority of women who attended the sessions were middle and upper class; as classes were usually held during the daytime, most working-class women could not attend.[31] Often the instructors were prominent politicians and community leaders. At a suffrage school held in 1914 in Madison, Wisconsin, organizers could attend classes taught by a variety of distinguished individuals, including sociologist E. A. Ross and novelist Zona Gale. In addition to courses on political organization, the Madison school offered a wide range of classes on women's history, the legal status of women, and the economic aspects of the woman's movement.[32]

To be effective in the field, the suffrage organizer needed to speak persuasively. Therefore, suffrage schools devoted much time and effort to elocution, debating, and oratory. These schools sought to discover women who had an "organizer temperament" with cheerfulness, optimism, and common sense. "Don't try to force your own opinion," cautioned WSP lecturer Mary Garrett

Hay, "you are teaching people to give!"[33] In practice, the schools attempted to train forceful speakers skilled in persuasion and argumentation. One school separated trainees into two groups, called the "agitators" and the "educators." Agitators were instructed to appeal to the emotions, while the second group was drilled in a more didactic style. Instructors reasoned that the educators could "reach a class the agitator could not get and fail utterly with the class the agitator can reach."[34] At another school, Anna Howard Shaw's seminar on "The Psychology of an Audience" prepared organizers to deal effectively with hostile, indifferent, and friendly audiences, while professional speakers and actresses coached pupils in voice culture and public speaking.[35] Many organizers doubtless followed the "brief," or outline, of a suffrage speech included in the woman suffrage volume of *Debaters Handbook*, embellished with some of the mannerisms and methods of professional public speakers.[36]

With training in both practical politics and public speaking, the organizers who were graduated from the WSP suffrage schools became the foundation of Catt's ambitious scheme to revitalize the movement. In spite of the identical training offered to all who enrolled, two distinct types of organizers emerged from the schools. For some, organizing was to be full-time paid employment. These professional organizers were often young single women employed by NAWSA or the WSP for a period of time that could extend from a few months to a year-long contract, for which they could expect to earn from one to two thousand dollars annually.[37] Some were sent to unorganized regions to work as troubleshooters or propagandists for the cause, while others were "loaned" to established clubs to work as executive secretaries or organizational specialists.

For other suffragists, organizing was a voluntary and often part-time occupation. Part-time workers were rarely paid a salary, although they sometimes received money for travel-related expenses.[38] More often than not, these organizers had familial obligations that prevented extensive travel, and therefore they confined their suffrage work to short trips.[39] College Equal Suffrage League members also served as volunteer organizers, working during college vacations and summer holidays. As one activist stated, "the chief service of the College League will prove to be a kindergarten for training workers for the regular association." After graduation, some CESL members took positions as professional activists, while others continued on a part-time basis.[40] Whereas the professional organizer might be sent thousands of miles from home to organize for suffrage, the volunteer worker would often make a day trip to a nearby town to hold a series of meetings and social gatherings. With the professional organizers, the volunteer workers provided the "motor" for Catt's suffrage machine and were largely responsible for the growth of the movement that occurred nationwide after 1910.[41]

Both professional and volunteer organizers engaged in a wide variety of activities. At the most basic level, their work was divided into two fields of endeavor: generating new converts and managing state suffrage referenda campaigns.[42] The leaders of NAWSA, regardless of their attitudes toward non-partisanship, shared the desire for a mass membership and recognized the WSP as a means to this goal. Moreover, they believed that once a large constituency had been amassed, suffrage victories at the state level would follow. In this sense, the organizers were to play a critical role in both short-term and long-term goals by wooing new members to the movement and by steering suffrage referenda through state legislatures with the help of the new constituency.

Organizers tackled the problem of attracting new suffragists in a variety of ways. One of the most common methods was the so-called flying squadron.[43] The flying squadron was usually composed of two suffrage organizers who traveled together through a designated region to form new organizations and revitalize weak or inactive clubs. In an unorganized area, the organizers first contacted prominent clubwomen, ministers, and local reform activists to ascertain the level of prosuffrage sentiment present. If their contacts proved amenable, the organizers would call a meeting in the town hall or other prominent place and publicize the affair in the area newspaper. Posters, fliers, and lapel buttons were distributed as the organizers made a series of informal speeches heralding the event. At the organizational meeting, the flying squadron supervised the election of officers, reported on state and national suffrage plans, and if all went according to plan, left behind a group of confirmed, enthusiastic converts to the suffrage cause.[44]

Occasionally, however, the flying squadron faced less receptive audiences. One organizer discovered, much to her dismay, that her distinguished contact in Helena, Arkansas, was a leading antisuffragist, and she promptly abandoned her efforts to organize the town.[45] Other activists found little or no interest in their crusade in a given area. As flying squadron leader Zara Dupont recalled, "Many a time we stood up [to speak] with not a human being in sight, and we would get up on a box or a bench if it were in the park and start at the top of our lungs and gradually people would come. . . . The small boys would come up and they would give the adults a little courage, and they would come a little nearer."[46] Massachusetts organizer Florence Luscomb encountered great difficulties with apathetic suffragists who refused to cooperate with her plans to revitalize club spirit. Luscomb described the club president in one small town as "a suffragist with the energy, enthusiasm and executive capacity of an oyster." Upon investigation, Luscomb learned that the ineffective president had been selected to head the local league solely because she was the wife of a prominent factory owner, and since assuming the presidency, she had not called a single meeting. Luscomb busied herself with the task of reestablishing the faltering league and managed to hold a series of meetings and social functions without the help of the club president.[47]

Another problem centered on maintaining enthusiasm for the cause after the organizers had left the area. Local suffragists were often inexperienced in club work and often allowed their league to languish without the dynamic presence of trained suffrage workers. To counter this tendency, activists often relied on traveling suffrage libraries to foster movement solidarity and local interest in votes for women. For example, one organizer for the Kentucky Equal Rights Association established a book-loan program that featured the multivolume *History of Woman Suffrage,* biographies of prominent suffragists, feminist novels, and suffrage tracts.[48] To supplement state lending libraries, NAWSA provided *Woman Suffrage: History, Arguments, Results,* a collection of essays on a variety of subjects pertaining to votes for women.[49] Many local clubs used the essays in suffrage study and discussion groups, a tactic some organizers recommended in order to ensure continued activity within a revitalized league.[50] Lending libraries and study groups thus served a valuable purpose: they provided a steady dose of suffrage ideology and helped to sustain new or revitalized clubs after the departure of the trained organizers.

In addition to founding new clubs and reestablishing weak leagues, organizers worked in areas that boasted flourishing suffrage organizations. In well-established associations, the task at hand was to increase the size of the existing organization by enrolling all households as suffrage advocates. The WSP leaders envisioned the suffrage plan of organization as a three-fold operation, with the first stage — individual effort — already complete. The second stage, the development of groups based on residence, was to be accomplished through the WSP's precinct organization and political settlement work. Finally, the third stage featured the enrollment of every adult on a domicile basis and was largely dependent on WSP organizers for its success.[51] To accomplish this final stage of organization, suffragists employed the services of both professional and volunteer organizers. The work included canvassing every adult within a given locality and enrolling the prosuffrage constituents. In Massachusetts, five organizers were employed by the Cambridge Political Equality Association (CPEA) to canvass one ward. These workers earned twelve dollars a week for about thirty hours of canvassing and follow-up calls. At each dwelling the suffrage worker surveyed the adult residents' opinions on woman suffrage and asked those in favor of the reform to sign cards indicating their support. Suffragists considered anything in excess of thirty signed suffrage cards a week per worker to be a successful canvass.[52]

Canvassing could be exhausting work, especially to those organizers who covered the tenement districts in northeastern cities like Boston or New York. One organizer described her canvassing efforts in East Boston tenements in 1915: "We left home very early every morning—at least at 8:30—and went over to our section with our voters' lists. We each had a precinct and went into every voter's home and talked to the wife and left suffrage literature and found out whether or not the woman herself believed in suffrage. We worked through until 9 or 9:30 in the evening. . . . For the first three days the calves of our legs just ached and it was slow going."[53] There were other obstacles in addition to physical exhaustion. Many organizers were well-to-do women who were unaccustomed to, or indeed unaware of, the poverty in Boston's immigrant wards. Ward Organization Committee Chairman Gertrude Halliday Leonard's report to the Massachusetts Woman Suffrage Association on the 1910 canvas of ward 8 offers testimony to the trepidation with which many organizers ventured into working-class districts: "It took some sense of duty, some sense of devotion to our cause, to push us through the first unguarded front door, up the dim and unattractive staircase, to knock at any one of the several noncommittal doors on the first shabby landing. Probably the woman who answered knew no English, and stared uncomprehendingly. No matter—you did as well as you could."[54] Leonard's revulsion at the immigrant tenements did not prevent her from welcoming the foreign-born into the suffrage fold—at least as nonactive members. Shortly after the canvass of ward 8 was completed, organizers staged a rally for the "greenhorns." After an evening of patriotic speeches and songs, suffragists collected more than two hundred suffrage cards, although no immigrant women were enlisted in active suffrage work.[55] The NAWSA organizers clearly drew a distinction between canvassing work in the tenements and their efforts to found suffrage clubs in middle- and upper-class communities. Suffragists spared no effort to enlist the active support and financial cooperation of elite women, whereas in the working-class and immigrant districts they often merely recorded the names of those favoring the reform. Some suffrage associations like the CPEA made careful distinctions between active, dues-paying suffragists and "associates," who simply signaled their support by signing suffrage cards. The CPEA, for example, could attest to only 537 "actives" in 1916, but it listed more than 4,000 associates on its membership rolls.[56]

Canvassing and enrollment helped to determine suffrage support within a given area and provided a growing number of nonactive converts to the votes for women cause. Like the Boston area suffragists, the president of the Kentucky Equal Rights Association reported a dramatic increase in the membership rolls after a statewide canvass and enrollment campaign. Canvassers recorded 4,665 members in November 1913, but by December of the next year, a total of 10,577 members had been enrolled. This association had the benefit of a professional organizer on loan from NAWSA to oversee the canvas and supervise the workers. In addition, five volunteer organizers worked during the summer to address ninety-four teachers' institutes and fifty citizens' meetings. By December 1914, Kentucky suffragists could boast more than ten thousand signed suffrage cards, forty-eight newly established leagues, and some type of organization in 119 of Kentucky's 120 counties.[57] The KERA membership totals could have soared higher, had its leaders sought to enroll black as well as white suffrage advocates. State president Madeline McDowell Breckenridge knew that suffrage sentiment was strong among black women in Kentucky but followed a policy of nonintervention regarding the recruitment of black suffragists. Like most southern suffragists, Breckenridge believed that the fight for the vote should be for whites only, although she defended the right of black women to the ballot after the battle was won.[58]

The canvass and enrollment procedure was but one facet of suffrage organizers' work. Another critical function played by the activists was that of conducting open-air or street meetings. Their goal was to reach the literal "man on the street," the unconverted citizen who would refuse to attend a suffrage meeting but who might be induced to listen to a suffrage speech on a street corner. Street meetings had the added advantages of being inexpensive and easily organized. A group of organizers would arrive at a busy corner in the early hours of the evening, climb up on a park bench or soap box, and begin to speak. In Boston, the Boston Equal Suffrage Association for Good Government (BESAGG) held street meetings in the foreign-born wards of the city during the summer of 1910. Speaking to crowds of immigrant men and women, organizers relied upon the services of interpreters who translated their speeches into Italian, Yiddish, Arabic, and other languages. While one organizer spoke to the crowd, others passed out brightly colored suffrage leaflets and accepted donations for the local club.[59]

Although open-air or street meetings became increasingly popular among suffrage organizations in the years after 1910, this form of propaganda initially caused some suffragists great anxiety. When the Pennsylvania Woman Suffrage Association (PWSA) embarked upon a series of open-air meetings in the summer of 1911, not all the organizers faced the task with equanimity, especially when the possibility of police interference was broached by Open-Air Committee Chairman Alice Paul. Paul and her close friend Lucy Burns had recently returned from England, where they had taken part in the militant suffrage campaign led by Emmeline Pankhurst. Paul and Burns planned to resist any attempt on the part of police to disrupt the suffragists' meeting, and they even designated an individual to post bail after the anticipated arrest.

Together with a young organizer named Caroline Katzenstein, the would-be militants hired a horse cart adorned with a yellow sateen "Votes for Women" banner and drove to a busy corner in Philadelphia. Katzenstein recalled the moment: "As we neared the corner selected for our meeting, I am frank to confess that I seemed to develop a sort of Jack and the Beanstalk complex, because the policeman on the beat near our corner seemed to grow taller and taller and bigger and bigger the closer we got to him. To me he seemed to be not just the arm of the law but the whole body of it!"[60] Despite Katzenstein's fears, the women conducted their meeting without interference. Lucy Burns closed the event with a rousing speech before a crowd of about three hundred, with the policeman reportedly listening attentively. By the summer's end, street meetings were an accepted part of Pennsylvania suffrage propaganda. When PWSA held its final open-air gathering in September 1911, eighteen speakers took turns speaking from five platforms to more than two thousand spectators.[61]

In addition to open-air meetings, suffragists attempted to win support for woman suffrage through a variety of publicity stunts. To celebrate the anniversary of the first woman's rights convention, organizer Florence Luscomb donned the dress of pioneer suffragist Lucy Stone and drove a carriage around the New England countryside, holding suffrage meetings along the way.[62] Parades were also popular with suffragists eager for publicity. Boston-area suffragists organized a modest Columbus Day parade in 1913 that featured several floats and numerous marchers.[63] Encouraged by the favorable response to the endeavor, organizers staged a larger event the following year. The 1914 parade boasted mounted parade marshals, marching bands, and elaborate floats. Rows of marchers clad in colorful costumes followed pioneer suffragists who waved handkerchiefs from open cars. Groups of professional women bore banners that announced their occupations: dentist, doctor, artist, farmer, minister, teacher.[64] One report estimated that at least a thousand men and women from Cambridge alone marched in the procession that wound up Beacon Hill. So congested was the parade route that one well-wisher had to be boosted above the heads of the crowd in order to spot his marching suffragist-wife.[65] Along with the thousands of suffrage advocates who watched the 1914 parade were a vocal contingent of antisuffragists. Antisuffragists responded to their opponents' publicity stunt with one of their own: they distributed one hundred thousand red roses — the official antisuffrage flower — to bystanders and claimed that those who donned their symbol outnumbered suffragists two to one. Parade marshals countered by ordering the marching bands to strike up "The Last Rose of Summer," while ushers and aides from Radcliffe and neighboring colleges passed out yellow "suffrage jonquils" to the crowds. This so-called war of the roses generated an unprecedented amount of newspaper coverage, and Boston organizers considered the 1914 parade to be a rousing success.[66]

Organizers eager for publicity occasionally embarked upon large-scale spectacles. Nashville suffragists staged a May Day fete in 1915 that called for a one-hundred-car procession, "aesthetic dances," and tableaux. Held at the city's Centennial Park, which featured a full-scale replica of the Parthenon, the tableaux included notable women from antiquity in addition to the twentieth-century embodiments of Motherhood, Nature, and Joan of Arc. The highlight of the festivities was the arrival of a statuesque matron representing Bodicea, who whirled up to the Parthenon in a chariot drawn by four white steeds.[67] The six thousand plus spectators reportedly watched with fascination as various "spirits" popped from behind the Parthenon's pillars to dance and sing; one observer was heard to remark that "the Greeks might have envied the entire scene."[68]

Suffrage organizers also sought to draw attention to their reform by emulating the publicity maneuvers used by political parties. Some clubs sold novelty items that were supplied by NAWSA for a small fee. Suffrage stationery, posters, calendars, seals, stamps, lapel buttons, and the like were hawked by ardent activists on street corners, at factory gates, and in city subways.[69] Others sold everything from suffrage dolls to peanut brittle at county fairs, Grange halls, and conventions. Organizers also appealed directly to other organizations for support. One worker created an elaborate card index for a three-state area, noting the agricultural societies, fair associations, trade unions, chambers of commerce, professional and scholarly groups in each county. Suffrage organizers used the index to circularize each association's membership and to recruit a well-heeled constituency.[70] The card index idea became, in time, a favored organizational tool of activists both on the state and local level and, by 1916, of those whose task it was to lobby Congress for the vote.

Organizers made sure that other reform, business, and professional groups received the suffrage message by arranging speaking engagements with a wide variety of organizations. The Massachusetts Woman Suffrage Association, for example, sent an organizer to speak before the Council of Jewish Women, the Nurses' Association, and other civic clubs and church groups.[71] Sometimes suffragists arranged for activists in other reform work to add a plea for the ballot to their speeches on such subjects as temperance, child labor, or international peace. Others, like Madeline McDowell Breckenridge, joined women's clubs and civic groups and lobbied for official endorsement of woman suffrage. Breckenridge was a longtime member of the Kentucky Federation of Women's Clubs, and in 1911 she chaired that group's Legislative Committee. She saw to it that suffrage speeches were delivered to a host of ancillary clubs and associations, distributed votes for women literature from the women's club booth at fairs and teachers' institutes, and sent out a leaflet on school suffrage to more than one hundred Kentucky newspapers.[72] Organizers thus reaped a double harvest: they received additional publicity for their issue while attaching it to the coattails of respected organizations active in other civic and reform work.

In a sense, organizers tapped a ready-made audience when they worked from within other women's organizations. Clubwomen and civic reformers were often predisposed to favor suffrage, and the organizers encountered little resistance, especially after the General Federation of Women's Clubs officially endorsed the cause in 1913. Associations with traditionally male membership rolls, however, were more resistant to suffrage propaganda. One tactic for recruiting males was first used in New York when Max Eastman founded the Men's League for Woman Suffrage. Eastman drew up a list of one hundred prominent men, enlisted their support, and then held an organizational meeting, at which the men joined the league with much pomp and circumstance. Eastman managed to extract the maximum publicity from the event and tied the issue of woman suffrage to such distinguished names as George Foster Peabody, John Dewey, and Oswald Garrison Villard.[73] Men's leagues proved successful in reaching the denizens of community chambers of commerce and fraternal organizations, and male suffrage clubs spread throughout the country.[74]

Trade unions were sometimes less tractable to NAWSA persuasion. In order to convert union workers, some state associations resorted to the use of male organizers. Connecticut suffragists hired Richard Kitchelt, a lithographer and union member, for twenty-five dollars a week to make suffrage speeches and canvasses. Kitchelt's duties were similar to those of his wife, who was also an organizer, but he was instructed to focus solely on trade union recruitment. Thanks to his efforts, 111 Connecticut unions ultimately passed suffrage resolutions, and the Connecticut Federation of Labor endorsed the federal amendment with only one dissenting vote.[75] Other clubs hired male organizers to canvass in immigrant neighborhoods, on the assumption that the so-called greenhorns would pay more attention to male workers.[76]

Female organizers also worked the trade union and immigrant circuits. Massachusetts Woman Suffrage Association organizer Florence Luscomb made a guest appearance before the workers of the Boston Rubber Shoe Company. With much trepidation, Luscomb spoke in a "dingy tobaccoey room" to about twenty-five workers: "Men are the funny things! There were all the sacred rites to be punctiliously observed, — being met by the Guardian of the Gate, ushered by the Grand Marshall up to the dais, ceremoniously presented to the High Muck-a-Muck — but it didn't occur to the dear creatures to let you lay aside your coat and hat in an ante-room, where you can pat up your hair into its pristine puffiness, or even, after you have undressed upon the platform to provide any place for you to put your hat and gloves. Then you get introduced with a flourish, but like or not the chairman hasn't informed himself what your name is or, as this afternoon, what is your subject." In spite of Luscomb's anxiety, the rubber boot workers presented her with a bouquet "as big around as a dishpan" and a standing ovation, and they told the startled suffragist that whenever she saw the hubmark of a rubber boot to think of them! Luscomb's triumph was complete when she assured the workers that they could smoke in her presence: "So they passed around cigars and every man lighted up with a sigh of relief. . . . And then one man said he'd like all the men present who believed in suffrage to stand up, and every blessed one of them stood."[77]

Luscomb's account points to the difficulties middle- and upper-class suffragists faced when speaking to a male working-class audience. In addition to class differences, organizers had to adapt to the rites and mannerisms of the male fraternal milieu. Whereas Luscomb's innate good humor proved infectious to the rubber boot workers, there is little doubt that less charismatic speakers could easily fail to win over similar audiences. And although NAWSA made some effort to organize both immigrant and trade union constituencies, these efforts varied widely according to locality and to the personal initiative of individual organizers. No official policy on the recruitment of these groups was ever handed down from the NAWSA Executive Board, nor were any special tactics developed to cope with organizing different ethnic groups. In an organization that, under Carrie Chapman Catt's leadership, made a speciality of bureaucratic micromanagement of every aspect of organizing, the lack of a specific policy on recruiting working men's and ethnic groups indicates the degree to which NAWSA concentrated its efforts on middle- and upper-class constituents.[78] What this meant in terms of the movement's ability to reach diverse class and ethnic audiences was that if an organizer like Florence Luscomb wanted to arrange meetings with boot workers and other industrial or immigrant groups, she was free to do so — but the association leadership did not particularly care if she spent her time in other venues.

While some organizers tackled street meetings, speaking engagements, and other publicity measures, other activists concentrated on the second primary objective of suffrage organization: the state referenda campaigns. By 1910, only five states had won woman suffrage, and of those, only three had achieved the reform by popular vote.[79] California was added to the list of full suffrage states when a referendum passed in 1911.[80] Encouraged by this victory, NAWSA strategists embarked on five referenda campaigns the following year in

Oregon, Kansas, Arizona, Ohio, and Wisconsin. Michigan was added to the list at the last moment, when the state legislature unexpectedly passed a suffrage amendment and scheduled it for the upcoming November election. Association President Anna Howard Shaw despaired over the untimely Michigan campaign because NAWSA funds had already been allocated to the approved five campaign states. The harried president offered a paltry two hundred dollars' worth of literature for Michigan suffragists and promised to try to raise money for the beleaguered workers, but she held out little hope of success.[81]

The organizers and state suffrage workers in Oregon, Kansas, and Arizona made good use of their time and resources and mounted successful publicity campaigns to bring the issue to the voters' attention. On election day, the three states reported narrow victories; in Kansas, suffragists celebrated their new status as voters by burning their old bonnets on a symbolic victory bonfire.[82] In the other campaign states there was little to celebrate. Suffrage was not the only issue before the voters in Ohio, Wisconsin, and Michigan, where it shared the ballot with the bane of the suffrage movement — prohibition. An active prohibition movement often spelled disaster for the cause of votes for women. Wets, believing that all suffragists favored temperance, opposed both reforms vehemently. With the addition of prohibition to the 1912 referenda, the chances of success for woman suffrage looked bleak. Wisconsin, for example, was second among the states in its output of malt liquor, and the brewing industry was an important part of its economy. Suffragists could expect a hard fight if the Pandora's box of prohibition were opened in 1912. Ohio also was a wet state with an active prohibitionist movement. In the 1912 referendum Ohioans would vote not only on woman suffrage but also on a liquor license amendment advocated by the temperance workers.[83] In Michigan, as well, the WCTU planned a heated campaign for reform, much to the disgust of NAWSA strategists. Learning of the prohibitionists' plans, Anna Howard Shaw exclaimed: "Now, if there could be anything worse than that, I don't really know what it is!"[84]

In spite of the NAWSA leaders' pessimism, organizers waged a vigorous campaign in Wisconsin and Ohio in the spring and summer of 1912. Suffragists were aided by an organizer on loan from the Boston Equal Suffrage Association for Good Government of Boston, Massachusetts. Traveling under the auspices of the College Equal Suffrage League, another organizer made thirty addresses to college audiences totaling more than seven thousand, and she also spoke to business meetings, union gatherings, and conferences. In early summer, BESAGG sent three additional activists to the region who led flying squadrons into unorganized parts of Ohio and also formed an Ohioan men's suffrage league.[85] Encouraged by the organizers' work, Ohio suffragist Harriet

Taylor Upton remarked, "There's nobody sliding down mail chutes or climbing out coal holes to get away from us—even the men who 'ain't jes' tellin' where they stand give us respectful hearings.' "[86]

The campaigns in Ohio and Wisconsin proceeded apace, but there were problems in Michigan from the outset. Before the campaign of 1912, Michigan suffragists lacked the tight organizational structure that strengthened suffrage societies in Ohio and Wisconsin. Little precinct work had been done, and many rural counties remained unorganized for suffrage. Moreover, the Michigan Equal Suffrage Association (MESA) did not have aggressive leadership and organizational expertise to mount a successful campaign. Symptomatic of the organizational woes that plagued MESA was the existence of not one but three "official" headquarters scattered across the state. To the disgust of NAWSA officials, MESA turned over the direction of the referendum campaign to a male minister. Suffragists outside the state feared that the presence of a male campaign director would be construed by antisuffragists as proof that women were not capable of organized political participation.[87]

Poor organization and bad strategic decisions took their toll, but perhaps the major obstacle was one of morale. "The difficulty in Michigan," Anna Howard Shaw explained, "is not with the attitude of the public toward this question but with the attitude of the suffragists toward it." She continued: "So far there has been a feeling that it was impossible to carry it, that the people were not ready for it and that it will happen some time in the future, and all that sort of thing. To go into a campaign with that kind of a spirit, presupposing defeat before we begin, if there is anything we should not do it is to fail to recognize the importance of a hopeful spirit toward the work."[88] Shaw went on to report that many prominent Michigan suffragists had refused to cancel their summer vacations, although the need for continuous organization and publicity was urgent.

Results of the referendum disappointed suffragists everywhere. In spite of thorough canvassing and good publicity in Ohio, the amendment lost by a margin of 87,456 votes. Organizers were gratified to learn that more Ohio votes had been cast in favor of suffrage than were cast on both sides when the amendment was passed in the 1911 California referendum. As the press chairman for Ohio stated, "Not a penny, not a day's work which has been done in Ohio in the past months, has been lost [because] . . . Ohio is today organized."[89] Prohibitionists had more reason to celebrate; the liquor license amendment passed by 84,536 votes. Ohio workers were firmly convinced that the temperance struggle and the ensuing publicity generated by the heated wet-dry debate cost Ohio women the vote. As one organizer reported, their attempt to avoid entangling alliances only led to greater difficulties: "We tried to keep out the liquor question. We might as well have tried to do our campaigning in aeroplanes! The liquor interests lined up with everybody who was against us, we shied off from everybody who was for us. We did not cooperate with the Socialists because it might antagonize the propertied class; we kept off the WCTU and the Anti-Saloon League because it might alienate our damp suffragists; we kept away from the Prohibitionists and Progressives so as not to give offense to our Democratic and Republican friends. In short, we were like Ishmael, a 'wild ass in the wilderness' by ourselves."[90] In Wisconsin and Michigan, too, woman suffrage amendments were defeated by the voters. The Wisconsin brewers allied with the antisuffragists to wage a campaign against both suffrage and prohibition, forecasting the economic ruin of the state if either reform passed. Some evidence of election fraud was discovered as well, and suffragists in Wisconsin saw months of hard work negated by a variety of unscrupulous maneuvers.[91]

The worst blow fell in Michigan. The first returns seemed to promise certain success, but the margin of victory slipped away. Defeat, however, was neither quick nor painless. Before nightfall, suffragists became convinced that fraud had been perpetrated; they received story after story of corruption. Suffrage ballots had been printed on separate slips of paper, to be handed out at the polls and initialed by election board members. Some ballots were printed incorrectly, while others, lacking election board initials, were ruled void. A common ploy was the failure to distribute the special suffrage ballots at all. In one ward, suffrage organizers reported that at least ninety votes were cast before a voter was even offered a woman suffrage ballot. As the Michigan votes were tallied, other irregularities quickly surfaced. In one county, eleven precincts failed to report their count, claiming their tally sheets had been lost. Ballots in another area were burned to prevent a recount, and in yet another, the ballots were removed from the polling place and then returned mysteriously two hours later.[92] One district reported vote totals in excess of registered voters. Moreover, suffragists were kept in suspense over the final outcome; thirteen precincts in the city of Detroit held back their tallies for a full month. After public outcry, including appeals by the governor for honest election returns, the Michigan woman suffrage amendment was defeated by a slim 760-vote margin.[93]

So close was the margin of defeat that MESA, with the approval of NAWSA leaders, elected to resubmit the amendment to the voters in a special referendum the following April. As the only campaign state in spring 1913, MESA expected and received the undivided attention of the national association. Unlike their previous half-hearted efforts at organization, MESA activists now set about their work with unmatched zeal. "Missionary teams" composed of an organizer, a speaker, and a financial expert were assigned to each congressional district. Each team scheduled house-to-house canvasses, undertook publicity stunts, and stationed poll watchers to guard against election fraud. In addition, MESA received the help of twelve NAWSA organizers for a total of twenty-nine weeks and distributed an abundance of printed matter donated by the national association. By election day, seventy-five of eighty-three Michigan counties had working suffrage committees or active leagues, and MESA workers joined activists nationwide in expecting success for their cause.[94]

It was not to be. The results of the 1913 Michigan referendum were a disaster, with the amendment losing by 96,144 votes. More disheartening was the fact that suffrage garnered 78,637 fewer votes than in 1912, while the number of opposing votes increased by only 16,747, despite a well-organized and financed antisuffrage campaign. Of these 16,747 excess opposition ballots cast, 13,000 were polled in counties where a prohibition contest was also being decided. This fact led most suffrage advocates to conclude once again that temperance and suffrage were not to be mixed.[95] Others saw the Michigan defeat as the work of a more ominous enemy than simply antisuffragists. One activist maintained that: "the Antis merely serve as a screen for the National Vice Trust to work behind. May God forgive them, they know not what they do. Perhaps sometimes some of these prosperous Antis may suffer enough in mind or body from the liquor traffic, the white slave traffic, the gambling interests, or the "black plague" to realize that these great evils never can be eliminated from society without the help of women's votes."[96] Other suffragists agreed. "We have a clear demonstration there of the Powers of Light against the Powers of Darkness," Carrie Chapman Catt wrote shortly after the April 1913 Michigan disaster. "The Darks won, but in the long run I say the Sun will drive them out."[97]

Anna Howard Shaw was less optimistic. Shaw, too, believed that the vice trust had conspired against the suffrage crusade in Michigan, but she recognized that antisuffragist propaganda and organizing efforts had taken their toll. Despondent, the NAWSA leader brooded to a friend: "We will never win another easy victory. The forces of evil are organized nationally. Never again can we carry on a campaign unless it is systematically and thoroughly planned and properly managed. If the defeats in the last two years have taught us anything, it is the necessity of proper management and proper organizing, especially in States which are largely populated."[98]

When suffragists took stock of their movement in fall 1913, however, some came to the conclusion that too much rather than too little organizing was at fault; they argued that the state-by-state method of winning the vote was an outmoded strategy doomed to failure. In spite of the addition of full suffrage in ten states and one territory, prospects for success in the South and East remained grim, and the temperance issue continued to cast a pall over hopes in the Midwest. In addition, a few activists were convinced that the presence of an energetic and vocal organization in some states had actually provoked the enemies of suffrage to greater efforts to ensure the reform's defeat. Was a state amendment campaign, no matter how well organized, an asset or a liability to the ultimate objective of the national association? Or was the strategy pioneered successfully in Oregon of the "still hunt" worthy of consideration?[99] Should attention be focused instead on a federal amendment, or would this avenue be blocked by southern extremists?

As NAWSA leaders pondered these questions, the state associations continued to pursue the elusive vote by the state referenda method. Without firm policy decisions from above, leagues on the state and local levels persisted in organizing, canvassing, and publicity measures that had been endorsed by the parent association. Between 1912, when Oregon, Kansas, and Arizona won the vote for women, and 1917, when suffragists in New York finally proved successful in their referendum campaign, only two lightly populated states achieved the reform, despite a plethora of amendment campaigns.[100] But regardless of these disappointing results, the role played by the new cohort of organizers and activists proved to be highly significant to the movement's momentum after 1910.

First, the new organizers could report dramatic results in the areas of membership and publicity. Thanks mainly to the Woman Suffrage Party method of district canvassing and enrollment techniques, NAWSA recorded impressive membership gains. Although the dues-paying members of suffrage societies increased only from 26,400 in 1909 to 28,700 in 1911, the number of enrolled — or nonactive — suffrage advocates experienced massive growth. The association reported approximately 65,000 non-dues-paying members in autumn 1911, but the following year the number stood at a staggering 171,000, an estimate based on only one-third of the suffrage societies' reports.[101] New organizing efforts also led to more publicity for the movement. When the WSP was launched in 1909, NAWSA expenditures for press work totaled less than $200 for an entire year's work. Three years later, the association boasted a full-fledged press bureau with a publicity budget of more than $3,000. The national organization also increased its state campaign support, from a little over $4,000 in 1909 to more than $18,000 by 1912.[102] The association's enhanced membership figures and increased expenditures on publicity and campaign work reflected the successful efforts of the suffrage organizers.

In addition to the organizers' achievements in enrollment and publicity, their work was of lasting personal significance to the activists themselves. That suffrage work was important to individual suffragists seems to the modern observer almost a triviality, unworthy of comment. Nevertheless, every archive that boasts even a small suffrage collection testifies to the importance of suffrage work as a formative personal experience. Boxes of memoirs, suffrage memorabilia, and aging photographs capture the lasting appeal and memories that the movement created for its ardent activists. But why did the organizing experience mean so much?

To understand the significance of organizing, it is necessary to look briefly at the circumstances and prospects of educated young women of the elite classes in early-twentieth-century America. For middle- and upper-class white women at the turn of the century, the future too often meant only marriage, motherhood, and the tedium of bridge club or church socials once a month. Although more women than ever before attended at least one year of college, graduation was too often an end rather than a beginning. Although a few ambitious graduates entered the professions, many more found their personal and economic independence at an end. In contrast, elite white men of the time could expect to conclude their education or professional training with a Grand Tour — if not to Europe, then to New York, Chicago, or another cosmopolitan center. Moreover, most males typically pursued the career for which they had been trained, and they were often able to combine the beginning of a career with an extended period of bachelor freedom. Single or married, young men could enjoy an active social life and peer companionship in clubs, lodges, professional societies, athletic associations, and public taverns.

For young women, there were far fewer options and greatly reduced opportunities for fulfilling independence. Other than club work, philanthropy, or marriage, the most common career alternatives for elite women were low-paying secretarial work or teaching, and these were often considered short-term stopgaps for the "true vocation" of marriage.[103] Female social life was further constrained by Edwardian notions of decorum. Unlikely to travel alone and too frequently bored with the confines of domesticity, some young elite women found a respectable outlet for their talents, their ambitions, and their wanderlust in the woman suffrage movement.

The suffrage cause provided an avenue for youthful idealistic enthusiasm and for the high moral purpose inculcated through education. Suffrage rhetoric and symbols stressed the progress of women, a theme that found a receptive audience with college and career women. Organizing work, in particular, tapped skills and sentiments honed in college and put away after graduation. Bookkeeping, secretarial, and office management skills allowed organizers to remain in the workforce with a small salary and postponed indefinitely the need to marry or to find permanent employment. Campaign strategies and management provided scope for imagination and initiative of sorts that had usually been reserved for men only. In a sense, suffrage organizing became a profession in its own right, rendered respectable by the high moral tone of the cause.

Because of the nature of organizing work, the suffrage movement provided many young women with an unaccustomed opportunity for work, travel, adventure, and camaraderie. In many cases, serious work could be combined with high adventure. On a flying squadron jaunt through a rural area of Ohio, organizer Maud Wood Park encountered a traveling circus in the process of setting up for an afternoon show. With an eye for publicity that P. T. Barnum would have admired, Park obtained permission to join the circus parade in a car decorated with streamers and "Votes for Women" placards. The circus manager extracted the maximum publicity from the situation (while perhaps revealing his own lack of sympathy for the reform) by stationing the suffrage car directly behind the elephants. Arriving at the big top, Park attempted to give a suffrage speech, only to be drowned out by a troupe of trained dogs in the next ring. All was not lost, however, for the ringmaster took her suffrage leaflets and instructed two clowns to distribute them to the cheering crowd.[104] Park's experience at the circus was but one of hundreds of instances in which the serious work of organizing gave way to exciting and unexpected adventures.

Travel in itself was a liberating experience. Professional organizers visited every region in the nation, sometimes traveling thousands of miles a year, and volunteer organizers savored their short day trips and found adventure in unlikely places. For example, Florence Luscomb and another young worker once arrived late at night in a small town, only to learn that the hotel was too seedy to accommodate them safely. Back in the car, they discovered their vehicle wouldn't start. After they had made numerous futile attempts to crank the car, six drunken young men emerged from the hotel's back room where they had been embroiled in a game of poker. Each took a turn cranking, but in vain. At last, a plan was hatched to start the car. With Luscomb behind the wheel, the drunken men pushed the car up a slope; as it raced down she popped the clutch and the engine roared to life. The two suffragists then sped away into the night as their besotted benefactors waved a sentimental farewell.[105]

For a young man of the time, this incident would hardly provoke a second thought; for a young woman, however, such an escapade could symbolize a new and tantalizing freedom. Alone in the night, far from home, confronted with six drunks and a stalled car, Florence Luscomb clearly was having the time of her life. Like Maud Wood Park's encounter with the big top,

Luscomb's account is simultaneously humorous, dramatic, and infectiously exciting. At the very heart of the organizing experience, then, was this quest for adventure, drama, and excitement. Organizers were drawn to the movement in part because it offered them experiences tantamount to those offered to young men under the guise of "sowing wild oats." In place of the Grand Tour, suffragists toured America, and like their male counterparts, they found excitement and liberation.

Although the old adage, "travel broadens," proved true for many organizers, life on the road had its disadvantages. Physical discomfort was too often the rule rather than the exception. "I measured my hot little room last evening and it is just 8 x 8 feet with one small window opening upon the [tin] roof of a shed, the sun pouring down on it fairly dazzles your eyes out," veteran campaigner Anna Howard Shaw complained, "oh, but campaigning is fun!"[106] Another organizer made an unwelcome discovery during a flying squadron trek across Illinois. "In one county seat . . . dainty Mrs. Bacon and I found the bed in our hotel had numbers of other little occupants," explained Catharine Waugh McCulloch, "so we sat up most of the night and plastered their little carcasses on the sheets."[107] Even Carrie Chapman Catt groused to a friend: "I don't like washing off the soil of travel in ice water out of a bowl. I don't like cold houses. . . . I don't like creaky springs in my bed and all the rest of it. I am homesick and want to creep back to my own nest. I don't want to be a reformer today."[108] One organizer recorded her sentiments in this humorous sonnet to the New York state WSP Chairman Vira Whitehouse:

> Oh Vira, when that eye so bright and black
> Turns on me while deciding I must go
> From Yaphank to Schenectady and back,
> From Warren County west to Buffalo,
> I do not any longer plead and weep,
> Nor say these trips are very long and far,
> Nor urge that now and then I like to sleep
> At home, instead of in a sleeping car;
> I do not, for I know your point of view —
> That suffrage work is never sacrifice,
> That going foodless, sleepless, seems to you
> If done for suffrage really rather nice;
> I dare not murmur with my failing breath,
> If *this* be Liberty, then give me Death.[109]

In addition to the physical hardships organizers encountered on the road, the work itself sometimes led to disillusionment and frustration. Of one small town, an organizer wrote: "All the inhabitants are dead, but unburied — it was like sitting down and talking to one lump of dough after another."[110] Another, describing her work in Iowa, complained of the naive attitude of the women she tried to enlist for suffrage: "They say, 'Why really, I never thought about it at all — but I guess there is no reason why I shouldn't vote.' — Imagine!"[111] Another activist exclaimed in frustration, "We may simply have to wait for my generation of women to die off, because they don't know how to do anything but buy clothes and go to card parties!"[112]

In spite of the frustrations and inconvenience of organizing, the women who took part in suffrage organization gained tangible benefits from their work. Shared hardships, as well as adventures, served as a bonding experience that tied organizers to the movement and to each other. Hardships were recounted at suffrage headquarters in much the same vein as returning veterans related their service experiences. Loyalties and friendships forged during the long road trips and state campaigns often lasted for decades after the suffrage crusade ended. In addition, the spirit of shared adventure and affection that marked the organizing experience led to a heightened sense of cooperation. "We are actually learning team work," one organizer exclaimed, and she insisted that even if the vote was not forthcoming, "I should still think the Cause worth working for if only to teach women the splendid development that comes from cooperation in a great work."[113] While some developed a stronger allegiance to the cause, others found in their work a symbolic meaning more profound than the vote itself. After defeat of the 1912 Ohio referendum, one organizer speculated on the significance of woman suffrage. "If it just meant votes it would hardly be worth working for. . . . The progressive men of Ohio would accept it as readily as the other progressive ideas," she wrote, "but they didn't accept it, so it must be that it stands for a more significant change than just casting votes. It symbolizes equality."[114]

For many, the organizing experience brought a new sense of self-respect and confidence. Although most suffragists shared at least a theoretical belief in female equality, perhaps tempered by race or ethnic prejudices, in actuality women in the new century were far from equal. Suffrage work offered a new field of endeavor, controlled by women and for women, outside the grasp of the male sector of society. After a long talk with a fellow organizer, one suffragist wrote: "In the last few years I [have met] more men of an advanced order than women. And men can't fill in all the chinks. . . . 'Men ain't exactly people,' and sometimes I think that's true. I can truthfully say and not in a spirit of egotism that I often suffer from a kind of sex-loneliness. . . . It's fine to talk with one with such a range as yours — especially as you just start to begin where I leave off."[115]

At its most basic level, the movement proffered the gifts of gender solidarity and individual self-esteem in exchange for service to the cause. After joining the WSP as an executive secretary, one suffragist remarked, "Seriously, I did develope [*sic*] a new kind of consciousness, a sort of respect for myself and a feeling that I can do any old end of suffrage job that falls my way to do hereafter."[116] Another professed, "For the first time I've seen something within the bounds of possibility in my life that makes me able to bear the thought of it to the end."[117] "Ought women to have less self respect than men?" yet another was prompted to ask, and she concluded, "Women are just beginning to gain self-respect, and it is in that that the symbolism and the chief value of the ballot lies."[118]

This new sense of self-confidence found expression in a variety of ways. Women who had once been too timid to address a parlor meeting found themselves speaking on street corners to hundreds of listeners.[119] Others learned new skills, like the District of Columbia society woman who taught herself to drive a car in order to take part in a flying squadron.[120] Still others found suffrage organizing to be a rite of passage. Once initiated, the organizer could find a surrogate profession, adventure, and a cure for "sex-loneliness" through shared experiences and hardships. "Oh, it is good to be alive at this particular time in the world's history," one organizer exclaimed, "and it is even better to feel one's self a part of a great movement for the emancipation of one half of humanity."[121]

The organizer experience bound its initiates to the crusade and to each other, creating a movement identity and zeal that would fuel the suffrage machine. But as organizers brought new converts into the NAWSA fold, the association's leaders increasingly turned their attention away from the state referenda campaigns. With the suffrage machine assembled and, after 1915, a new driver behind the wheel, NAWSA set its sights on Congress and accelerated for a head-on collision with the Washington political elite.

PART **II**

The Politics of Suffrage

5

The Front Door Lobby

The years between 1912 and 1915 were ones of organizational conflict and resolution for NAWSA. Although membership and finances rose to an all-time high, poor leadership, inefficiency, and factionalism prevented the organization from capitalizing on these gains. As a result, NAWSA suffragists replaced their longtime president Anna Howard Shaw, a champion of universal suffrage but an inefficient administrator, with Carrie Chapman Catt.[1] Catt's election was in part a response to Shaw's poor leadership and a need to reunify the organization around a clearly defined strategy, but her ascendancy also marked an acceleration of the trend away from the egalitarian spirit of the movement in its earlier days. Nevertheless, Catt's reliance on efficiency, centralization, and modern political tactics promised the reorganization that NAWSA needed. Many suffragists welcomed the change in leadership and hoped that Catt could solve the factional problems that Shaw had allowed to develop.

Two sources of conflict had emerged within NAWSA that threatened the organizational unity so carefully constructed in the first decade of the century. First, Alice Paul, returning from her apprenticeship in the militant British suffragette movement, joined NAWSA as the head of its virtually defunct Congressional Committee.[2] Paul was successful at raising large sums of money and gaining favorable publicity for the cause; in 1913, she organized a massive parade in Washington, D.C., that upstaged newly elected President Woodrow Wilson. By 1914, however, Paul had alienated the NAWSA leadership. Eager to try more militant tactics and impatient with NAWSA, she formed her own organization—the Congressional Union (CU)—to work side by side with NAWSA's Congressional Committee as well as independently in the states. Anna Howard Shaw refused to hide her anger at Paul's actions. In a series of letters to suffragists across the nation, the NAWSA president fumed that Paul was competing directly with the parent organization and accused her of stealing recruits from NAWSA. Other suffragists blamed Shaw for the rift and called for new leadership within NAWSA to match Paul's charismatic style.[3]

The dissension over Paul and suffrage militancy was quite disruptive to NAWSA. As the split worsened, some NAWSA activists tried to persuade the Executive Board to work toward compromise with the Congressional Union. When this failed, some of NAWSA's most talented members defected to join Paul. Many of those who left made up what might be called the feminist wing of NAWSA. Mary Beard, Inez Haynes Irwin, Lavinia Dock, and Florence Kelley were perhaps the most prominent of those who joined the CU. They associated suffrage with a larger vision of feminism that many suffragists of the time did not share. In addition to their feminism, they were also strong supporters of working and immigrant women's issues; several had been members of Harriet Stanton Blatch's Equality League of Self-Supporting Women and the WTUL.[4] Their defection silenced an important source of support for class and gender issues within the NAWSA leadership. Such issues as equal pay for equal work, equality of opportunity, industrial safety, and legal equality for women that once formed important planks in the suffrage movement's overall reform platform were quietly allowed to disappear from the NAWSA agenda after the departure of this cohort of women.[5]

Citing conflict of interest, Shaw, Catt, and other NAWSA leaders maneuvered the militants into severing their ties with NAWSA.[6] From then on, the two groups followed different strategies. Congressional Union activists instigated a variety of militant tactics, including attempts to defeat the Democratic Party in the elections of 1914 and 1916. The CU campaigned solely for the federal amendment; it charged that NAWSA had abandoned the amendment route to the vote in favor of gradualism and education. Alice Paul's charismatic style of leadership, coupled with her flamboyant use of militant tactics, gained national publicity for her group. One new convert explained: "Partly it was perhaps a kind of violence that seems inherent in me. The other was a kind of sinister despair that was growing in me. Nobody in the world welcomed the militant movement in England as I did. I have always said that when they threw the first brick, my heart was tied to it."[7] Indeed, by 1914 NAWSA members' frustration with gradualism had reached a crisis point. Organization by the Woman Suffrage Party had increased membership rolls and finances, but the organization lacked fresh leadership and a renewed sense of purpose to match these advances. Suffragists increasingly felt a combination of frustration, jealousy of Paul's exciting style of leadership, and a sense that NAWSA was being shunted aside as the young and vital Congressional Union took control. Carrie Chapman Catt's rise to power was in part a response to these events.

A second faction that would trouble NAWSA emerged in 1913: the Southern States Woman Suffrage Committee (SSWSC) led by Louisiana's Kate Gordon. The SSWSC opposed the federal amendment on the grounds that its enforcement would expose the South's election laws to federal supervision and disrupt the racial settlement adopted throughout Dixie in the late nineteenth and early twentieth centuries that disfranchised most black males and many poor whites. Although not all white southern suffragists agreed with Gordon's states' rights suffrage, she claimed to represent the southern states and worked tirelessly to thwart the federal amendment campaign.[8] In truth, Gordon's organization was too small to challenge NAWSA's federal amendment policy when the association voted on policy each year at the convention. More troublesome was the negative propaganda that her group distributed concerning the amendment and the race issue, an issue that NAWSA sought to avoid at all costs.

Gordon took no pains to hide her vehement racism, and through New Orleans newspapers, letters to NAWSA board members, and eventually her own newsletter, the *Southern Citizen,* she injected racism into the federal amendment debate and forced NAWSA to address the issue. Thus, while Alice Paul called for abandoning the state route to suffrage in favor of the federal woman suffrage amendment, Gordon objected to the vote by federal amendment and insisted on state suffrage referenda as the proper course of action. Clearly the carefully constructed suffrage coalition was unraveling. If the organization were to continue, new leadership was essential to quell factionalism and realign the movement behind clearly defined goals.

With Catt's ascent to the NAWSA presidency, the association completed its evolution into a single-issue pressure group. And while suffrage education continued in a few areas, the organizational focus shifted from educating the public to convincing politicians at the federal and state levels of the inevitability of votes for women. After 1915, when Catt took steps to end factionalism and set the course for NAWSA, the suffrage movement increasingly turned to what some activists called *practical politics.* Catt introduced bureaucratic centralism to NAWSA and forged a suffrage machine that became one of the most successful pressure groups in American history. As the suffrage machine brought the "century of struggle" to a victorious conclusion, NAWSA underwent internal changes that compromised its democratic heritage and shaped the fate of the twentieth-century women's movement in ways the suffragists of NAWSA never expected.

Torrential rains and gale-force winds beat down on the streets of Chicago on June 7, 1916, as newly elected NAWSA president Carrie Chapman Catt asked the Republican National Convention's Resolutions Committee for a woman suffrage plank in the 1916 party platform. While the politicians listened to Catt's appeal, six thousand suffragists assembled in parade formation several blocks away, ready to do battle for their cause.[9] Leading the parade were two elephants resplendent in rubber blankets, with a Highland piper and two fife and drum corps following closely behind. Music from twenty-four bands competed with the din of the storm as the suffrage forces stepped forth into the downpour. The rain washed over the marchers, and white dresses soon bore streaks of yellow as the color rinsed from the women's parade sashes. Spectators crowded into windows and doorways to cheer the women, and two — Mrs. Gifford Pinchot and journalist Arthur Brisbane — abandoned shelter to join the parade.[10]

As the marchers neared the convention hall, Catt concluded her remarks. Her place on the podium was taken by an antisuffragist who urged the Resolutions Committee to reject any prosuffrage plank. Just as the antisuffragist proclaimed, "Women do not want the vote," the doors of the hall flew open, and the storm-battered suffragists marched in to the tune of "Hail, Hail, the Gang's All Here." The "sodden six thousand" stood shoulder-to-shoulder along the walls and down the aisles, then turned to face the assembly and the stunned speaker in absolute silence. Under the collective gaze of the suffrage army, the antisuffragist's voice faltered; quickly concluding her statement, she turned and fled. At her retreat, a demonstration began, and the delegates watched as the suffragists cheered for their reform.[11]

The Resolutions Committee, however, remained unconvinced. After a bitter dispute that lasted long into the night, Senator Henry Cabot Lodge appeared before the convention the next day to read the plank. To the suffragists, the plank was a mixed blessing: it endorsed woman suffrage but contained a rider that left the question up to the states to implement as they saw fit. The NAWSA leaders had hoped the committee would recommend the federal suffrage amendment, but Lodge and Senator James Wadsworth, the husband of a leading New York antisuffragist, managed to cast the plank as a states' rights issue. In spite of the suffragists'efforts, a week later the Democratic National

Convention followed suit by approving a watered down suffrage plank, which also specified state action. During the debate, Texas Governor James Ferguson presented an impassioned minority report against a woman suffrage plank, and although his report was voted down 888 to 181, his allies were powerful enough to block a more comprehensive endorsement.[12] Texas Equal Suffrage Association President Minnie Fisher Cunningham was so angry at Governor Ferguson's performance that she cut up her black crepe dress, used the pieces to drape over the Texas state flag, and led a parade of Texas activists past Ferguson's hotel.[13] Cunningham was not alone in her wrath. The *New York Times* reported that when the plank passed, "It was like the French Convention of the revolution, gallery ruled, and the women . . . suggested the knitting women of the Reign of Terror."[14]

Not all suffragists were displeased with the party planks. In 1913, some white southern suffragists had rallied behind the Southern States Woman Suffrage Conference. Vehemently opposed to federal intervention in southern elections, SSWSC members objected to the federal suffrage amendment's enabling clause, which required governmental supervision to ensure its enforcement. A small minority of Dixie activists, the SSWSC represented the most vocally racist element of southern white suffragists. Other white southerners favored the so-called Shafroth-Palmer resolution, a substitute amendment introduced in 1914 that provided for popular initiative for state suffrage referenda. This procedure would allow suffragists to bypass hostile state legislatures and take their reform directly to the electorate.[15] By whatever means, many southern advocates were committed to a states' rights approach. Thus, SSWSC president Kate Gordon and other Dixie activists rejoiced at the Democratic Convention's woman suffrage plank. The SSWSC issued a jubilant report taking credit for the plank, and Gordon's own suffrage society, the ERA Club of New Orleans, sent a congratulatory message to Woodrow Wilson urging him to throw his entire support behind his party's platform.[16]

Although NAWSA leaders heard some favorable reaction from a few northern Democrats and an occasional Republican, the majority of suffrage advocates outside the South disagreed with the states' rights perspective.[17] Personally disgusted with both Republican and Democratic party efforts on behalf of woman suffrage, Carrie Chapman Catt held a meeting of the NAWSA Executive Board on the afternoon that the Democrats adopted the disputed plank. In order to plan an effective political strategy for the federal amendment and to discuss the widening sectional split over states' rights, she called for the association's annual meeting to be rescheduled from December to September. In addition, Catt planned to invite both presidential candidates to speak to the convention in hope of winning them over to the federal amendment. The Executive Board overwhelmingly supported her suggestions, and the annual convention was slated to convene in Atlantic City in September 1916.[18]

When Catt had assumed the presidency of NAWSA in December 1915, the association boasted a total membership of over two million, with forty-four state auxiliaries and a yearly budget of more than $110,000. Nevertheless, her first priority was the recruitment of politically astute activists to serve as her advisers. "We must look for women who have political talent," she explained. "We who have come down from the last generation are reformers, but reformers are poor politicians."[19] Catt had accepted the office of president on the condition that the association adopt a new method of selecting its Executive Board. The board had previously been elected by the delegates at each yearly convention; Catt demanded and received permission to name her own board, a move that undercut the democratic foundation of the association while increasing board efficiency. Unlike traditional board membership, composed of women from all sections who rarely met face-to-face during their terms of office, Catt selected eight women of independent means who could afford to attend the numerous work sessions she scheduled.

With the help of her new Executive Board, Catt spent the three months following the June party conventions planning the September meeting's agenda. In response to the southern shift away from the federal amendment, she wanted to pull state and local associations tightly under centralized NAWSA control. Although she maintained an attitude of ambivalence toward the state versus federal route to victory, her unspoken commitment lay fully with the federal amendment. Fearing that "Congress would hide behind those states' rights planks and shut us out from Congressional action forever," Catt laid plans to put the association "securely on the Amendment trolley."[20] But first, a major obstacle had to be overcome: the recalcitrant South. Southern suffragists were wary of Catt's plans. As word spread of the new date for the convention, some Dixie activists expressed reservations over the break with NAWSA tradition. Others, like Kate Gordon and her Kentucky friend Laura Clay, believed that Catt and her allies intended to unite the national association with the Republican Party. Although Catt repeatedly denied partisan endorsements, Gordon remained unconvinced and insisted that such a move would be the "death knell of the NAWSA."[21] The sectional rift worsened in August when Catt informed southern suffragists that the September convention would include open debate on what she called the "Three Cornered Question" — whether to pursue state, federal, or dual routes to victory. Aware of SSWSC threats to support only state suffrage work, Catt also proposed to debate NAWSA policy toward associations that refused to follow the national association's directions. One sentence in particular in her letter to state and local associations seemed directed to the sswsc: "If a State fails to co-operate in the National [federal amendment] campaign, can the National Association organize a State Association which will?"[22]

Kate Gordon and her sister Jean, the president of the Louisiana Woman Suffrage Association, immediately grasped the hidden agenda of Catt's plan: to force a showdown between states' rights advocates and activists favoring the federal amendment. The Gordons retaliated quickly. Their ERA Club voted to stand firm on the southern interpretation of the NAWSA Constitution, which they believed protected a state association's right to choose the type of suffrage work it engaged in, and unanimously elected Kate Gordon as delegate to the September convention.[23] In order to placate southern delegates, the Atlantic City convention included a "Dixie Evening," with speeches from prominent southerners on such topics as the "Southern Temperament as Related to Woman Suffrage."[24] And when President Woodrow Wilson, a southern Democrat highly regarded by Dixie suffragists, spoke to the delegates, many found reassurance for their states' rights stand in his words. Telling his audience that "the [suffrage] tide is rising to meet the moon," Wilson continued, "We feel the tide, we rejoice in the strength of it, and we shall not quarrel in the long run as to the method of it."[25]

Despite such auspicious beginnings, the serious questions facing the delegates resurfaced the next day. When Catt presented the assembly with three platforms to consider, she already had the backing of the Executive Board and Executive Council (composed of all state association presidents) securely behind the first platform.[26] Platform I, in support of the federal amendment, included a provision that would enable the Executive Board to dictate state associations' work and to assume direction of that work if the state refused to comply. Additionally, Platform I called for a far-reaching agenda of publicity, education, and financing directed by NAWSA headquarters and its Washington lobby. Platform II left all decision-making power to the states and defined NAWSA as a "clearing house for information" without responsibility for campaigns, state or national. The third, or middle-of-the-road, platform allowed the national organization a more positive role in state campaigns, with it serving as an umbrella for various educational, financial, and organizing activities.[27]

The majority of delegates favored Platform I. When the assembly voted to concentrate all forces on the federal amendment and pledged to support the takeover of noncomplying state associations, the southern delegates sat in stunned silence. Kate Gordon slowly rose from her seat, her face pinched and white. "And if a state association refuses to be bound by this resolution, [and] refuses to support the federal amendment," she asked a silent audience, "what will the national board do about it?" Carrie Catt stepped to the edge of the stage and replied, "The national board would deal very leniently with that state branch." Slowly Gordon resumed her seat, and hissed to a companion, "A well-oiled steam roller has ironed this convention *flat!*"[28]

After the controversial vote, Catt outlined her plan for a "nation-wide campaign of agitation, education, organization and publicity" in support of the federal amendment. Included in these lofty goals were concrete proposals: a national press bureau, a publicity council with departments in each state, at least four campaign directors with a corps of two hundred organizers, extensive state organization, a professional congressional lobby, and a million dollar fund to finance the program. State work was not forgotten, with provisions for state referenda if associations met strict NAWSA guidelines. Without the approval of the Executive Board, however, states hoping to enter into campaigns would find themselves cut off from the national association's coffers. This safeguard gave NAWSA leaders ultimate control over the direction of state work, and it helped reduce the number and expense of poorly planned contests that were doomed from the start.[29] In addition to endorsing this so-called Winning Plan, the assembly pledged $818,000 toward the million dollar campaign fund and adjourned firmly committed to the federal route to victory.

The resolution of the Three-Cornered Debate and the implementation of the Winning Plan were to have dramatic consequences for the woman suffrage movement. First, after the Atlantic City debate, suffragists nationwide were united behind a single political goal: the federal suffrage amendment. Sectional disputes were put aside, and the organization's energies were focused on one rather than two roads to victory. Second, the move away from state referenda to total commitment to the amendment significantly increased NAWSA's chances for success by 1920. Had the association continued to seek state contests, there was an excellent chance that southern legislatures would have continued to block the reform indefinitely. With ratification of the federal amendment, however, all states would fall under its jurisdiction, regardless of the southern legislators' wishes. Although the federal amendment required the approval of three-fourths of the states, a difficult process at best, suffrage strategists reasoned with justification that ratification could be achieved without the help of the South. Third, efficiency gradually took the place of confusion. With an all-powerful Executive Board, ill-conceived referenda campaigns were avoided as state and local workers adhered to plans handed down from a centralized authority. Finances now could be allocated to clubs or areas with the best chance of success instead of the old policy of financing any group that asked for funding.

In spite of the numerous advantages of the Winning Plan, its implementation carried with it certain ominous implications for the movement. The reforms and resolutions passed at Atlantic City increased organizational efficiency and unity but at the expense of traditional democratic procedures. From Catt's handpicked Executive Board to the loss of policy-making power by the states, the Winning Plan stripped NAWSA rank-and-file members of their voice in the formation and execution of suffrage work and turned power over to a small group of nonelected officials. Centralized authority does not in itself constitute an abuse of power, especially given the fact that in the case of the suffrage movement, a representative body had sanctioned that authority. Yet the new reforms initiated at the convention held the seeds of abuse. As the Winning Plan was put into effect, southern fears of a "NAWSA oligarchy" became a reality.

Within days of the convention, the Executive Board began to implement the plan of work adopted at Atlantic City. One of its first actions was to issue a statement to the state associations. "Owing to the lack of time for more discussion at Atlantic City," the letter read, "the details of several items of the constructive policy adopted were left out. Under the circumstances, the most practical and time-saving plan seems to be to issue instructions from our National Headquarters for the next few months, as though these details had been agreed to, in the hope that each state will do its utmost to carry them out."[30] With this blanket statement, and in contradiction to NAWSA bylaws providing for delegate approval at the annual convention for the yearly plan of work, the Executive Board assumed control of all policy decisions for the association.

Another shift away from NAWSA tradition occurred almost imperceptibly. At a meeting of the Congressional Committee held during the convention, newly appointed chairman Mrs. Frank Roessing asked a group of state suffrage leaders if their organizations were willing to undertake efforts to defeat all antisuffrage congressional candidates. Although no state activists were prepared to act on the suggestion at that time, Roessing, Catt, and the NAWSA board had clearly discussed the idea at length.[31] This was a departure from the traditional policy of convincing candidates to endorse woman suffrage while avoiding attacks on those who refused. And despite a hurried note to state leaders shortly after the convention reaffirming the national organization's nonpartisan stand, Catt took the occasion to hint at future partisan activity. Although suffragists should refrain from endorsing a given candidate or political party, she explained that "they must merely let the world know where each candidate stands and then ask the voters to choose a candidate who is favorable to the Federal Amendment."[32] Thus Catt opened the door for more direct and possibly partisan participation by suffragists in individual congressional races. This was the first step in NAWSA's descent from the lofty plane of positive exhortation into the hurly-burly of negative campaigning.

Catt followed this directive with a long list of instructions to the state association presidents, including plans for two "Federal Amendment Days," report blanks to be returned to NAWSA headquarters on the state of organization required, and sample letters for all county and local workers detailing the Winning Plan.[33] Moreover, each state was to circularize rural and urban voters, church leaders, businessmen, and political machines on a county-by-county basis, in addition to members of state legislatures, county officials, and precinct chairmen. An Efficiency Squad composed of press, field, and headquarters directors would be made available to plan fund-raisers, publicity stunts, and suffrage schools for local and state chapters.[34] These measures resulted in a new level of standardization for suffrage work; over time, suffrage clubs nationwide increasingly resorted to ready-made propaganda material and trained organizers from the national headquarters at the expense of their own less professional publicity and organizational endeavors. Without doubt, the new services were superior, but they lacked the spontaneity and exuberance that characterized local initiative in the past.

State activism was not the only avenue for victory; the Winning Plan also contained plans for a professional lobby based in Washington, D.C. Although NAWSA had operated a Congressional Committee in the nation's capital for many years, poor funding and a widely scattered membership had left it weak and lacking in influence. In 1910, for example, the national association failed to appropriate any money for the committee, a fact bitterly resented by former chairman Emma Gilette. Shortly before the Atlantic City convention, Gilette brought Carrie Catt up-to-date on her experience with past NAWSA officials: "I was advised by a former member of the board that if I submitted my plan of questioning candidates for Congress to the national board, I would probably be stopped as independent work of this kind was not approved. I have had a long experience of rebuffs from National officers whenever I attempted any work in Washington to further national legislation."[35]

In 1916, however, Catt was determined that things would be different. One of the first moves that she made upon assuming the presidency was to investigate the condition of the Congressional Committee; what she learned left her in a state of despair. Illinois Progressive Ruth Hanna McCormick had taken over the committee in 1913 when Alice Paul, its former chairman, left to found the Congressional Union. Under McCormick's leadership, the committee conducted polls, interviewed congressmen, and supported the introduction of the controversial Shafroth-Palmer amendment.[36] In fall 1915, McCormick resigned, leaving a less qualified, querulous coworker in charge. By the time of the Atlantic City convention, the committee's affairs were in disarray. "It really is in a pitiful condition," Catt reported to Maud Wood Park, "and we are tremendously hard pressed." In a letter posted the next week, Catt continued to urge Park to take over the committee: "The situation is new to me and I may not analyze it right, but it seems to me that the National Association is losing its Federal Amendment zealots to the Congressional Union merely because we do not work on that job hard enough. . . . [NAWSA] never has really worked for the Federal Amendment," Catt concluded. "If it should once do it, there is no knowing what might happen."[37] After some hesitation, Park agreed to serve on the re-formed Congressional Committee; she arrived at committee headquarters in December 1916.

Maud Wood Park had an impressive suffrage vita. As a student at Radcliffe, she had helped establish the College Equal Suffrage League, which she served as an organizer and as executive secretary. She had also held executive positions in the Massachusetts Woman Suffrage League and the Boston Equal Suffrage Association for Good Government. Yet when she arrived at the committee's Washington headquarters, she inwardly quailed at what lay before her. The office was crowded with file cabinets bulging at the seams with 531 folders, each bearing the name of a member of Congress. Executive Secretary Ruth White, the one holdover from the McCormick years, had devised a system for cataloging all known information on the representatives and senators. What Park found waiting for her was White's masterpiece: fact sheets on the lawmakers' personal, political, business, and religious affiliations; printed biographies; voting records; and interviews conducted by previous committee members with individual congressmen.[38]

In addition to the organizational talents of Ruth White, Park had the services of Helen Hamilton Gardener. Nicknamed the "diplomatic corps" by coworkers, Gardener had intimate knowledge of a host of prominent Washingtonians through her many social contacts.[39] One of her confidants was her next-door neighbor, Speaker of the House Champ Clark. Gardener often waited in her parlor in hat and coat until she heard the door slam next door. Then she would saunter out, as if by accident, fall in step with the Speaker, and discreetly pump him for useful information. Through these seemingly casual conversations, the suffrage lobby learned many important tidbits of information.[40] Thanks to Clark and other sources, Gardener "knew the things that could be done, and she knew the things that couldn't be done—she *knew* official Washington."[41]

Gardener was also responsible for setting the professional tone of the committee. "National work has to be learned from a national outlook," she cautioned, "free from any and every state 'pull' of bias or thought." Stressing the need for an objective outlook from every member of the committee to avoid charges of partisanship or sectional bias, Gardener taught her coworkers to appeal to politicians on the basis of a national woman suffrage constituency. She also insisted that the Congressional Committee handle all press releases and other news stories concerning the amendment in order to assure a dignified, accurate picture of their work.[42]

As Park's able lieutenant, Helen Gardener used her influence and her political ability to help create what would soon be called "the Front Door Lobby." A wit in the press gallery gave the Congressional Committee this sobriquet because, as he explained, the suffragists never used "backstairs" methods.[43] Few would have dared to accuse such prominent women as Mrs. J. Borden Harriman, Mrs. Winston Churchill, Mrs. William Jennings Bryan, and Mrs. Charles W. McClure of indulging in shady politics. As members of the committee, they added legitimacy and prestige that less influential workers failed to match.[44] Past Chairman Ruth Hanna McCormick returned to the committee in 1917, and through her contacts within the Progressive Party she persuaded many congressional wives to devote time to suffrage work.[45] Additionally, the Front Door Lobby acquired the services of Dr. Alexander J. McKelway as temporary publicity director and legislative adviser. McKelway had impeccable progressive credentials, having served as the legislative representative of the Child Labor Committee when the first child labor bill passed successfully through Congress. With this impressive array of talent and influence to call upon, Maud Wood Park assumed command of the Congressional Committee that was to play a vital role in the passage of the Nineteenth Amendment.

The general division of work fell into four broad categories: legislative, publicity, office work, and Suffrage House activities. On one occasion, Park itemized her duties: "to keep our friends in the Congress active for the Amendment, to direct pressure of every sort upon doubtful or opposed men, to make an accurate poll, . . . to study the floor situation and be ready to take advantage of favorable opportunities and to avert threatening action, to keep in touch with friendly politicians and with leaders of the political parties, to bring delegations from the states . . . [and] to stimulate the sending of letters and telegrams at the right moment."[46] As this description indicates, suffrage lobbying was a full-time job. Lobbyists lived in a rambling, rundown mansion on Rhode Island Avenue that they nicknamed "Suffrage House." The former home of such dignitaries as cabinet members, ambassadors, and philanthropists, Suffrage House provided dignified and spacious accommodations for the suffrage lobbyists. The house boasted sixteen bedrooms, all on the third floor, with the second floor given over to a huge drawing room, a smaller parlor, and a state dining room with rows of high-backed chairs covered in red velvet. Suffragists could also wander into the music gallery, where on a dais stood a velvet seat with gold-fringed canopy; waggish workers referred to the gallery as "the throne room."[47] On December 17, 1916, the house was formally opened to the public with the dedication of the Susan B. Anthony room, furnished with Anthony memorabilia and other inspirational items.[48]

The routine at Suffrage House revolved around the legislative agenda for the day. At breakfast each morning, the suffragists gathered to hear their assignments for the day's interviews. After long hours of knocking on office doors, interviewing, and recording their findings, the group reassembled after dinner in front of a huge fireplace in the formal drawing room. There they heard daily reports, shared political gossip, and occasionally howled with laughter at droll imitations of congressmen. On some occasions, the permanent residents of Suffrage House made room for visitors from the state associations who came to lobby individual politicians before a crucial vote. At times like these, the third-floor lights shone late into the night as suffragists visited up and down the halls.[49]

Suffrage House was also the scene for weekly teas and other social events presided over by the committee's "housemother," Mabel Willard. Willard saw to it that prominent society women from the area served as guest hostesses, and sometimes she maneuvered the wives and daughters of antisuffrage lawmakers into passing the cakes and sandwiches. During World War I, the women executives of the War Department, Food Administration, and various nursing corps used the Suffrage House facilities for their monthly luncheons, with Willard catering the gatherings.[50] Willard, like all other lobbyists, paid a low fee for room and board at the house. The revenue generated from room rentals and catered luncheons, however, did not meet the committee's expenses, which were in excess of $17,000 for the year 1917–18.[51] Suffrage House members were forced to look to NAWSA to make up the deficit.

After December 1917, a second source of support became available: the Leslie Woman Suffrage Commission. The Leslie Commission was the legacy of heiress Frank Leslie (née Miriam Follin). The wife of publisher Frank Leslie, the former Miriam Follin took her husband's name at his death, invested her inheritance shrewdly, and by her death in September 1914 was a millionaire in her own right. In her will, she left the bulk of her fortune to Carrie Chapman Catt to "apply the whole thing as she thinks most advisable to the furtherance of the cause of woman's suffrage." In addition to a cash amount of more than one million dollars, Leslie bequeathed to Catt her jewelry, appraised at more than $34,000. When informed by her lawyers that disgruntled relatives planned to contest the will, Catt replied, "We can afford to wait!" Even the thought of an antisuffrage jury finding in favor of the relatives failed to shake her. "If it could be proved that the case was lost on that issue," she maintained, "the publicity it would give to suffrage would be of as much value to the movement as the money."[52]

After many delays, mounting court costs, and out-of-court settlements, Catt at last received a little more than $900,000 on February 1, 1917. Several days later, the Leslie jewels were brought under guard to Suffrage House, and Catt poured a shower of rubies, emeralds, diamonds, and pearls out on a table. The gems had been appraised at $34,785. Without a moment's hesitation, she sold them all and invested the money in her favorite reform: woman suffrage. In March 1917, the newly created Leslie Woman Suffrage Commission met in furnished headquarters to "educate the people on the principles and operation of woman suffrage by means of literature and press work." One of the commission's first acts was to underwrite the rent and expenses for Suffrage House. In addition, $25,000 went to various suffrage clubs in New York for their 1917 suffrage referendum campaign.[53] In a press release shortly after the first meeting of the commission, Catt announced that NAWSA and its auxiliaries now had at their command about a million dollars a year.[54] She pointed out that this figure was all the more impressive when compared to the two and the two-and-a-half million dollar budgets, respectively, of the Republican and Democratic National Committees.[55]

The Leslie fortune enabled Catt and the NAWSA Executive Board to fulfill their dreams of a high-powered, professional lobby. Maud Wood Park and Suffrage House lobbyists could draw on the vast resources of the Leslie Bureau of Suffrage Education, founded by the Leslie Commission in spring 1917. Director Rose Young envisioned the bureau as "the news purveyor, publicity expert, and propaganda carrier" for the suffrage movement, and she set in motion a winning plan of her own. Under her guidance, the Leslie Bureau was divided into six departments, with a staff of twenty-five trained publicity experts and journalists.[56] The news department held daily interviews with reporters for dailies and syndicated presses; issued a weekly bulletin; and ran a news, photographic, and clipping service. Special features was responsible for supplying special stories, interviews, personality sketches, and biographical information to magazines and journals. Between the two, a typical yearly output of 250,000 words of suffrage propaganda was circulated in the nation's newspapers and periodicals. The departments also produced their own plate material and prepared "canned" suffrage special editions and Sunday supplements during state referenda campaigns.[57] In the victorious 1918 South Dakota campaign, for example, 284 papers used bureau-supplied plates.[58]

In addition to these services, the Leslie Bureau also included divisions of field press, research, editorial correspondence, and magazines. Of particular importance to the Front Door Lobby was the field press department, for it was this department that coordinated the work of the state press chairmen. Under the direction of Rose Lawless Geyer, the press chairmen polled the leading newspapers of their state on the issue of woman suffrage, and they exerted great pressure on stalwart editors to include news of the movement's work in Washington. Rose Young also ran what she jokingly referred to as a "sort of correspondence school of suffrage journalism" by writing on a regular basis to the press chairman with professional tips and encouragement.[59] "Detail, Truth and Timeliness" was the motto of the research division, an appropriate slogan for a department that collected data, statistics, and historical facts about woman suffrage. Journalist and historian Ida Husted Harper oversaw the work of the editorial correspondence department, wrote editorials, and answered attacks mounted by antisuffragists. Lastly, one of the most effective bureau activities was the magazine department, which produced the *Woman Citizen,* a political magazine for women.[60]

The Front Door Lobby used the various research, editorial, and news services provided by the Leslie Bureau to publicize their work in Congress. Moreover, the bureau's work with state press chairmen proved to be invaluable to the lobby. For example, when a lawmaker made a particularly impressive speech in favor of woman suffrage, the bureau instructed the press chairmen to distribute copies of the speech free of charge to his constituency. State press workers also played an important role when a concerted barrage of state and lobby pressure was needed to sway votes before a critical roll call in Congress. At times like these, press chairmen flooded area newspapers with suffrage stories, then relied on other state activists to send the clippings to the congressman along with letters and telegrams. This one-two punch proved to be very effective in convincing congressmen that their constituents favored woman suffrage. Added to the $16,000 for the rent and expenses of Suffrage House, the Leslie Bureau's press and publicity work turned Frank Leslie's fortune into tangible advances for the Front Door Lobby and for the movement in general.

In December 1916, however, when Maud Wood Park and the other Suffrage House residents set out to lobby Congress, the Leslie Bureau existed only in the imagination of NAWSA leaders. And in spite of the hundreds of files and interviews on members of Congress in the committee's office, Park and her coworkers faced the daunting prospect of learning five hundred thirty-one names, faces, and voting records. In the House of Representatives, the Democrats sat on the left of the center aisle, with the Republicans on the right, but the members rarely kept to their seats. Watching from the visitors' gallery, the suffragists were dismayed at the prospect of keeping the men straight, especially on learning that it was forbidden to take notes. The Senate, too, was a formidable challenge, with ninety-six members who drifted in and out of the chamber in a constant stream. Speeches in both houses were difficult to hear, and too often they proved to be inconsequential. "Before long," Park explained, "I acquired the useful senatorial habit of not listening to much that was said and yet of catching promptly an interesting or important turn of debate."[61]

After a stint of gallery observation, the Front Door Lobby took to the halls of Congress in what would become the ultimate daily challenge of their Washington experience: catching congressmen. Working in pairs, the women prepared for interviews by reading files, reviewing voting records, and, most important of all, learning the name of each member's secretary. Arriving at a lawmaker's door, the pair would knock and then quickly enter to prevent the wily politician from slipping out a private exit. All too often their quarry got away. Then, doorkeepers and elevator personnel, aides and secretaries would be called upon to find the elusive prey. "Our task was like a game of hide and seek," Park recalled years afterward, "though we were too firmly impressed with the seriousness of it to get the full benefit of the absurd idea."[62]

On some occasions, the lobbyists were rewarded for their diligence. Interviews were conducted in a professional manner, with the women attempting to extract from the congressman a positive endorsement for their cause. Park drew up a set of guidelines for her coworkers' conduct that underlined the ladylike standards they aspired to:

> Don't nag
> Don't boast
> Don't threaten
> Don't lose your temper
> Don't stay too long
> Don't talk about your work in corridors, elevators or streetcars
> Don't tell everything you know
> Don't tell anything you don't know (i.e., don't repeat rumors)
> Don't do anything to close the door to the next advocate of suffrage[63]

In spite of these rather genteel instructions, the suffragists were occasionally startled by ungentlemanly conduct. One lobbyist filed the following report after a visit to Oklahoma Democrat William H. "Alfalfa Bill" Murray: "Called on Congressman Murray. Sat, hat on, feet on the table, and expectorated tobacco juice through most of our visit. Said Governor Haskel's wife had said that women vote to satisfy love or hate, and that in [a] school election she had voted for a bar-room bum, rather than [for] one of her old professors, whom she personally disliked."[64] Others, like Democrat Martin Dies of Texas, launched into oratory. Believing that "woman dwells apart from man" in nature, Dies told his stunned audience to "look at the barnyard, at the cockerel who protects his hen" to justify his stand against woman suffrage.[65] Another Texas congressman, future Speaker of the House Sam Rayburn, argued his case for male representation of women more eloquently. When the lobbyist replied that she was a widow and thus lacked representation, Rayburn gallantly offered to personally represent her. "The fact of his living in Texas and my residence being in Kentucky did not dismay him at all," the suffragist noted angrily, "but the proposition was most unsatisfactory to me!"[66]

Not all those interviewed by the Front Door Lobby were against woman suffrage. The lobby sought out New York's Fiorello La Guardia, for example, who said "I'm with you; I'm for it; I'm going to vote for it — now don't bother me!"[67] To keep track of those for and against, the suffragists kept a continuous poll of both houses. Poll sheets were organized alphabetically by state and contained the voting records of all representatives and senators, as well as the dates of previous interviews and suffrage votes. Thus, when the Front Door Lobby compared the House suffrage vote of January 12, 1915, with a poll of January 29, 1917, and learned that the number of ayes had only increased by eight after a four-week intensive lobbying effort, they realized that their reform would not be won easily.[68] Long after the disappointment of the January poll, Park recalled the lessons that failure taught: "I came to understand that trifles cannot be ignored in reckoning the factors that lead to a given result. A badly digested luncheon in the stomach of a senator or representative, an ancient prejudice or animosity lurking in his sub-consciousness, a small stupidity on the part of advocates or opponents of a measure, may change the course of history, at least temporarily."[69]

The January poll taught the Front Door Lobby another lesson as well: the need for "home pressure." Many activists like Mrs. Frank Roessing and Park became convinced that the Washington lobbyists could do nothing to persuade reluctant congressmen without the aid of the state associations.[70] Home pressure linked the Congressional Committee to workers all over the country by utilizing the Woman Suffrage Party organizational scheme. Under the WSP system, each state association included a congressional chairman with a corps of district and precinct captains for each congressional district. "Each congressional district chairman should make herself an authority upon the man who represents her district," instructed Catt, shortly after the January 1917 vote. "She should know his religion, his business, his associates, his history, his character, and especially the influences that elected him."[71] Congressional workers then contacted influential constituents who responded with a steady stream of letters, telegrams, clippings from hometown newspapers, and occasional personal deputations to Congress in support of suffrage. In addition to the state congressional activists, NAWSA appointed ninety-five congressional aides to stir up recalcitrant members. Selected strictly on the basis of their prominence in state social or political life, aides harried local editors into writing prosuffrage editorials, pressured the business associates of the congressmen, and saw to it that important constituents wrote in favor of a vote for suffrage. State congressional workers and congressional aides were also welcome at Suffrage House, where they stayed while conducting personal visits to Capitol Hill.[72]

Home pressure and lobbying, however, were to prove ineffective in the face of an unprecedented event that took place in April 1917. Throughout the early spring, relations with Germany had worsened, and on April 2, newly inaugurated President Woodrow Wilson gave his war message to Congress. Four days later, America was at war. Would the war impede the federal amendment's progress, NAWSA leaders wondered, or was there a way to use their resources to serve the country — and the movement as well? And so, as America geared up for the national emergency, the suffrage machine also went to war.

6

The Suffrage Machine

The suffrage machine's last struggle with Congress took place against the backdrop of World War I. America's participation in the war both helped and hindered the suffrage cause. Congress's preoccupation with military concerns meant that, for a time, lobbying for the vote was suspended. And like most other organizations, NAWSA redirected some of its energies toward war work and patriotic service. The war also provided a forum for militancy; the National Woman's Party picketed and mounted hunger strikes to underline the contradictions between government pronouncements on world democracy and women's lack of democratic rights at home.

World War I offered NAWSA suffragists a chance to demonstrate their formidable strength in a show of public-spirited war work. Ironically, they were so successful at patriotic service that commentators would later claim that the war won suffrage for America's women. This raises the question of the importance of World War I to the woman suffrage crusade. Were congressmen and the president so grateful to women for their patriotic service that they granted the vote as a reward? In fact, rather than representing an indispensable boon to the movement, the wartime situation was turned to advantage by NAWSA's shrewd political efforts. Besides the goodwill earned by war work, suffragists gained leverage over politicians through electoral success and political coercion—two hallmarks of the mature suffrage machine.

America's entry into World War I did not catch NAWSA leaders unprepared. Plans had already been laid to convert suffrage societies into an army of volunteers to be placed at the government's disposal. In late February 1917, Executive Board and Council members met in Washington to debate the association's course of action if war with Germany occurred. Unlike previous meetings, this executive session was a stormy one; Catt and a few prominent board members were pacifists, while others believed strongly in preparedness. Finally a compromise was reached, and the group agreed on a dual role for NAWSA of patriotic service and suffrage work, but with patriotic service taking a decidedly second place.[1]

Wartime presented both problems and opportunities for the woman suffrage crusade. Like the NAWSA leaders, not all suffragists were united on the issue of suffrage war work. Some, like the members of the Pennsylvania Woman Suffrage Association, believed that all suffrage agitation should be suspended until the hostilities ceased. Catt quickly silenced the criticism: "Suffragists are quite capable of speeding up and conducting the proposed campaign, and also of doing all the war service that is likely to come their way. They are also quite capable of sitting down to take a rest upon very slight provocation. This is the time for speeding up, not resting."[2]

The time for speeding up began in March, a full month before America's entry into the war. Following up on their February resolution, NAWSA leaders formed plans for war service that included Americanization classes, food production and distribution, waste elimination programs, and cooperation with the Red Cross. Each state organization received copies of the plan, and after an appeal by Catt to put aside sectional differences, thirty state presidents began to implement the suggestions at once. When hostilities actually began, the suffragists were well on their way to a wartime footing, and they quickly volunteered their impressive resources to the government.[3]

The Front Door Lobby was forced to drop its federal amendment drive, previously scheduled for early April, when Congress passed a resolution curtailing debate on all nonemergency measures.[4] Like the NAWSA board, the Congressional Committee was sharply divided on the issue of what, if any, suffrage work should be done in time of national emergency. Ruth Hanna McCormick was particularly outspoken in her opposition to suffrage work in wartime. As a compromise, Catt and Maud Wood Park agreed on a plan to suspend congressional lobbying temporarily in favor of working to build up the state congressional committees, which were originally created to provide home pressure for the Front Door Lobby. Under the Catt-Park scheme, lobbyists would tour the states and lecture on the necessity of home pressure until Congress again took up the issue of woman suffrage. "When and if we are really caught in the throes of a real war, we shall probably be forced to drop suffrage activities," Catt mused. Until that time, however, she remained convinced that suffrage should not be sacrificed for patriotic service.[5]

Like their rivals, antisuffragists were determined to use the war for their own propaganda purposes. Seizing upon NAWSA's dual program of war service and suffrage as evidence of disloyalty, the antisuffragists charged that suffragists failed to aid their country in time of national emergency. According to one observer, the antisuffragists used "every devilish art to befuddle the public"; they even charged Carrie Catt with harboring pro-German sympathies. Catt's friendship through the International Woman Suffrage Alliance with Hungarian feminist and pacifist Rosika Schwimmer led antisuffragists to proclaim that all suffragists were disloyal. So persuasive were their charges that Schwimmer was accused of being a German spy. The fact that Catt's compromise stand on NAWSA war work had cost her her membership in the New York Peace Party, an organization she had helped to found in 1915, failed to convince antisuffrage critics of her patriotism.[6]

Unlike Catt, who abandoned her convictions concerning militarism in order to curry favor for woman suffrage with the government, other women felt a sense of betrayal at the NAWSA board's decision to engage in war work. For example, conflicts over patriotic service provoked anger among suffragists who were also pacifists. The association traditionally had supported antimilitarism, and there was a sizable faction of pacifists within the suffrage movement. Some, like Jane Addams, did not officially resign from the suffrage organization but rather withdrew from active participation. Others joined the National Woman's Party, which disassociated itself from war work completely.[7]

Radical women, in particular, were outspoken in their disgust with the association's stand on the war. Crystal Eastman dropped her involvement in suffrage to concentrate her efforts on pacifism. "I believe," wrote Eastman, "[that] a great many suffragists who are not pacifists felt decidedly aggrieved that their services had been so lightly pledged to a government which has denied to them for forty years a fundamental democratic right."[8] Even before the outbreak of World War I, many radicals had formed only loose ties with NAWSA because of their distrust of the movement's elitism and disinterest in working women's issues. Radical suffragist Sarah Colvin recalled NAWSA activists' class biases in her 1944 memoir: "They all looked upon themselves as highly competent people engaged in a fundamental movement, and were quite serious in their belief that they knew what should be done; all they needed was to be given the power to carry out their plans. Never did I hear a discussion about economic inequalities, never any anxiety expressed over the double work women did when they had to carry the two burdens of keeping a home going and earning a living."[9] The association's stand on pacifism, combined with its reaction to wartime militancy by the National Woman's Party, severed forever the fragile link between the middle-class suffrage movement and radical women.[10]

The leaders of NAWSA urged pacifists to remain within the suffrage movement, yet those who did were sometimes charged with disloyalty because of their aversion to patriotic service. Massachusetts activist and pacifist Wenona Pinkham faced a vicious attack by Boston area suffragists when she attempted to run for office in the MWSA. "I desire with all my heart both to make the world safe for democracy and to guard and extend such measure of democracy as exists in our country," Pinkham argued in defense of her principles, "When freedom is cut off, democracy is slain."[11] After much discussion and the intervention of the NAWSA Executive Board, Pinkham and other pacifists were given the option of service in areas that were unrelated to the war. Thus, pacifists could continue to be suffrage activists while avoiding the stigma of disloyalty.[12]

During the war years, NAWSA leaders spent much time and money rebutting antisuffrage charges of disloyalty and settling local disputes over pacifism. The association also faced criticism from the other extreme of the political spectrum, the militant National Woman's Party. Founded in 1916 by Alice Paul, the NWP advocated coercive tactics, including partisan attacks on the political party in power. At the outbreak of hostilities, Paul steered her followers along a path of total commitment to suffrage, eschewing patriotic service in favor of work for the federal suffrage amendment. "We will not bargain with our country for our services," a NWP official stated, "We will not say to our government: 'give us the vote and we will nurse your soldiers,' but we will insist on suffrage now."[13] The NWP leaders were also outspoken in their scorn for NAWSA's war work, asserting that their rival had forsaken suffrage for patriotic service. For the remainder of the war, NAWSA was forced to steer a narrow course between the shoals of disloyalty to the woman suffrage movement, on the one hand, and disloyalty to the nation, on the other.

For most NAWSA activists, however, the decision to engage in war work posed no problem, nor was there any significant degree of protest over the association's treatment of pacifists. More troublesome to many activists was the slow process by which the government doled out the work. Women's groups nationwide competed for choice assignments, and in the confused early days of the war, chaos reigned. Some groups, including the antisuffragists, had joined an umbrella organization founded in February 1917 and called the National League for Woman's Services (NLWS), which offered its services to the government for census taking and other war work. The NLWS competed bitterly with NAWSA for war work and repeatedly urged government officials to shun the aid of the suffragists in favor of that of their own membership. In late April, the Council of National Defense appointed a Woman's Committee (WCCND) to coordinate the activities of women's groups, and antisuffragists were enraged to learn that suffragist Anna Howard Shaw had been chosen to head the new organization.[14] In addition to Shaw, NAWSA leaders Antoinette Funk, Katharine McCormick, and Carrie Chapman Catt found places on the executive committee.[15] Moreover, six of the nine-member committee were active in the movement, giving the WCCND a decidedly suffragist tilt.[16]

Under Shaw's guidance, the WCCND formed divisions in the states much like those created under the Woman Suffrage Party organizational scheme. Americanization, food conservation and production, canvassing, and studies of camp life were but some of the WCCND's concerns, but its primary function remained the coordination of women's organizations involved in patriotic service. The National American Woman Suffrage Association exploited Shaw's connection with the WCCND throughout the war, claiming that suffragists did more for their country than any other group. But poor funding, red tape, and little real authority made the work difficult for Shaw: "I thought women were bad enough," Shaw groaned to a friend, "but oh my—deliver me from the pettiness of public officials!"[17]

Under the WCCND, suffragists took part in a variety of war-related jobs. The Patriotic Committee of the New York State WSP staffed Red Cross booths in department stores, collected money for the United War Work drive, sold thirty-five thousand dollars worth of War Savings Stamps, and donated hundreds of knitted garments to the Red Cross. The group also conducted the military census for the state, using their precinct and electoral district organization to carry out the work. The chairman of the WSP, Vira Whitehouse, called the census "the most effective suffrage propaganda possible."[18] The propaganda value of war work was not lost on antisuffragists. When a Massachusetts weighing and measuring campaign was turned over to the state suffrage association, local antisuffragists refused to cooperate and charged their rivals with using war work to gain political capital for their reform.[19] Unmoved by their argument, suffragists pointed out that the campaign was to be conducted by their nonpolitical Child Welfare Committee, at which point the criticism subsided.[20]

The Boston Equal Suffrage Association for Good Government was another society that took full use of World War I as a vehicle for prosuffrage publicity. The BESAGG created thirteen war-related committees coordinated by the organization's War Service Committee. In addition to holding food-conservation lectures and operating community kitchens and canteens for enlisted men, the group sold Liberty Bonds, ran a convalescent hospital, and made surgical dressings.[21] One of BESAGG's many successful projects was an Americanization program, designed to assimilate Boston's immigrant population into American society. After taking a survey of the foreign born to determine such factors as nationality, work conditions, and eligibility for citizenship, the suffragists used their precinct and district organizations to form local outreach programs.[22] At the local level, activists staged a series of mass meetings, such as the one held for Italian immigrants in Boston's North End in early 1918. On the night of the meeting, the local community hall was decorated in the national colors of Italy, with both Italian and American flags gracing the podium. After speeches in Italian on woman suffrage and citizenship, girls dressed in old-world costumes danced the tarantella. Similar meetings conducted in other ethnic districts featured lantern slides, literature on child care, and job counseling. The Americanization Committee of BESAGG was also responsible for an Americanization Station in the North End, which ran a free employment bureau for agricultural labor and, through its connections with the Red Cross and state Board of Education, offered classes on American history, literature, and English for neighborhood residents.[23]

Other suffrage societies used the wartime emergency to implement a variety of progressive programs. Kentucky suffragists took command of a neighborhood school in a black section of Lexington and turned it into a community center much like Chicago's Hull House. At night, the women offered swimming and gymnastics classes for children, ran the neighborhood's first library, and sponsored a number of youth groups and activities for adults.[24] Americanization programs and other progressive reforms, however successful and necessary, were implemented almost exclusively by state and local suffrage societies. The national leadership of NAWSA took no part in these activities, nor did it include such ventures in its strategic planning.

More to NAWSA leaders' liking were activities that were directly war related and well suited to generate favorable publicity for the movement. Kentucky activists bought their own ambulance, christened the "Laura Clay" after the state's pioneer suffragist, as their contribution to NAWSA's most ambitious wartime venture, the Overseas Hospital.[25] The Overseas Hospital, adopted as a "war baby" by NAWSA's 1917 convention, was in reality two fifty-bed hospitals and a gas unit in France. The project was funded at a cost of $125,000 a year through donations from state and local NAWSA chapters.[26] Twenty-four female doctors, nurses, and other medical personnel initially staffed the institutions, although by the end of the war, a total of seventy-four women had served there. One hospital located in Chateau Ognon was bombed three times during the course of the war, and the unit's three surgeons and head nurse were decorated for bravery under fire with the Croix de Guerre. The only suffrage casualties occurred when NAWSA vice president and director general of the Overseas Hospital Mrs. Raymond Brown led a band of doctors and nurses to France to set up a gas unit in Cempius. Two of the young nurses contracted influenza while en route on a crowded troop ship and died soon after arriving in France. In spite of this setback, Brown managed to establish the unit, and with the arrival of the latest anti-gas equipment from the States, left the staff at work hosing down gassed soldiers.[27]

Patriotic service served the woman suffrage movement well. As Ida Husted Harper wrote to the editor of a Dallas, Texas, paper, the suffragists' war work "has not been equalled by that of any organization of women in the United States."[28] Census taking and other government-sponsored jobs gave the suffragists the official government sanction they had long coveted. Much of the WCCND correspondence at the state and local level used the stationery of NAWSA, connecting the association with governmental relief efforts.[29] As the *Woman Citizen* boasted in fall 1918, "The leaders in women's work in the Red Cross, YMCA, Liberty Loan, Food [Administration], are almost without exception women who have been trained in their work in our Association."[30] Thus the change in public opinion toward the movement, begun in the first decade of the twentieth century with the society plan, reached new heights during World War I. In wartime NAWSA found a nonmilitant lever with which to pressure the government to grant woman suffrage. A NAWSA flier summed up the suffrage position by contrasting a long list of "services that the country is asking of women" with the sole war measure — enfranchisement — that women desired in return.[31]

But did the war win suffrage for women? Antisuffragists also engaged in war work and publicized their patriotic services. Weighing only women's patriotic service, Congress might have defeated the federal amendment as a favor to antisuffrage activists as readily as it passed it to honor suffrage war work. And despite the propaganda purposes of patriotic service, there were real drawbacks to the women's war work. As one suffrage activist reported: "In order to do all this work and more, we have had to lay aside much of our suffrage work. . . . This important but grinding work was the first to be sacrificed. We have had to abandon the suffrage street meetings, we have abandoned the great pageants, we have postponed the suffrage motor tours with meetings and parades. We have abandoned the money-raising campaigns we had organized for every district in the state."[32] In addition to a slowdown in state suffrage activism, the Front Door Lobby had suspended all work in Washington throughout spring 1917. By early summer, however, the Congressional Committee formulated a new strategy designed to induce the House to create a Woman Suffrage Committee. Previously the federal amendment had been under the jurisdiction of the Rules Committee, chaired by an opponent of votes for women. The lobbyists reasoned that a new committee chaired by advocates of suffrage would facilitate the amendment's passage. When Speaker Champ Clark supported the idea and representatives from Western suffrage states promised to petition the Rules Committee for action, the women's hopes rose.[33] In May, the hostile Rules Committee received President Wilson's endorsement and a petition for a vote on it signed by eighty-five representatives.[34]

The suffragists had not counted on the action of the National Woman's Party. In early January 1917, the NWP had embarked on a new technique to call attention to the federal amendment and simultaneously to exert pressure on President Woodrow Wilson and the Democratic Party. National Woman's Party pickets appeared at the White House gates bearing banners that asked: "MR. PRESIDENT, how long must women wait for liberty?"[35] Alice Paul explained her strategy this way: "If a creditor stands before a man's house all day demanding payment of his bill, the man must either remove the creditor or pay the bill."[36] President Wilson at first refused to do either, choosing instead to ignore the pickets. Many congressmen, however, were not amused. After a May 18 hearing on the proposed Woman Suffrage Committee, Rules Committee member Pat Harrison issued a statement declaring: "I shall never vote to create a special committee on woman suffrage so long as any suffrage organization continues the practice of picketing the White House and the Congressional office buildings."[37]

Upon reading Representative Harrison's statement, the NAWSA Executive Board, together with the Front Door Lobby, immediately conceived of a two-pronged plan. First, in an effort to persuade Alice Paul to abandon the picketing, Catt wrote to the NWP leader urging her to reconsider her strategy. Calling the NWP maneuver "an unwarranted discourtesy to the President and a futile annoyance to the members of Congress," Catt pointed out that the pickets were blocking the creation of a woman suffrage committee.[38] The NAWSA leaders had little sympathy with militancy or other tactics devised by Alice Paul. To Catt and her coworkers, militant displays threatened the careful alliances and insider strategy that the Front Door Lobby had built; eager to win Wilson's endorsement by offering him their support, NAWSA activists watched with horror as the NWP pickets tried to embarrass the president into suffrage advocacy. Convinced that the NWP would refuse to remove the pickets, Catt and other NAWSA leaders embarked on a scheme to lessen the impact of their militant rivals.

On the same day that Catt wrote to Alice Paul, she also prepared letters to all press correspondents in the nation's largest cities. The letters laid out the congressional situation in regard to Harrison's statement and the woman suffrage committee stalemate and expressed disapproval with NWP tactics. "We feel most keenly the handicap and injustice to the suffrage cause," the letter continued, "when suffragists as a whole are blamed for the action of a small group . . . which is in no real sense representative of the suffrage movement generally. I am asking you therefore to assist us in making plain through the newspapers the fact that the pickets do not represent suffragists in general. Will you not emphasize the distinction between the two organizations, and their relative size and importance in anything you write regarding the suffrage issue?"[39]

In response to Catt's request, numerous journalists agreed to distinguish between the two organizations. David Lawrence, Washington correspondent for the *New York Evening Post* and *Washington Times,* assured NAWSA strategists that their suggestion "fits in with the policy I have been pursuing in my dispatches." Another member of the Fourth Estate, *Washington Post* correspondent Thomas Logan, also promised to clearly define "your representative organization from the offshoot."[40] At least one state NAWSA affiliate also petitioned the press to emphasize that the organization did not endorse militancy.[41]

But journalists alone could not turn the tide of publicity that eddied about the National Woman's Party. On June 20, the White House pickets greeted a delegation from the Alexander Kerensky government with a banner that proclaimed: TELL OUR GOVERNMENT THAT IT MUST LIBERATE ITS WOMEN BEFORE IT CAN CLAIM FREE RUSSIA AS AN ALLY.[42] After the Russians had passed, a group of enraged bystanders attacked the pickets and tore their banner to pieces.[43] After the Russian banner riot, the president's passive policy toward the NWP suddenly altered. The following day police arrested two pickets for obstructing the sidewalk and ordered that the picketing cease. Every major paper on the East Coast carried reports of the riot and arrests, often on the front page. National Woman's Party members were also pleased with photographs of the event that pictured two young women surrounded by a mob of rowdies.[44] In a press release, Alice Paul commented: "The responsibility is with the government and not with the women of America, if the lack of democracy at home weakens the government in its fight for democracy 3,000 miles away."[45]

As a result of the excess publicity, NAWSA lobbyists found themselves unable to persuade the House Rules Committee to act on the woman suffrage committee. "Had it been men who did it," fumed one NAWSA lobbyist after the Russian banner incident, "they would have been behind prison bars so quick their heads would have been swimming!"[46] On June 23, when Park, Gardener, and Congressional Committee secretary Ethel Smith met with the Speaker of the House, the women were discouraged to hear Clark advise delaying tactics; "this would be a very bad time" for a vote on the woman suffrage committee, the Speaker cautioned the women.[47] Several days later, the three lobbyists spoke with Senator A. A. Jones, chairman of the Senate Woman Suffrage Committee, and learned that he, too, believed that the picketing had jeopardized action by that body. Jones had been eager to issue a favorable report on the suffrage resolution, and he had previously assured the lobbyists that his committee would endorse the measure unanimously. But with the White House arrests and subsequent publicity, two Senate committee members reversed their stand, and another refused to attend committee meetings until the pickets decamped. "I only mildly express my feelings," Jones wrote in a letter to Maud Wood Park, "when I say that the present situation is giving me real concern."[48]

Perhaps it was the Front Door Lobby's mounting sense of frustration that led them to formulate a scheme in late June 1917 to silence the militants once and for all. On June 26, the same day that the women interviewed Senator Jones, Ethel Smith wrote jubilantly to Catt: "I have good news, I think! I am told this morning in confidence, which I am permitted to pass on to you, that a train has been laid by certain newspaper men who are our friends, to apply the remedy of silence to the picketing performances. . . . I went to see a representative of one such newspaper yesterday and found him very receptive to the idea of voluntary censorship of this subject on the grounds of public policy. He has a direct line to the big press associations and he seems hopeful that these associations will request Mr. Creel's committee to pass along the word to other papers."[49]

Smith's scheme was quickly endorsed by lobbyists Maud Wood Park and Helen Gardener. The first stop on the Front Door Lobby's new agenda was the White House, where Smith, Park, and Gardener discussed their idea of a conspiracy of silence with President Wilson's secretary, Joseph P. Tumulty. Aware that the president was annoyed with the pickets, Tumulty agreed to think the matter over for a few days. Fortune smiled on the women, however, as they left the secretary's office. Outside they encountered George Creel, the chairman of Wilson's newly created censorship agency, the Committee on Public Information (CPI). Creel immediately endorsed the scheme of press silence, and he suggested that the women approach the various press associations with their plan. Moreover, Creel offered to arrange the visits. Several days later, he notified the lobby that appointments had been made for them to interview Associated Press, International News Service, and United Press correspondents.[50]

Creel aided the suffragists in another way as well. On July 3, 1917, his office issued an official bulletin to all newspapers, post offices, government officials, and public agencies. The statement defined NAWSA as "the great body of organized suffragists [that] deplores as absurd, ill-timed, and susceptible of grave and demoralizing suspicion the tactics of the isolated handful of suffragists at the national Capitol." Pointing out that the picketing was "but a detail of a publicity campaign," the CPI memorandum urged press and public alike simply to ignore the National Woman's Party activists.[51] At the same time that Creel's bulletin circulated through Washington, Park and Smith embarked on a series of calls to influential journalists. The lobbyists requested that the newspapermen omit the word *suffrage* from all coverage of the National Woman's Party. "To call them suffragists," explained Park, "brands all supporters . . . with a stigma which is utterly undeserved." All the correspondents agreed to the women's request, and one, David Lawrence of the *New York Post* and *Washington Times,* promised to cut back on the publicity given to the militants.[52]

By late July, the NAWSA plan for press censorship of National Woman's Party activities had found a new ally in the person of President Woodrow Wilson. When Washington journalist Arthur Brisbane broached the scheme to Joseph P. Tumulty, the secretary laid the matter before the president. Wilson responded in an undated memorandum: "There is a great deal in what Mr. Brisbane writes about entire silence on the part of the newspapers. . . . My own suggestion would be that nothing that they do should be featured or put on the front page but that a bare colorless chronicle of what they do should be all that was printed. That constitutes part of the news but it need not be made interesting reading."[53] Although a few papers followed Wilson's wishes on day-to-day coverage of the militants, there is no conclusive evidence about the extent of compliance with the scheme by the press. A check of newspaper coverage on three dates when significant militant activity occurred indicates that most journalists were loath to pass up a good story, even if their actions angered the president.[54]

At NAWSA's instigation, President Wilson and the wartime censorship agency abridged the freedom of the press. This episode illustrates some of the forces at work within the suffrage machine. More concerned with ends than with means, suffrage leaders connived at undemocratic manipulation of the press and public opinion in the service of avowedly democratic goals. These events posed one of the dilemmas of modern politics. Increasing reliance on public opinion to shape political processes invited popular participation in policy making, while attempting to mold rather than to educate that opinion.[55] Although the NAWSA leaders had evolved a strategy for victory based on an ostensible outpouring of popular support, they did not trust the people to provide that support if presented with all the facts.

The erosion of the national association's internal democratic structure that began in 1915 with Catt's elevation to the presidency was by 1917 projected into the movement's tactics as well. The association had become an oligarchy in pursuit of democratic reform. Not surprisingly, it developed an institutional aversion to such democratic values as unrestricted debate and freedom of the press. By allying with Creel's Committee on Public Information, for example, NAWSA not only worked to damage the credibility of other suffragists, but, given the wartime censorship function of the CPI, also unintentionally linked the mainstream suffrage movement with a government committee notorious for persecution of radicals and Socialists. For example, *The Masses,* a vocal advocate of woman suffrage, was censored by the CPI; Socialists like Eugene V. Debs and Max Eastman, both lifelong suffrage supporters, were jailed in the backlash of ethnic and political hatred generated by the wartime censorship agency.[56]

The alliance with the CPI was symptomatic of the gradual narrowing of the movement itself. Over time, the association excluded blacks, working women, and socialists; during World War I, feminists, radicals, and to some extent pacifists were added to the list. As policy making became the province of fewer individuals, the goals of the organization also became narrow and restricted. When Front Door Lobbyist Ethel Smith began to include in her weekly press releases stories that related the poor pay and bad working conditions of American women during wartime, Catt angrily objected to the lobby "putting its fingers into every pie." In addition to her work with the Front Door Lobby, Smith was the chairman of NAWSA's Industrial Protection of Women Committee, charged with "securing women workers to fill the place of men called for military service" and protecting their rights in the workplace. Smith had the sanction of the NAWSA convention to use the Washington lobby's publicity bureau to supplement her Industrial Protection Committee's efforts.[57] Insisting, however, that the lobby concentrate solely on the federal amendment, Catt tersely summed up the NAWSA Executive Board's position on "outside" reforms: "We do not care a 'ginger snap' about anything but that Federal Amendment at present."[58]

Throughout summer 1917 the fate of the federal amendment remained uncertain. The Congressional Committee had suspended all lobbying activity after the Russian banner incident, and despite efforts to silence news coverage of the NWP pickets, the group had accomplished little in regard to the creation of the woman suffrage committee.[59] Therefore, when prosuffrage advocates in the House suggested pushing the amendment as a war measure, thus avoiding the congressional dictum on nonemergency legislation, suffragists quickly agreed to the plan. State suffrage delegations appeared at politicians' doors, and telegrams and telephone calls flooded in as the Washington lobby geared up for the fight. Even President Wilson took a hand in the issue by writing Rules Committee Chairman Edward Pou that the proposed committee would be "a very wise act of public policy."[60] When the House of Representatives prepared to debate the creation of the committee on September 24, 1917, prosuffrage sentiment was running at fever pitch. After a two-hour debate, Chairman Pou, a former opponent of the measure, summed up the opinion of many congressmen: "A word to the wise is sufficient; this, Mr. Speaker, is a question that will not go down."[61] Conceding to the pressure for action, the hostile Rules Committee issued a favorable report on the new committee, which was subsequently adopted by a vote of 180 to 107. Chaired by Representative John E. Raker and with ten of its thirteen members committed to woman suffrage, the new Woman Suffrage Committee was a welcome relief to suffragists who had feared that their reform would remain tabled forever in a hostile Rules Committee.[62]

The Front Door Lobby rejoiced in their victory over the Rules Committee, but the problems of shepherding the amendment through both houses of Congress and the states still lay ahead. "The rest of the game is political," Catt wrote to a friend in October 1917. "I am not a politician and politics is no place for a reformer. That is why I can see no opening of the Red Sea of political messing for us to walk through. It is the symptom of the end stage of the argument. What next? We are in the stage of surrender, but how to bring the actual throwing up of hands, the handing over of the sword, is too much for a reformer mind."[63] In spite of her protestations, Catt's political sensibilities were more than a match for her adversaries in Congress. Additionally, suffragists at the state level were finding their own path through the Red Sea of politics. Ohio, Indiana, Nebraska, Michigan, and Rhode Island women won the right of presidential suffrage in 1917, and with a primary suffrage victory in Arkansas, the solid South was broken at last. The most important victory of the year, however, was in New York. Two years earlier, activists there had lost a heartrending battle for the vote, despite intensive organization and publicity drives, a campaign chest in excess of fifty thousand dollars, and the support of more than two hundred thousand women.[64] Therefore, the 1917 New York contest was doubly important, both as a crucial test of the suffrage machine's new wartime publicity efforts and as revenge for its loss in 1915.

The New York campaign was a two-year-long effort that began two days after the 1915 defeat with a mass meeting at Cooper Union. Woman Suffrage Party leaders divided the city into campaign districts and established headquarters in each borough. In the first campaign district, for example, eight organizers interviewed ninety-eight candidates for Congress, canvassed house to house, and distributed more than three thousand leaflets before the November 1917 vote.[65] Other activists passed out suffrage buttons and fliers at county fairs and baseball games in an effort to raise public awareness, while suffrage training schools drilled new recruits in suffrage history, organizing tactics, and public speaking.[66] As a result, endorsements poured in from the major political parties, President Wilson, and a host of New York associations and organizations. As New York State Woman Suffrage Party Chairman Mrs. Norman Whitehouse reflected, "the change in sentiment in regard to women, because of the assistance they have given the government at war, has been enormous."[67]

An important factor in the suffragists' 1917 New York victory was the work of Mary Garrett Hay, chairman of the WSP first campaign district. A longtime resident of New York and a student of local machine politics, Hay recognized that chances for success were slim without the cooperation of Tammany Hall. Resolved to win Tammany to suffrage, Hay recruited the wives of several machine bosses and installed them as officers in the local WSP. When Tammany Hall called a meeting to debate the issue shortly before the November election, the New York suffragists were well represented. Moreover, Hay managed to convince Tammany boss Charlie Murphy that the Democratic Party would be held responsible for the fate of the woman suffrage amendment after women were eventually enfranchised. Murphy apparently recognized that the issue could not be avoided indefinitely, and he instructed the machine to adopt a "hands-off" position during the contest. Without the opposition of the New York City machine, victory was assured in the Tammany-controlled wards of the city.[68]

Upstate New York, however, remained firmly against the amendment. Even a statewide house-to-house canvass and enrollment campaign in the summer of 1917 failed to win over the rural sectors. Thus it was voters in New York City who carried the day for woman suffrage.[69] In addition to the Woman Suffrage Party's organizing efforts, Socialist women worked tirelessly to organize working-class and immigrant neighborhoods for suffrage, despite poor funding and inadequate support from the Socialist Party. Assistance also came from the Women's Trade Union League, which took control of the WSP Industrial Section and formed the Wage Earners Suffrage League to stimulate working-class support and to act as a liaison between women workers and the suffragists. Pacifists and German Americans joined the so-called radical coalition to rally those groups so long neglected by NAWSA and its affiliate the WSP. So effective was this ad hoc coalition that the antisuffragist *New York Times* proclaimed that the Socialists were responsible for the 1917 victory.[70]

The efforts of the Socialists, WTUL, pacifists, and German Americans, as well as the votes of the immigrant and working men of New York City, were ignored in the victory celebration held by the WSP. Among the women present at WSP headquarters when the election results were announced, ex-NAWSA President Anna Howard Shaw was perhaps the most affected by the long-awaited victory. The elderly orator had often been called on to address suffragists after bitter defeats. In victory Shaw's voice failed her, and she sat with tears streaming down her face.[71] Later Shaw expressed to a friend the conflicting emotions she felt: "It is undoubtedly true that the organization in New York State was magnificent and the campaign was directed in a splendid manner, but when I realized that they had hundreds of thousands of dollars to put into it and thousands of people ready to assist them in every possible way, I could not help thinking of the old days when we had almost no money and but few workers and slight encouragement. And somehow those old days are dearer to me than the later ones, and those old friends and workers seem to have a different kind of consecration. . . . Now that the end is so nearly in sight that we can see it just over the hill, it does not take so much courage."[72]

Shaw's commentary reflects the state of the woman suffrage movement in its twentieth-century incarnation as political pressure group. With the society plan, vast organization, and oligarchical control came the long-desired success, but the price of victory proved high. From the standardization of propaganda to the loss of local and state decision making, the modern suffrage movement had moved slowly away from its democratic and heroic origins. The initiative of solitary reformers over time was replaced by an impersonal bureaucracy composed of professional crusaders lauded for their work in the popular press and public arenas of the nation. "I don't see people much nowadays who care about Miss Anthony or real suffrage," one elderly activist grumbled, "they are gallivanting out for war work and all sorts of things."[73] For some of the movement's pioneers, success proved bittersweet without the heroic sacrifice and individual exertion of days gone by.

Others, like Carrie Chapman Catt, greeted the New York victory with unqualified enthusiasm. "The battle of New York," Catt proclaimed in an address circulated to the state legislatures of America, "was the Gettysburg of the woman suffrage movement."[74] In Washington, the Front Door Lobby rejoiced as the number of electoral votes in states with woman suffrage jumped from 172 to 215 after the New York contest. Maud Wood Park also noticed a positive effect among that state's congressional delegation within days of the election. "Most of those listed as 'doubtful' on our poll promptly changed to supporters, as did several of those previously opposed," Park remarked, "because the carrying of New York was accepted by the politically wise as the handwriting on the wall."[75]

Park's observation proved correct. With the New York victory the political situation was suddenly altered; lobbyists faced not a lack, but rather too much congressional zeal for their reform. The rising tide of suffrage sentiment threatened to break prematurely when Representative Claude Kitchin rashly scheduled a vote on the federal amendment on December 17, 1917, the day before Congress was to address the prohibition resolution. Kitchin's action caused great concern among the suffrage forces, who feared that any association with the controversial prohibition amendment would spell defeat for their measure. After a series of hastily scheduled meetings with Kitchin and other friends in Congress, Park concluded a "gentlemen's agreement" satisfactory to all parties. The congressmen agreed to name the members of the Woman Suffrage Committee, which would assume jurisdiction over the amendment, and the amendment would be reported out of committee in time for a vote in early January. Park also agreed that if at that time the amendment was defeated, no further vote on it would be attempted during the current session. True to their promise, House members created the committee during the second week of December and staffed it with a prosuffrage majority.[76] The lobbyists' fears of a prohibition backlash were put to rest, and their hopes rose for a successful House vote when the lawmakers returned from their holiday break.

One obstacle to the smooth passage of the federal amendment was the southern wing of the Democratic Party. Lobbyists turned to President Woodrow Wilson for help. He had proved amenable to votes for women as early as 1915, when he cast his vote for a state suffrage amendment in a New Jersey referendum. Although initially an advocate of the state route to woman suffrage, by late 1917 Wilson had become convinced of the inevitability of the reform by the militancy of the NWP; the pickets, jail terms, and hunger strikes had forced him to treat the issue seriously. The president's conversion to a supporter of the amendment, however, was also attained by the skillful persuasion of Helen Hamilton Gardener. Gardener used her contacts with White House secretaries Joseph Tumulty and Rudolph Forster to press home the wisdom of bringing the Democratic Party into line behind the suffrage resolution and thereby stealing political thunder from the GOP. On occasion, she resorted to plying the president with flattery as well.[77] Wilson at last issued a declaration in favor of the federal amendment on the day before the House vote. Although his influence on the southern wing of his party proved negligible,[78] both NWP and NAWSA activists counted his support as a symbolic victory, indicative of the turning tide of suffragism that would eventually produce success.

In spite of the president's efforts, Front Door Lobby polls showed a majority of only one on the morning of January 10, 1918, when the House members assembled to debate the federal suffrage amendment. With no votes to spare, Park and her coworkers worked frantically to ensure the presence of each prosuffrage vote. When Illinois Representative Clifford Ireland was involved in a train wreck on his way to Washington, state suffrage leaders arranged to have a replacement locomotive sent to the scene of the crash. On board were suffragists who disembarked long enough to secure Ireland's signature authorizing a pair, then rushed on to the next town to cable the news to the capital. Two representatives were hospitalized in the district; both appeared for the vote, although one — Representative Henry A. Barnhart of Indiana — called out "aye" from a stretcher. Another friend of suffrage, Tennessee Democrat Thetus W. Sims, fell and broke his shoulder on the way to Capitol Hill. Unwilling to have his shoulder set lest he miss the crucial vote, Sims went to the House where he cast his vote for suffrage through a grimace of pain.[79] When the votes were totaled, the federal woman suffrage amendment had passed the House by a bare one vote majority, 274 to 136.[80]

The leaders of NAWSA sought to capitalize on the House victory by pressing for a Senate vote as soon as possible. When the Front Door Lobby poll revealed that ten more votes were needed to assure success, activists turned again to personal interviews and home pressure to sway the senators. By February 1918, two Senate vacancies had been filled with prosuffrage advocates; when North Carolina won presidential suffrage in March, another vote was added to the senatorial roster.[81] In addition, WSP official Mary Garrett Hay turned her attention to key Republican leaders in an effort to woo the GOP to the cause. Hay promised the support of women voters in future contests in exchange for congressional support for the amendment, an action in direct violation of NAWSA's policy of nonpartisanship. As Hay and Carrie Chapman Catt shared living quarters and were close friends, it is doubtful this breach in policy went unnoticed by NAWSA executives. More probably, Hay embarked on a policy of partisan appeals with the full approval of the association's leaders (but not its members), and in doing so, she gave further evidence of the erosion of traditional goals and values of the movement.[82]

A handful of senators continued to block the vote on the federal amendment throughout spring and early summer of 1918. In May, Catt issued an urgent appeal to state presidents and congressional chairmen to remonstrate against the delay. State and local activists responded with resolutions, delegations, and telephone calls to recalcitrant senators, all couched in terms of indignation at the lawmakers' opposition to a "world-wide struggle for democracy."[83] An August poll showed the results of home pressure and Congressional Committee lobbying efforts: the number of favorable votes stood at sixty-two, with only four more needed to win passage of the amendment. In addition, two senators had shifted from "opposed" to "doubtful," giving the suffragists reason for optimism when the amendment debate and vote was scheduled for late September.

Park, Gardener, and other lobbyists continued to interview senators and meet with members of Congress for daily progress reports. Catt rallied state activists who deluged the Senate with a barrage of letters and telegrams from influential constituents; for "doubtfuls," fifty wires, each worded differently, were requested, while opponents of the measure received a thousand from their home district.[84] In addition to these efforts, Catt urged state and local activists to embark on a campaign of what she called "blowing our common trumpet." "Will you not try to draw the advocates of our cause closer together," Catt asked in a bulletin circulated among suffragists throughout the nation, "magnify the achievements and importance of our organization in order that the unity, aims and objects of our association may be set forth clearly to the public?"[85]

Catt's use of the word *magnify* is significant; her objective was to create the appearance of mass support for suffrage when in fact such support did not exist. In a Liberty Loan drive the previous spring, she had employed the same strategy when she urged activists to sell bonds at factories, workshops, open-air meetings, and movie theaters. In a bulletin to her Liberty Loan coworkers, Catt described the strategy that would later be applied to suffrage work. "It goes without saying," she instructed, "that most people who speak [for the Liberty Loan drive] will not be able, in the few minutes allowed at such times and places, to persuade those who come within hearing to go forth and buy bonds. The main object is not that. It is to create the momentum for the drive, and by continual repetition of the demand to buy bonds, to impress the mind of every citizen with the duty to do so."[86] In both cases and throughout her organizational work, Catt placed great tacit reliance on the bandwagon effect, the propensity of many people to associate themselves with a movement on the basis of its seeming popularity rather than through a rational analysis of its goals. Eschewing the traditional suffrage tactic of conversion of individual supporters through appeals to justice and gradual education, the NAWSA strategy by 1918 instead reflected the suffragists' growing emphasis on image over substance.

Congressional lobbying and home pressure created an avalanche of publicity for suffrage in the national press. The NWP, experts at publicity, and NAWSA flooded editors with suffrage stories and kept up a steady stream of home pressure from their state societies. In an effort to share the spotlight with the suffragists, Mrs. James W. Wadsworth, president of the National Association Opposed to Woman Suffrage, demanded a public debate over the issue with Carrie Catt. When Catt refused on the grounds that such a debate would be "like speaking to a motion after it has been carried," Wadsworth issued an angry response: "It may be that you are ready to admit to the American people that the organized violations of democracy practiced by the Political Machine of which you are president cannot be defended and ought to be suppressed. [Nevertheless] the American people must be converted to woman suffrage, if at all, by the results and reasonableness of woman's participation in politics. They cannot be commanded or forced to adopt woman suffrage by the mere coercion of politicians and the suppression of facts and fair discussion."[87] Others saw truth in Wadsworth's charge that NAWSA had become a political machine. So visible had the Front Door Lobby and its state-level publicity schemes become that during the September 1918 debate, one senator protested the undue influence exerted by the suffragists upon his colleagues. "We find a petticoat brigade awaits outside, and Senate leaders, like little boys, like pages, trek back and forth for orders," the senator fumed. "If you accept that office, Senators, then put on cap and bells and paint your cheeks like a clown . . . and do your truckling in proper garb."[88] In spite of the efforts of the petticoat brigade, however, the Senate defeated the suffrage resolution by two votes. Nevertheless, the vote, on October 1, 1918, showed a net gain of sixteen over the last Senate vote in 1914. Moreover, seven of the 1918 prosuffrage senators had voted or paired against it in 1914, and ten of the additional ayes came from senators from the seven states that had won woman suffrage in 1917.[89] The association leaders and lobbyists drew some hope from this new Senate vote, but within the organization itself dissension was brewing.

Early warning signs appeared in January 1918 with the publication of a *New Orleans Times-Picayune* article entitled "Federal Law Called Useless by the ERA Club." States' rights suffragists had watched the progress of the federal amendment and were angered by the very success that the majority of activists welcomed. When a *Times-Picayune* reporter asked Kate Gordon why she objected to the amendment, she explained that federal suffrage legislation would place black women on a par with white women. Gordon offered further proof of the amendment's detrimental effects when she pointed out that "while white men would be willing to club negro men away from the polls, they would not use the club upon black women."[90] Two months later, Laura Clay expressed her antipathy to the amendment in a letter to Gordon and proposed a states' rights suffrage coalition to resist the federal amendment.[91]

The NAWSA Executive Board's concern over the southern dissenters grew in April 1918 when Jean Gordon and the Louisiana State Woman Suffrage Association (LWSA) endorsed a vicious attack on the federal amendment printed in the *Times-Picayune*. In response to the LWSA's action, the board issued a stern reprimand to the Dixie activists.[92] In reply, Kate Gordon reaffirmed the Louisiana association's opposition to the federal amendment and pointed out that LWSA, as a NAWSA affiliate, was entitled "to fight a Federal Amendment if we see fit" according to the national association's states' rights policy.[93] Again the NAWSA board protested to the Gordons, but this time the message was severe: given that the LWSA was the sole suffrage organization working at cross purposes with the national association, would not the Louisiana group simply resign from NAWSA if it could not comply with its policy?[94]

The Gordons and Laura Clay met the request for resignation from NAWSA with stony silence, but they gave the question much thought. Kate Gordon's bitterness regarding the amendment's progress, coupled with a growing frustration over the failure to win suffrage at the state level in any Deep South state, led her to write to Boston suffragist Alice Stone Blackwell. "I suppose you are very happy over the Federal Amendment situation," Clay wrote. "We have one of two alternatives, to continue the frauds that made a farce of democracy or live under negro government. I always hoped that woman suffrage would come as a power for good but certainly it will not be an active agent here, handicapped as it will be with subterfuges. It is an awful thing to feel that a life work has borne such dead sea fruit."[95] Gordon's frustration grew when a Louisiana woman suffrage referendum was defeated by five thousand votes in November 1918. The LWSA had asked legislators for the vote in order to preserve suffrage as a state right and to allow the Democratic Party to take credit for the passage of the reform at the state level.[96] While Gordon believed that her association with NAWSA had "borne dead sea fruit," in reality her adherence to the principle of states' rights regarding woman suffrage and her virulent racism were also barren and moribund. Unable to face the failure of their strategy, the Gordons and Laura Clay resigned from NAWSA in fall 1918, severing ties and friendships that stretched back to the nineteenth century.[97]

With the southern problem temporarily out of the way, NAWSA leaders turned to the task of winning the two needed Senate votes. One tactic favored by the Executive Board was the use of mass petitions collected by state workers and sent to reluctant senators. In fall 1918, suffragists embarked on a nationwide petition campaign that included house-to-house canvassing and an ambitious publicity drive to display the documents in courthouses and county seats before forwarding them to Congress. Suffragists hoped not only to win the needed votes in the Senate but also to prepare the ground for ratification after the amendment passed Congress.[98] Catt was particularly anxious to assure a smooth and speedy ratification, and as early as November 1918, she adopted the slogan "a vote for every woman before the Presidential election in 1920."[99]

To ensure financial backing for an extended campaign, suffrage leaders also instructed state and local activists in fund-raising techniques, including pledge drives, public functions, and luncheons for prestigious citizens. Catt offered a useful tip regarding pledge drives in suggesting that large contributions be confirmed in advance but made public in such a way as to suggest spontaneous support for the cause.[100] The association's reliance on the bandwagon effect to stimulate interest in the movement thus was extended to fund raising, and manipulation of public sentiment once again replaced the organization's traditional reliance on reasoned and spontaneous popular support.

Petitions alone, however, were not sufficient to sway the Senate opposition coalition. Of those opposed, only two came from states west of the Mississippi, while seven hailed from New England, seven from the Mid-Atlantic states, two from the Midwest, and fifteen from the South. When Woodrow Wilson proved unable to budge the antisuffrage southern Democrats, suffragists searched for another lever to pry loose the needed votes. Maud Wood Park enlisted the aid of prosuffrage congressmen in the form of written pledges in support of the amendment, and she secured the promise of the Speaker of the House that no obstacles would be permitted to delay speedy passage by that body. Both actions failed to persuade the Senate coalition.[101] More effective, however, was a scheme devised by the NAWSA Executive Board in late summer and fall 1918. Targeting four opposition senators who faced reelection in November, suffragists laid plans to defeat the four and to replace them with prosuffrage men.[102]

Of the efforts to defeat antisuffrage senators, perhaps the most innovative was the campaign to defeat John W. Weeks, a Republican from Massachusetts, carried out by members of the Massachusetts Woman Suffrage Association and the Boston Equal Suffrage Association for Good Government. Massachusetts activists had long disliked Senator Weeks for his opposition to a number of progressive reforms. One of the women's first actions was to form the "Non-Partisan Committee to Defeat Weeks," chaired by Boston lawyer Teresa

Crowley and Grace Johnson, an area clubwoman and progressive.[103] The two women set about documenting Weeks's voting record on thirteen key issues, which revealed the politician's negative response to such measures as the Clayton Anti-Trust Act, prohibition, popular election of senators, taxation on war profits, and woman suffrage.[104] Their next step was to send a flier featuring the congressman's record to all registered Republican and Progressive voters in the state; mailings also went out to thirty-five thousand state suffragists, with the suggestion that each woman exert her influence on voting family members to defeat Weeks.[105]

Not content with waging a mail campaign alone, the activists sought to pull together an anti-Weeks coalition of disparate groups throughout the state. Organizer Margaret Foley turned to trade unions for support and spoke against Weeks at the gates of local factories and mills. Committee coworker Mabel Gillespie, area secretary of the Women's Trade Union League, drew on her many contacts among organized labor to back up Foley's efforts. Massachusetts trade unions responded with alacrity, and they willingly aided the Non-Partisan Committee in its work.[106] Many prohibitionists also joined the coalition when they learned of Weeks's opposition to their cause, as did workers from the state's rural areas who disliked the politician's vote against a rural credits bill. Another powerful bloc of voters swung into line behind the anti-Weeks banner when Massachusetts Jews learned of the senator's vicious opposition to confirmation of Louis D. Brandeis's nomination to the Supreme Court. The majority of the state's Jewish population voted the Republican ticket, and so the suffragists were gleeful when Jewish organizations pledged to vote against the incumbent.[107] By fall 1918, the Non-Partisan Committee had formed a powerful political coalition of organized labor, liberal reformers, farmers, and Jews to combat the acknowledged head of the state Republican machine. Ironically, the Massachusetts suffragists had united a nucleus of support that paralleled, although on a much smaller scale, Franklin D. Roosevelt's 1932 New Deal coalition.

Senator Weeks, however, had many resources at his disposal. He had the active support of the state's Republican leader Charles Sumner Bird. Bird in turn received aid from his wife, who was the newly elected president of the Massachusetts Woman Suffrage Association. Although she and the association pledged to defeat Weeks, Mrs. Bird refused to take an active part in the campaign and encouraged her associates to oppose the efforts of the Non-Partisan Committee.[108] Even Carrie Catt's appeal failed to change Mrs. Bird's stand, although she did agree to sponsor a letter drive among influential Republicans to pressure Weeks to change his vote.[109] More helpful than Mrs.

Bird's belated efforts were the interest and encouragement offered to the Non-Partisan Committee by NAWSA. When committee members Crowley and Johnson sought the aid of the Executive Board, the response was quick: Catt arranged for the Leslie Commission to donate more than $2,000 outright and to loan $2,500 more to finance the campaign. Moreover, the national association agreed to postpone payment of the annual Massachusetts pledge, allowing all MWSA and BESAGG funds to be channeled to the Non-Partisan Committee.[110]

The campaign to defeat John Weeks reached its climax the day before the election, when advertisements detailing the senator's voting record appeared in sixteen of the state's largest Republican newspapers. For additional impact, the record was validated in a statement at the bottom of the page by the editor of *Searchlight on Congress,* a highly respected magazine that monitored the behavior of congressmen.[111] In addition to the publicity generated by the newspaper advertisements, the Non-Partisan Committee also staged open-air meetings, circularized religious groups, and addressed moving picture audiences between features on the issue.[112] Despite their thorough organization, suffragists nervously waited while the ballots were counted on election day. At last the news arrived: Weeks had been defeated by nearly nineteen thousand votes.

Carrie Catt and other NAWSA officials were jubilant; they believed that the final obstacle for the federal amendment had been surmounted.[113] In Massachusetts, the Non-Partisan Committee's celebration was marred only by the dawning realization that state Republicans and, in particular, Senator Weeks were loath to attribute his defeat to a band of nonvoting women.[114] Committee Cochairman Teresa Crowley astutely realized the importance of claiming credit for Weeks's rout, and she wrote to Front Door Lobbyist Maud Wood Park of the importance of reaping the full benefits of his defeat: "A conviction on the part of Washington politicians that we did it would do more to swing all the wobblers both in the House and Senate in short and long term over to our side than any other one thing."[115] Crowley also sent Park copies of the anti-Weeks circular and urged her to circulate word of the women's efforts to recruit the Jewish and industrial sectors.

In Delaware the suffragists were also victorious in their effort to defeat Senator Willard Saulsbury. Employing tactics similar to those used in Massachusetts, lobbyist Mabel Willard enlisted the help of munitions workers and other sectors of the labor force to defeat the senator.[116] Willard's job was made more difficult by the timidity of Delaware suffragists. After consulting NAWSA leaders, Willard prevailed on Carrie Catt to rally the reluctant women. "They held up their hands in horror," recalled Catt many years later, "but a committee was finally organized and they went to work."[117] Subsequently, Saulsbury, like Weeks, went down in defeat on election day. In New Jersey and New Hampshire, however, efforts to defeat the incumbents failed.

By November 1918, then, NAWSA had severed the last link with its traditional adherence to nonpartisan politics. Although the committees formed to defeat the senatorial candidates had included representatives from all parties, the fact remains that by attacking one candidate the suffragists were implicitly supporting another. Moreover, by using negative campaign tactics and publicity to replace antisuffrage politicians, NAWSA used a new style of political behavior that transformed old-fashioned mud-slinging into a well-documented assault on the voting record of politicians. And although the association based its opposition on the single issue of woman suffrage, it drew support from a wide range of groups by appeals couched in terms of a variety of special interests. Ironically, some of these special interests, such as trade unionists and working-class women, were among those previously excluded from active NAWSA membership or serious recruitment efforts. When viewed from the perspective of the gradual narrowing of the movement to the single issue of woman suffrage, the extensive network of lobbyists and activists on the state level, and the use of negative campaigning and organized political attacks, NAWSA by December 1918 had completed its transformation into a modern single-issue pressure group.

With Weeks and Saulsbury defeated, suffragists believed that they had the votes to pass the federal woman suffrage amendment during the next session of Congress. In addition, when word spread of the campaigns waged against the two men, some congressional "doubtfuls" recognized the inevitability of the reform. Antisuffrage advocate Henry Cabot Lodge admitted privately that the amendment's passage was certain in the next Congress and might go through as early as December 1918.[118] War work contributed to this change in opinion, but the aggressive campaigns waged by suffragists in Massachusetts and Delaware were to be the crucial factors. The campaigns won needed senatorial votes, and it also served notice to foes that the suffragists were capable of beating them at such political maneuvers as coalition building and negative campaigning. The specter of coalitions and negative publicity moved the stalwarts in a way that education, entreaties, and petitions never could.

Suffragists' hopes rose after the November elections; not only had they managed to gain the two Senate votes, but three new states had been added to the suffrage map. In South Dakota, Michigan, and Oklahoma they had won crucial referenda, and the total number of electors drawn from states where women could vote climbed to 339 of a total of 435. Lobbyists and state workers alike were optimistic when the Senate scheduled a vote for February

10, 1919, but it soon became apparent that victory would not be forthcoming. According to Senate rules, unanimous consent was required to bring the resolution to the floor. When the so-called Unholy Alliance led by Senators James Wadsworth and Henry Cabot Lodge suddenly halted debate, lobbyists realized that the amendment was one vote short of unanimous consent.[119]

On the eve of the Senate vote, Catt was resigned to defeat. "Apparently our chances have not been changed," she wrote Maud Wood Park, "except by the additional earnestness of our friends and bitterness of our foes. . . . If fate perches victory on our bedraggled and outworn banner, we shall all be glad and perhaps we shall even feel jubilant. We shall shed no tears at any rate. But if our familiar experience is repeated, I want you to know that I am quite resigned. . . . In any event the delay cannot be long. Those who will eventually triumph can afford to be patient and forgiving."[120] Catt's seeming ambivalence concealed her growing depression over the fate of the amendment. Fearing a conservative backlash at the end of World War I, she agonized over the Senate roadblock. A week before the Senate vote, Catt dreamed that her trusted friend and coworker Maud Wood Park had died and awoke crying, "The federal amendment did it!"[121] So deep was her despondency that she made plans to close Suffrage House and abandon congressional lobbying if the amendment failed to pass on February 10.

In spite of memorials in favor of the amendment passed by twenty-four state legislatures, numerous petitions, and delegations, the resolution was defeated. No choice remained for the suffragists but to await the convening of the special session of the Sixty-sixth Congress on May 19, 1919. Even hopes of presidential pressure flagged; as one suffragist concluded, "[Wilson] is bringing home [from the Versailles Peace Conference] a pocket full of trouble all his own."[122] The National American Woman Suffrage Association turned once again to home pressure to bring about the needed votes. Delegations from state associations called on congressmen and their wives, a professional organizer was dispatched to the South in hope of winning the support of key Democrats, and press chairmen nationwide flooded newspapers with pro-amendment publicity.[123] One organization used a prosuffrage appeal from the late Theodore Roosevelt to an opposition senator and circulated the statement widely.[124] Suffragists at the state level secured petitions from twenty-four legislatures urging Congress to act.[125]

As home pressure in support of the federal suffrage amendment grew, so did NAWSA leaders' concern over opposition in the Senate. Lobbyists had assured board members that the House would pose no problem, but the Senate's Unholy Alliance had not retired from the field. With such masters of parliamentary procedure and political manipulation as Lodge and Wadsworth aligned against them, suffragists were forced to consider the possibility that victory would once again elude them. Consequently, some months before the new Congress was to convene, the NAWSA Executive Board reevaluated the amendment's chances. Catt toyed with the idea of demanding a national constitutional convention but concluded that such a plan would also fail.[126] Similarly she rejected an alternate amendment that would grant women the right to vote in congressional elections.[127] Increasingly frustrated with the Senate roadblock, Catt and other NAWSA leaders began to entertain the thought of making the amendment more palatable to the opposition.

Southern Democrats had opposed the federal suffrage amendment on the basis of its enabling clause, which stated: "Congress has the power, by appropriate legislation, to enforce the provisions of this article."[128] The enabling clause brought with it the possibility of federal election supervision in Dixie, and it revived white supremacists' fears that political rights would be restored to blacks if woman suffrage was enacted in the South. Disfranchisement of blacks depended on nonintervention by federal authorities, and any change in the status quo posed a threat to white supremacist politicians and citizens. Thus when Senator Edward J. Gay of Louisiana introduced a new amendment granting enforcement power to the states instead of to Congress in February 1919, many southerners hastened to Washington to press for the resolution's passage.[129] Two days later, a second senator proposed yet another substitute resolution that barred from suffrage immigrant women, regardless of their husbands' citizenship. Neither of these bills was endorsed by NAWSA's Congressional Committee, and they died in committee without the backing of a majority of prosuffrage senators.[130]

Although the Front Door Lobby refused to support these alternate resolutions, Catt had already laid plans to amend the federal amendment itself if needed. Writing to lobbyist Ruth White in July 1918, six months before the first efforts by senators to amend the suffrage resolution, Catt proposed a new amendment that "would provide that citizens only will be permitted to vote hereafter in the United States." In order to qualify to vote, she continued, "women cannot claim citizenship through marriage with their husbands, but must obtain a separate naturalization." Since nativist and good government groups had long called for voting restrictions for unnaturalized immigrants, Catt was convinced that such an amendment would "secure a quicker ratification and some friends it does not now possess."[131] In her proposal, the anti-immigrant sentiment that had lain dormant within NAWSA for years at last found expression.

By March 1919, with only one vote needed for the passage of the federal suffrage amendment, some NAWSA leaders had become persuaded that the only route to victory was to alter the original amendment. After several attempts, a draft was deemed acceptable by NAWSA lobbyists. Although no copy of this measure is recorded in annals of Congress or in the voluminous NAWSA records, readers today may speculate on its wording from a rough description provided by Carrie Chapman Catt.[132] In a March 1, 1919, letter to Maud Wood Park, Catt broached the subject in a paragraph headed "The Next Bill": "I believe that we better not do any talking with Senators or Congressmen about the Bill to be put in at the next Congress. . . . I think it will be advisable for us to bring it before the [NAWSA] convention for adoption and in the meantime it will be wise for us to ask that a Bill be drawn, *making some concession to the South, putting in our citizenship business, etc.* and that we make certain that it is legal and proper before hand" (emphasis added).[133] Clearly the Executive Board and the Congressional Committee were prepared to go to any lengths to ensure the passage of some form of federal suffrage amendment. In all probability, they went so far as to draft a substitute resolution that included the possibility of qualified, rather than equal, suffrage, reflecting the final abandonment of NAWSA's commitment to universal suffrage. The secrecy that shrouded the substitute amendment was eventually extended to the NAWSA convention. Catt had originally planned to seek the approval of both the Executive Board and the assembled delegates, but she apparently disregarded this notion in favor of a vaguely worded subterfuge. When the annual convention met later in March, the Executive Board proposed a resolution affirming that the association would "continue to support and endorse the Federal Amendment which has been pending before Congress for 40 years, *the wording of the amendment to be left to the Congressional Committee,* with the understanding that the vital principle be preserved in the text" (emphasis added).[134] No mention was made that a new amendment had not only been proposed but drafted as well. The delegates approved the resolution without debate. And although Maud Wood Park's Congressional Committee report to the convention contained a substantial section on the forthcoming congressional campaign, it, too, made no reference to the substitute amendment.[135]

The life of the substitute amendment, however, was brief. Although the altered bill was promptly introduced and referred to the Woman Suffrage Committee when the Sixty-sixth Congress convened in May 1919, House members sounded the death knell for the measure by denying the unanimous consent needed for the bill to be reported out of committee. The original federal amendment was then quickly acted upon and its undemocratic substitute forgotten. History, too, was quick to forget, in part because of the efforts of NAWSA leaders. In the hundreds of boxes of suffrage documents, correspondence, reports, and memorabilia in existence today, a large part of it assembled by the association's leaders, there is scarcely a trace of the substitute amendment. Carrie Chapman Catt's and Nettie Rogers Shuler's *Woman Suffrage and Politics* contains the sole published account of efforts to abandon the original amendment for a compromise measure, a four-sentence description that is remarkable more for its vagueness than for the information it reveals.[136] So thorough were suffragists in their attempt to purge the historical record of the ultimate betrayal of traditional NAWSA ideology that only a few scrawled fragments remain.

In addition to forsaking the organization's commitment to full and unrestricted suffrage for all women, NAWSA leaders again proved that they had been forced to come to terms with the reality of pressure politics. A large segment of the convention's delegates had protested the submission of the Shaforth-Palmer resolution in 1914, and without doubt they would have equally opposed further concessions to the South in the form of the substitute amendment. Rather than debate the issue, the Executive Board and the congressional lobby chose to elicit the approval of the convention by less than honest means, thereby making suffragists nationwide share in the responsibility for the substitution without their informed consent. Moreover, although few NAWSA leaders used the term *feminist* in describing their generation of women, the ideological foundation laid down by pioneer suffragists was based on the unswerving belief in the political equality of all women. This belief had its origins in the antebellum abolition crusade, and it survived in the hearts and minds of many — although not all — NAWSA suffragists well into the twentieth century. In a bold stroke, the movement's leaders shattered this commitment to full political equality. When the new bill died in committee, they attempted to destroy all evidence of its existence in the hope that their betrayal would be lost to posterity.

The opening ceremonies of the Sixty-sixth Congress helped divert attention from the ill-fated substitute resolution. Representative James R. Mann, the new chairman of the House Woman Suffrage Committee, saw to it that the original federal amendment was scheduled for debate in the early days of the session and pressed for its quick passage. When the House passed the federal suffrage amendment on May 21 and the Senate scheduled it for debate in early June, suffragists across the nation became convinced that victory was at hand.[137] Nevertheless, on the morning of the Senate vote, Maud Wood Park refused to read the daily newspaper lest she find that a prosuffrage senator had died in the night. Park's anxiety grew when she reached the Senate gallery. In spite of her rule that lobbyists refrain from any sign of disapproval while in the public eye, she muttered angrily at antisuffrage speeches on the floor of the

Senate.[138] She drew some consolation from the fact that the Republicans abstained from debating the measure. Under orders from the Republican whip to remain silent no matter what the Democrats might say, antisuffrage senators like Henry Cabot Lodge sat quietly, although a few voted against the measure.[139] Unlike Park and other Front Door Lobbyists, NAWSA president Carrie Catt did not witness the Senate deliberations. After the day in October 1918 when the Senate defeated the amendment and she had sat wringing her hands in anguish, the lobby had never asked her to come to Washington for a vote. "It was useless torment [for Catt]," one lobbyist remarked, "to sit in the gallery, listening to antisuffrage speeches and trying to follow roll calls."[140] When the Senate passed the federal woman suffrage amendment on June 4, 1919, by a vote of 56 to 25, Catt was not among those who celebrated the culmination of the long congressional battle.

Pioneer Ohio suffragist Harriet Taylor Upton's reaction may serve as an example of the joy and relief of those who were present. Catching sight of Upton in the melee that followed the vote, Belle La Follette shouted gleefully, "Well, Harriet, it's all over." Upton's mouth, usually stretched into a wide grin, began to twitch, and without warning the elderly suffragist was sobbing.[141] Mary Garrett Hay was also in the Senate gallery, and she hastened to relay the news to Carrie Catt at her home in New York. Upon learning of the victory, Catt "danced all over the place, and then settled down to think."[142] The federal amendment had passed through Congress, but ratification by three-fourths of the states lay ahead, and Catt's celebration was therefore brief. The roadblock of the solid South must be overcome, the border states brought in line, and the suffrage machine galvanized to greater efforts than ever before. With the end of World War I in sight and the possibility of a conservative backlash, ratification by the states must come quickly or not at all. To Catt and other suffragists, their celebration brought with it a growing realization that the final victory lay not at hand but somewhere in the future.

7

Ratification

When the United States Senate passed the woman suffrage amendment on June 4, 1919, the twentieth-century suffrage movement entered the final, or ratification, stage of its campaign. Histories of the movement have tended to gloss over the ratification campaign, focusing instead on the decades-long battle for state and congressional approval. Ratification, in contrast, was accomplished in a little more than a year and a half — a relatively short period when compared to the congressional fight. To many readers, ratification by the states seems almost an afterthought, easily accomplished after the gripping congressional drama was played out. In fact, this was far from true. Arguably, ratification was the most difficult political test NAWSA activists would face, and it posed a new and challenging set of problems for suffrage strategists.

Ratification required a shift in focus for those who masterminded the congressional campaign. For the amendment to take effect, it had to be approved by thirty-six state legislatures; in each state, suffragists had to grapple with different political agendas, coalitions, and personalities. Suffrage was not the only item before many legislatures, and unrelated and conflicting goals and factions sometimes threatened to postpone ratification indefinitely. Problems within the suffrage camp also disrupted the ratification process: states' rights suffrage associations refused to support the federal amendment, societies impatient with the slow federal route clamored for state amendment campaigns, and militants vied with NAWSA activists for control in several states. Moreover, the antisuffragists, sensing Armageddon, redoubled their efforts to defeat the amendment.

Given these difficulties, it is quite remarkable that ratification was achieved so quickly, or, perhaps, at all. The importance of NAWSA's ratification campaign, however, does not lie solely in its rapid resolution. Without NAWSA's suffrage machine operating at the federal, state, and local levels, the woman suffrage amendment might easily have gone the way of its late-twentieth-century offspring, the Equal Rights Amendment. Ratification was the ultimate test for the suffrage machine, and it reflects the strategy, political power, and ideology of NAWSA at the culmination of its great campaign.

The leaders of NAWSA had anticipated many of the problems inherent in the ratification process when they began planning for the final stage of the campaign in early 1918. That April the Executive Council had met in Indianapolis to make long-range plans for ratification.[1] One idea adopted by the group was for a massive petition campaign to commence at once: state and local suffragists would collect signatures of those favoring speedy action on the part of their legislators and would post the documents in public locations to advertise the strong support for the amendment. After the amendment passed in the U.S. Senate, the petitions would be forwarded to the appropriate legislature to further the impression that a large prosuffrage constituency demanded immediate action.[2] Suffragists also petitioned trade unions, women's clubs, and other reform groups and passed the results on to the state legislatures. "The sentiment of the country is with us," Catt explained to activists, "our duty is merely to secure its expression."[3]

In addition to petitions, the ratification plan adopted in Indianapolis called for the formation of suffrage ratification committees, composed of representatives from each suffrage society within the state. Based on the successful Empire State Campaign Committee that directed the New York campaigns of 1915 and 1917, the ratification committees elected officers, established headquarters in the state capitals, and drew up their own budgets. Activists could choose to serve on a variety of committees, such as organization, legislative, petitions, endorsements, press, finance, and publicity. Other committees were responsible for canvassing the industrial, rural, and church-going population of the state.[4] Adequate financing was essential for the amendment's success, and the Executive Council estimated that the ratification campaign would require in excess of $40,000 in certain difficult states, with a lesser amount allocated for states that had already won woman suffrage. The Executive Council approved what it termed a "graphic plan" for fund-raising, which called for the state ratification committees to levy county-by-county assessments based on the size and relative wealth of the population.[5]

With the favorable Senate vote in June 1919, NAWSA's ratification campaign began in earnest. One of the Executive Board's first steps was to close the Washington lobby. Suffrage House was disbanded and the Front Door Lobbyists, so successful in the congressional battle for woman suffrage, said their good-byes to the rambling mansion that had been their home. Although Carrie Catt had seldom visited the Washington residence, she directed the dismantling of Suffrage House from her New York office, even telling Maud Wood Park which typewriters to jettison.[6] Catt's depression had lifted after the amendment passed the Senate. "I never had so much enjoyment in all my life as I am getting now," she confided to Park several days after the Senate vote, "and I am longing for you to be here to share in it."[7] When the door to Suffrage House was locked for the last time, Park hastened to New York, where she served as Catt's lieutenant throughout the remainder of the campaign.

Many of the forty-eight state legislatures were slated to meet in fall 1919, and twenty-two were expected to ratify easily. A few states would need to call special sessions if ratification were to be obtained before the elections of 1920. Of the remainder, NAWSA strategists calculated that at least ten would require strenuous efforts on the part of state activists to ensure victory, and the Deep South states were considered all but hopeless.[8] The Executive Board had been loath to abandon the South altogether. In response to the pleadings of a delegation of Dixie activists in spring 1919, the Executive Board allocated funds to support suffrage schools and professional organizers for each state. Moreover, Catt planned to hold a series of conferences throughout the region to train new workers and bolster support for suffrage. In return, southern suffragists agreed to furnish workers to act under the direction of the NAWSA organizers, to create speakers' bureaus, and to embark on petition drives in support of ratification.[9] By fall 1919, however, the South had done little to fulfill its part in the agreement. Trained organizers came and went, but only one state out of thirteen took control of the work after they departed. No speakers' bureaus were set up, and of the three states that attempted petition work, none had completed the task. The proposed conferences had failed to take place as one state after another refused to participate. Two state associations neglected to respond to the NAWSA board's letters in time to schedule the events, nine never scheduled conferences, and two more failed to reply at all. In October, the Executive Board fired off a sharp remonstrance to the southern state presidents and essentially abandoned hope that Dixie would ratify the federal amendment.[10]

Without the southern and border states, NAWSA could afford to lose only two of the remaining states. Suffragists instead pinned their hopes on the West, a region where women had voted for decades and could bring pressure for quick ratification. The West, ironically, was so accustomed to woman suffrage that western women and their representatives felt little urgency. Most western suffrage societies had disbanded; NAWSA had to press for legislative action without the customary organization at the state level. To circumvent this problem, the Executive Board sent two commissions to the region to persuade leading politicians and influential party leaders to adopt the amendment quickly. A third commission attended the National Governors' Conference in Salt Lake City and lobbied western governors to call special sessions.[11]

The commissions' joint report was not encouraging. Although there was no doubt of the western states' commitment to ratification, a host of reasons threatened to postpone action on the amendment indefinitely. Some of the governors were candidates for the U.S. Senate, and they were reluctant to take a stand that would propel them into the political arena prematurely. Others were afraid to call special sessions, lest their political foes use the sessions to put forward their own agendas. Moreover, the commission reported that NAWSA could expect little help from voting women in the West. "They do not understand the national situation," Catt wrote to state presidents, "and take little interest in a speedy close of the century long struggle." In the same memorandum, the NAWSA president sketched the amendment's status as of September 10, 1919: seventeen states already ratified, fifteen states would almost certainly ratify when governors could be persuaded to call special sessions, and two states certain to ratify during their regular sessions in January. Totaling thirty-four, her estimate revealed that the federal amendment would fall two states short of acquiring the necessary three-fourths majority needed for success. In a letter to a Connecticut coworker, Catt speculated that the additional votes must come from two of four states: Vermont, New Jersey, Delaware, or Connecticut. "The situation in each of these is pretty bad," she confided, and she urged Connecticut suffragists to wage a vigorous campaign to assure success of the amendment.[12]

Of the full suffrage states in the West, only Utah had ratified by September 1919. Instead, the amendment's first successes came from the Midwest and the Northeast. The ratification committee in Massachusetts formed the Cambridge Council of 100 to lobby the legislature on behalf of the amendment. On the council were city dignitaries, labor leaders, prominent businessmen, and educators. Because of their efforts, the state legislature ratified the amendment in record time.[13] Pennsylvania, too, adopted the amendment quickly. When the vote was taken and the results read out, suffragists were startled when members of the legislature actually "burst forth in joyful song."[14]

In spite of these early gains, the battle for the vote was not yet won. While NAWSA leaders concentrated all of the vast resources of their organization on ratification of the federal amendment, some state activists with strong organizations grew increasingly impatient for success. State referenda, if successful, would give immediate results and guarantee that at least some women would vote in the 1920 elections, regardless of the fate of the federal amendment. As the Senate concluded its deliberations in spring 1919, suffragists in Arkansas began to lobby for a state woman suffrage referendum.[15] Catt acted quickly to dissuade the Arkansas association, pointing out that any state action would draw needed funds and workers away from the upcoming ratification campaign.[16] When other state leaders appealed to NAWSA for aid in order to submit similar resolutions, Catt advised against such action. The national association, she concluded, "can give no assistance whatever to any state campaign unless friends and other state associations provide money from which to draw."[17] Most activists, including those in Arkansas, heeded Catt's admonition and chose to abandon state referenda in favor of amendment work.[18] The national association was not so fortunate when it came to Texas.

A close look at the Texas story demonstrates the complexities NAWSA faced in ratifying the woman suffrage amendment. A renegade band of San Antonio suffragists disregarded the advice of Texas Equal Suffrage Association (TESA) leaders and pressed for the introduction of a state suffrage referendum. When the legislature complied with the San Antonio group's wishes, scheduling the contest for May 24, 1919, TESA and NAWSA executives alike were dismayed at the prospect of waging a state amendment campaign. "It is quite possible that a defeat of that amendment in Texas would throw us out of suffrage for some years to come," Catt lamented to Minnie Fisher Cunningham, and she concluded that "it is an awful tragic situation." Both Catt and Cunningham, who had served a stint in Washington as a Front Door Lobbyist, believed that the Texas women faced strong opposition within the state and were not optimistic about the state amendment's chances for success.[19]

Consequently, the NAWSA strategists eagerly endorsed an idea put forward by NAWSA official Nettie Rogers Shuler. Shuler observed that in a recent South Dakota campaign, suffragists had added a clause that limited suffrage to those who had attained American citizenship to their resolution, a move that had helped their amendment to carry. Because Texas's large Hispanic and German populations were permitted to vote without completing the process of naturalization, Shuler reasoned that a citizenship restriction clause might also push the Texas amendment over the top.[20] Acting on the advice of Shuler and the NAWSA Executive Board, the Texas suffragists prevailed on their friends in the legislature, and a citizenship clause was duly added.

Throughout spring 1919, while the federal amendment awaited the convocation of the Sixty-sixth Congress, Texas suffragists prepared for the May referendum. Catt recommended petition work, house-to-house canvassing, suffrage schools, and ample publicity to ensure a favorable vote; Cunningham and other state activists agreed with her but faced a crucial shortage of funds and workers.[21] Of thirty-one senatorial districts, TESA could provide only twenty-five with district chairmen. Moreover, volunteers were in scarce supply for canvassing and petition work. There was a desperate need for money with which to finance their work, but activists could raise less than half of the $40,000 that NAWSA executives recommended for a successful campaign. Nevertheless, TESA workers endeavored to overcome these liabilities. The organization's press department flooded the state's newspapers with prosuffrage propaganda and sent weekly bulletins to county press chairmen to place in local papers. Petition work and canvassing were attempted in areas where volunteers were available, and a flying squadron toured the state in early May, speaking in schoolhouses and town squares on the amendment. The churchgoing population was not forgotten; letters went out to ministers urging support for the reform from the pulpit.[22]

In spite of these preparations, Texas suffragists remained concerned over the fate of the state amendment. Corruption was an ever-present danger, and TESA leaders feared that victory might be stolen from their grasp by dishonest election officials. One friend of suffrage cautioned TESA Treasurer Jessie Daniel Ames about the need to assure a fair count. "The counting is what counts and gets result," cautioned a political friend. "Just count and then count some more and you will be sure to win. Now if you Ladies are as adept in vote counting as some of you are in ordinary games, why, if the male population of China was arrayed against you, you would win."[23] On the eve of the May 24 contest, Cunningham issued stern instructions to TESA precinct chairmen to guard against election fraud at all costs. Each precinct chairman was to "secure in writing a statement from the Election Judge as to the result of the election in her precinct BEFORE SHE SLEEPS," Cunningham admonished, "we must have figures in order not to lose after we win."[24]

In addition to corrupt officials, Texas suffragists encountered yet another group who hoped to see their reform fail. Antisuffragists knew of their opponents' activities, and they were determined to prevent the passage of the state amendment. The Texas Association Opposed to Woman Suffrage (TAOWS) was organized in Houston in March 1916 with the stated goal of defeating equal suffrage in the state. Like the TESA, TAOWS organized along district lines, appointing both district and precinct chairmen to oversee the work.[25] Led by Mrs. James B. Wells, wife of a Brownsville, Texas, political boss, the antisuffragists also drew support from ex-governor James E. Ferguson, who had been impeached for financial misconduct with the help of TESA activists and other state progressive reformers. While the ex-governor worked against woman suffrage through his remaining political contacts, Wells chose a more direct method of attack. Several weeks before the May election, county Democratic chairmen across the state received a circular from the TAOWS that linked woman suffrage to socialism and closed with an appeal to the officials to "help save Texas from the 'Dawn of the Red Day.' "[26]

In addition to Wells's letter, antisuffrage propaganda flooded into the state, much of it addressed to state politicians. Some of the literature bore the imprint of the Texas antisuffrage association, but a large amount circulated anonymously. On receiving a bundle of unsigned literature, one prosuffrage state senator passed the material along to Jane Y. McCallum, chairman of TESA's ratification committee. One of the circulars the senator had received pictured two black women outside a polling place with the caption "Majorities Win at the Polls." An unsigned, handwritten note at the bottom of the document warned: "These 'ladies' will sit on the jury with your wife — then it will be too late for regret."[27] Another circular, cleverly constructed to resemble a prosuffrage handbill, featured quotations from prominent suffragists advocating such southern taboos as racial equality. "These women are spending millions to put suffrage over Texas, break the solid South, and put us all in Hell again," proclaimed the senator's anonymous correspondent, "The women of Texas do not want Suffrage, not the *real* women, and the South must stand together on this."[28]

When the votes were counted on May 24, 1919, the Texas woman suffrage amendment lost by the sizable majority of 25,120.[29] Suffragists learned too late of uncounted ballots that disappeared in the night and polls that never opened in towns where support for the measure was strong. "We have been defeated not in a fair fight, but by fraudulent ballot and the massed vote of the deceived ignorant," Cunningham charged.[30] A few activists blamed TESA's poor funding and shortage of workers for the loss, but others laid the defeat at the door of the so-called aliens, who voted against the amendment on the grounds that it would deprive them of the vote by altering the citizenship requirement for suffrage.[31] Without doubt, many of the opposing votes were cast by German immigrants; some counties with heavy German populations voted ten-to-one against the state amendment.[32] Coupled with TESA's shortage of volunteers, the citizenship clause suggested by NAWSA hurt the Texas woman suffrage campaign. Discouraged but determined, TESA members concentrated their remaining energies and money on ratifying the federal amendment; they met a week after the defeat to plan the campaign.[33]

The Texas Equal Suffrage Association activists felt confident that the Texas legislature would ratify quickly; in addition to scheduling the May state referendum, a majority of the legislators had simultaneously supported a resolution urging speedy ratification of the federal amendment. Moreover, suffragists had strong support among many representatives as a result of their long opposition to impeached governor James Ferguson. Cunningham, for example, had been in the forefront of the campaign to oust Ferguson, and she had also been a vocal supporter of governor-elect William P. Hobby. Because the legislature was composed of a majority of anti-Ferguson men, Cunningham could count on a degree of reciprocity from this faction.[34] Equally important to the suffragists' chances were the strong factions of prosuffrage prohibitionists and Progressives in the Texas legislature.

The strongest support for the woman suffrage amendment lay in the house, and suffragists were not surprised when it easily passed that body by a vote of ninety-six to twenty on June 24, 1919.[35] Polls showed a narrow margin for success in the senate, and when a prosuffrage senator suddenly changed his vote the week before the special session convened, the poll stood at sixteen favorable to fifteen opposed. Another vote was lost when a prosuffrage lawmaker was killed in a gunfight on the eve of the house deliberations, and the prospect of a tie vote threw reformers into near panic. Cunningham next learned that antisuffragists planned to introduce a substitute amendment calling for a popular referendum on the issue. More alarming news followed: the lieutenant governor, pledged to vote for ratification in case of a tie, had also promised to vote for the antisuffragists' resolution if it was introduced first. Rumors circulated that two other senators would follow the lieutenant governor's lead.[36]

Suffrage strategists wisely sought to bring the senate into line by postponing the amendment's introduction until after the house vote had been secured. When the resolution passed the house by a large majority, TESA members were hopeful that the upper house would be swept along in the current for reform. Only a few minutes after the lower house acted, the senate committee began its deliberations on the federal amendment. Despite four long, hot hours of antisuffrage speeches, the committee reported the resolution favorably, and as Ratification Chairman Jane Y. McCallum recalled, "then the real fight was on." Antisuffragists attempted several schemes to break the quorum, including efforts to spirit the opposition lawmakers out of town. Suffragists patrolled the train stations and senate offices to catch the fleeing men before they made their escape.[37]

At last, with a quorum assured, the senate voted on the woman suffrage amendment on June 28, 1919. "I lived a million years while they were voting,"

Minnie Fisher Cunningham recalled several weeks later. When the count was read, Cunningham drew a deep sigh of relief: the amendment was ratified by a vote of nineteen to ten. Even news that ex-governor Ferguson had plans to contest both ratification and the state's primary suffrage law could not dim the suffragists' joy at the successful conclusion of their hard-fought battle.[38] The Texas victory was welcome news to NAWSA leaders who fully recognized the difficulties that the TESA had overcome. Ratification followed on the heels of a bitter defeat by popular vote in the May 24 contest; Texas suffragists seemed to be more successful with the politicians than with the public at large. Given the citizenship clause of the state amendment and factionalism in the legislature caused by ex-governor Ferguson and political issues outside the suffrage campaign, it remains unclear whether the suffragists managed to convince either politicians or the populace of the justice of their reform. External factors played a large part in both the May 24 referendum and the ratification procedure a month later. Whether the suffragists prevailed over legislative opposition or whether the anti-Ferguson faction prevailed over the ex-governor to the benefit of suffragists, the result was the same: Texas ratified the woman suffrage amendment, and both TESA and the Texas political reform faction were satisfied with the result.[39]

Ratification proved less difficult in states that had already achieved suffrage by state amendment. Women in Arizona had voted since 1912, and when that state's special legislative session convened on February 12, 1920, the woman suffrage resolution was introduced by that state's four female legislators. Antisuffragists from outside the state appeared before the senate, but their speeches drew only smiles from the lawmakers. To no one's surprise, the amendment was easily ratified without a dissenting vote.[40] In Idaho, a state that had adopted woman suffrage in 1896, ratification was also accomplished with little fanfare.[41] Prior voting experience, however, did not always ensure a speedy ratification. Although women had exercised school suffrage in Kentucky since 1912, the issue of states' rights complicated the ratification process in that state. States' rights champion Laura Clay, although once the leader of the Kentucky Equal Rights Association, had resigned from the organization when Congress passed the federal amendment. She then formed her own Citizens' Committee for a State Suffrage Amendment in opposition to the federal route to reform. Despite Clay's work, the federal amendment was ratified by a narrow margin in January 1920.[42]

One of the suffragists' most hard-fought victories came in Oklahoma, where in 1918 suffrage activists had won a state referendum against staggering odds. As in Texas, the Oklahoma campaign provides a good example of the complexities of a ratification fight. To secure the passage of a state amendment, the Oklahoma Constitution stipulated that any such resolution must win a majority of the highest number of votes cast in the previous election. Thus in 1918, NAWSA spent $18,000 on the referendum campaign and sent eleven professional organizers to the state to oversee the work. With money and workers the state woman suffrage measure carried, leading NAWSA strategists to assume that ratification of the federal amendment would pose no problem.[43] Unfortunately, they were mistaken. The Oklahoma Woman Suffrage Association (OWSA) was in favor of the state-by-state route to enfranchisement, and it refused to endorse a proposed resolution to the state's congressmen in support of the federal amendment. The amendment's enabling clause would "vote every darkie and abolish the Jim Crow law," one state suffragist insisted, and the organization upheld her position by majority vote.[44]

In addition to the vocal opposition of the state suffrage association, NAWSA had to contend with the peculiarities of Oklahoma politics. In order to proceed with ratification, Governor J. B. A. Robertson needed to call the legislature into special session. Mysteriously, Robertson steadfastly refused to do so in spite of NAWSA organizer Marjorie Shuler's prompting. Shuler then obtained pledges of support from a majority of the representatives, as well as an offer from the state Republican Committee to pay all GOP legislators' expenses to the special session. With these levers she extracted a promise from the reluctant executive to reach a decision by September 27, 1919.[45]

As the twenty-seventh dawned, suffragists anxiously awaited the governor's response, but again Robertson refused to commit himself to a special session. Baffled by his mysterious conduct, lobbyists sought to unravel the puzzle. By the second week in October, the women had their answer: Governor Robertson's refusal to call a special session came, not out of opposition to woman suffrage, but because he feared the assembled legislators would institute impeachment proceedings against him. Shuler immediately relayed the news of the governor's predicament to Catt and the NAWSA board and requested that a National Democratic Committeeman be sent to the state to "sound the party tocsin and unite the party behind the Governor." With the Oklahoma campaign still unsettled, Shuler moved on to Colorado. Vastly relieved to be on the road again, the organizer wrote to Catt, "After Oklahoma, hell has no terrors."[46]

After Shuler's departure, the Oklahoma ratification campaign fell into the capable hands of Aloysius Larch-Miller, an exuberant young woman who was active in the state Democratic party. Because the state suffrage association opposed the federal amendment, Larch-Miller could count on little aid from Oklahoma suffragists. To build a suffrage constituency, she toured the state. She later reported on her adventures to a friend: "I am thoroughly ill after a week of torture. The Boy Scouts lost my bags . . . and I sat down in a Baptist pew and tore the Christian seat out of my onliest tailored skirt. All meetings were held in a dismal little church with a poor thorn-crowned Jesus (listening to the emptiness of a multitude of speeches). Twice a day we were led to the whitewashed basement and fed cold chicken and deadly pie, and deadlier cold [*sic*] slaw by the church ladies. As you love me and wish to reward me, take steps to secure me a Carnegie medal."[47] Larch-Miller's recruitment efforts proved ineffective, and the majority of Oklahoma suffragists remained committed to state action. Instead, she increasingly turned to NAWSA for money and organizers. The national association's interference was not appreciated by Governor Robertson. In a press release on January 17, 1920, the chief executive declared that most of the agitation for suffrage came not from Oklahoma women, but rather from "he-women from the north."[48]

But the so-called NAWSA he-women could not entirely relieve Larch-Miller of the full weight of the campaign. In late January, the exhausted young organizer contracted influenza. Before her recovery was complete, she attended a county Democratic convention to debate the state attorney general, who opposed not only a special session but woman suffrage in general. Thanks to her eloquent oration, the convention voted to ask the governor to call a special session to ratify the amendment. The effort proved too much for her; in the early hours of February 2, Aloysius Larch-Miller died at her home in Oklahoma City. Contrite over his part in the tragedy, the attorney general requested that the flags at the capitol be lowered to half mast in her honor.[49] Larch-Miller's death prompted NAWSA strategists to redouble their efforts in Oklahoma. On the day of the young suffragist's funeral, Minnie Fisher Cunningham wired Oklahoma Senator Robert L. Owen asking him to use his influence to pressure the state Democratic convention to demand a special session.[50] Owen responded with alacrity, firing off seventeen telegrams to opposition state senators. While the governor continued to stall, other forces were at work. Influential Democrats within the state had become convinced of the inevitability of woman suffrage, and they took steps to bring their party into line. When Governor Robertson suddenly announced he would call the special session on February 23, 1920, suffragists concluded that his change of heart had been the result of their efforts.[51]

When the Oklahoma legislature convened on February 23, the woman suffrage amendment was quickly introduced. What followed gives modern readers a good glimpse of the suffrage machine in action. When antisuffragists attempted to insert an emergency clause calling for a popular referendum, NAWSA organizers relayed the news to national headquarters. Carrie Catt hastily called on President Woodrow Wilson for assistance, and he duly wired his support for the federal amendment to the Oklahoma speaker of the house and the president of the senate. Moreover, U.S. Senator Thomas P. Gore and Representative Scott Ferris returned to their native state to lobby for ratification, along with Homer Cummings of the National Democratic Committee.[52] The NAWSA Executive Board also sought to supply pressure from the more cooperative western and southern governors: wires went out to the chief executives of Arkansas, Missouri, Tennessee, Texas, Montana, Nevada, and Utah, requesting them to ask Governor Robertson for his support.[53] Home pressure from the South was particularly important because the antisuffragists' propaganda often linked woman suffrage with racial equality in an effort to stir up states' rights opposition to the measure. "We need every ounce of strength the National can put on from the South," one NAWSA organizer confided, "It is strictly a States' right fight."[54]

Thanks mainly to the political pressure brought to bear on the Oklahoma governor and state party leaders, suffrage advocates were victorious in Oklahoma. On February 25, house members passed the amendment with the antisuffragists' emergency clause, but they rescinded the rider three days later after a telegram in support of the unabridged amendment arrived from President Wilson. The same day, the Oklahoma senate passed the federal woman suffrage amendment, and Governor Robertson reluctantly signed the document. A reporter had once remarked that the governor would "probably not change his mind [on woman suffrage] until a rock falls on his head." Together with a few state activists, NAWSA had provided the political pressure needed to activate state and national party leaders, who in turn supplied the "blow to the head" that forced the governor into compliance.[55] As in Texas, however, party factionalism and external issues played a role in the suffrage victory. Although Oklahoma women already enjoyed state suffrage, there was little support for the federal amendment — even among state activists. Ratification was accomplished more by the combined forces of external political pressure, local issues and factions, and NAWSA strategy than by state suffrage activism and legislation that reflected the public sentiment. In the case of Oklahoma, woman suffrage was won over the objections of the state suffragists themselves.

Oklahoma became the thirty-third state to ratify the federal amendment, and when the governors of West Virginia and Washington signed those states' ratification proclamations in late February and early March of 1920, NAWSA leaders realized that the end was in sight. But which state would provide the thirty-sixth vote? The Executive Board had originally believed that the Connecticut Woman Suffrage Association (CWSA), although faced with stiff opposition, could be counted on to bring about ratification. The Connecticut association had begun its efforts in January 1918 with the formation of a joint legislative committee for ratification, composed of the state NAWSA affiliate and the National Woman's Party. Although CWSA executives were reluctant to ally with the NWP, they recognized the difficulties inherent in a divided campaign.[56] Together the two groups agreed on a plan calling for the election of county chairmen, as well as senatorial district and township leaders. Additionally, the committee created the position of "political leader" to oversee the political work in each section of the state.[57] Unfortunately, this joint committee was abandoned in March 1919 when the leadership disagreed over tactics. Although the two groups agreed to adopt a position of peaceful coexistence, further attempts at unity were jettisoned.[58]

In place of the joint committee, CWSA formed its own ratification committee, which approved an elaborate month-by-month program that included circularization of influential political, church and business leaders, interviews with candidates, press work, and town caucuses. Open-air meetings, poster displays in shop windows, and mass rallies also helped bring the suffrage message to the public. The committee lobbied both incumbents and prospective candidates and raised $30,000 to pay for campaign work.[59] Suffragists hoped their work would rouse public support and force the governor to call for a vote on ratification as soon as the amendment passed the U.S. Senate.

The Connecticut Republican machine, led by Chairman of the State Central Committee J. Henry Roraback, opposed ratification. In addition to the machine's stand on the suffrage issue, state reformers were outraged as the Republican-dominated legislature repeatedly voted down a wide range of progressive bills.[60] When a progressive majority was returned to the General Assembly after strenuous campaigning in 1918 by suffragists and other reform-minded residents, CWSA officers felt confident that their issue would be given a fair hearing. But their hopes were dashed when the 1919 legislature adjourned without acting on the issue. As that body would not meet again until 1921, state suffrage forces faced the task of persuading the governor to call a special session to ratify the federal amendment.[61]

The final stage of the Connecticut battle for ratification began in April 1920 when CWSA strategists launched a full-scale assault on the governor to demand a special session. Forty-five out-of-state organizers, whose expenses were paid by NAWSA, toured the state in flying squadrons. Local committees backed up their efforts with meetings, rallies, and press work. At the conclusion of the tours, the organizers converged on Hartford to stage a rally and hearing with the governor.[62] When the governor remained hesitant, CWSA activists voted to oppose the Republican party in the coming elections, with the exception of prosuffrage candidates. In desperation the women polled all gubernatorial candidates on the issue of the special session and published the results in state newspapers; additionally, a committee of prominent Republican women issued a statement containing a "no vote, no money" pledge. Others met with Republican National Committee Chairman Will H. Hays to protest the Connecticut situation and to urge that he pressure the state party officials to act.[63]

In spite of the excellent organization and publicity efforts of the CWSA, the Roraback machine continued to block a special session.[64] With the Connecticut campaign deemed hopeless, NAWSA strategists grew increasingly pessimistic. Delaware, another state with both NWP and NAWSA activists hard at work, had offered good prospects of ratifying the previous March, but again the suffragists were doomed to disappointment. Catt traveled to the state capital to speak at the legislative hearing as did out-of-state antisuffragists, but the amendment failed to pass after the legislators debated the issue for two months. "It doesn't matter much," reflected the dejected NAWSA leader after the Delaware votes were counted, "only I feel so ashamed of our conservatism and ignorance. I feel that we have repudiated the aims of the war and set ourselves up as the Chief Reactionary among Nations."[65]

In June 1920, NAWSA was gratified to learn that both parties had endorsed ratification of the federal amendment at their national conventions.[66] When Democrat Carter Glass read the pro-ratification plank to the party delegates, he added, "And if there is anything else the women want, we are for it!"[67] With the additional support of the national conventions, along with a host of congressmen and governors, Catt and the NAWSA board readied themselves for a showdown in the most unlikely of states: Tennessee.

When suffragists realized that the last battle for the vote would be fought in Tennessee, few were optimistic. Although the legislature that had granted presidential and municipal suffrage to the state's women the previous year would also act on ratification, there were other factors that canceled these advantages. Both the Democratic and Republican parties in the state were split into opposing factions, a rift that was duplicated within the Tennessee suffrage movement. As one state suffragist exclaimed in frustration, "Ratification was an insignificant pawn in the local chess game."[68] Party factionalism also threatened to postpone ratification indefinitely because Governor Albert H. Roberts was reluctant to call the legislature into special session without legislative consensus. Moreover, many legislators insisted in abiding by an archaic provision in the state constitution that required the election of a new legislature before the state could ratify a federal amendment.

In addition to these problems, suffragists quickly learned that state representatives were equally divided on the question and would require extensive lobbying to ensure passage of the amendment.[69] This process was made more difficult by the geographic contours of the state. As a NWP organizer explained in a letter to Alice Paul: "Many of the counties in the mountains and hills of the eastern and middle sections are almost inaccessible, with no railroad facilities and bad dirt roads. . . . There are ninety-seven counties and one hundred and thirty-two members of the legislature [to lobby]. . . . The presidential bill received only a bare majority so that the loss of any Republican votes or of any votes because of states' rights opposition would cost us ratification."[70] In an attempt to overcome one obstacle, NAWSA leaders resolved to contest the Tennessee constitution's provision regarding ratification of federal amendments. Long before the battle had shifted to Tennessee, Helen Hamilton Gardener had persuaded President Wilson to request a judgment on the provision from the Justice Department, which ruled that a recent Supreme Court decision rendered the constitutional point invalid. Wilson then telegraphed the governor, who at last relented and called the Tennessee legislature into special session on August 9, 1920.[71] With the promise of a special session, suffragists and antisuffragists converged on the state capital to lobby legislators and publicize their respective positions on the upcoming ratification procedure.[72] Throughout July, both groups toured the state, speaking in rural villages and urban centers. Carrie Catt spoke for suffrage in the larger cities, returning to her temporary home at the Nashville Hermitage Hotel between engagements. In addition to Catt and Harriet Taylor Upton, the elderly Ohio suffragist who served as Catt's lieutenant for the Tennessee campaign, states' rights advocates Laura Clay and Kate Gordon used the Hermitage as home base for their lobbying efforts against the amendment. When the suffragists met their estranged coworkers in the lobby, the Dixie dissenters pointedly refused to make eye contact with their onetime friends.[73]

For two hot weeks, the Tennessee legislature debated the woman suffrage amendment. The resolution quickly passed the senate, but house members remained divided on the issue. Catt refused to attend the debates; instead she sat alone in her hotel room, listening to the distant sounds of cheering and applause that drifted out of the capitol windows. Meanwhile, suffragists constantly polled the representatives at the statehouse and patrolled the nearby railway station to intercept fleeing antisuffrage legislators who intended to break quorum by boarding trains for hillside hideaways. "[The legislators] were threatened with loss of jobs, ruined careers," Tennessee activist Mrs. Guilford Dudley recalled later, "and they fell away from us like autumn leaves in a high wind."[74] In an effort to counteract the antisuffragists' maneuvers, suffragists spirited favorable legislators away to movies and drives in the country.[75] "With all the political pressure, it ought to be easy," Catt wrote to a friend on August 15, "but the opposition of every sort is here fighting with no scruple desperately. Women, including L. Clay and K. Gordon are here appealing to Negrophobia and every other cave man's prejudice. Men, lots of them, are here. What they represent, God only knows. We believe they are buying votes. I've been here a month. It's hot, muggy, nasty, and the last battle is desperate. Even if we win, we who have been here will never remember it with anything but a shudder. Verily the way of the reformer is hard."[76]

Catt's assertion that the antisuffragists were out in force to block ratification was correct. In addition to Clay and Gordon, Mrs. James Pinckard, president of the Southern Women's League for the Rejection of the Susan B. Anthony Amendment, also traveled to Nashville to lobby the Tennessee legislature.[77] Besides lobbying, the antisuffragists distributed posters and fliers throughout the city. Antisuffrage handbills were particularly inflammatory, with such titles as "Mrs. Catt and Suffrage Leaders Repudiate the Bible" and "Woman Suffrage Means Reopening the Negro Question." Another flier, printed by the Selma, Alabama, United Daughters of the Confederacy (UDC), featured a UDC resolution condemning the "slander of Robert E. Lee by Susan B. Anthony and others."[78]

Eager to combat the antisuffragists' negative influence, the suffragists looked for ways to win support with wavering legislators. When a group of representatives approached Catt for a fifty dollar donation so they could rent the last hotel room in town for use as a prosuffrage conference room, she quickly gave them the money. Harriet Taylor Upton, however, made a more realistic appraisal of the politicians' motives. Convinced that the money was in fact being spent on spirits with which to lubricate doubtful decision-makers, Upton exclaimed "If they are as pegged out as I am, I hope it's good stuff!" When a female reporter overheard the jovial suffragist's remark, she promptly bought a bottle of moonshine and hid it under the pillow of Catt's bed as a joke. Later in the day, when the NAWSA leader lay down for a nap, she discovered the bottle and jumped to the conclusion that an antisuffragist had placed it there in order to discredit the suffragists. Catt eventually smuggled the contraband out of the hotel in a locked suitcase and, driving miles out of town, deposited the bottle in a stone wall covered with poison ivy.[79]

At the end of two weeks of stormy debate, the speaker of the Tennessee House of Representatives at last called out, "The hour has come!" Tension grew as a poll of the house revealed that the amendment fell two votes short. Speaker Seth Walker, an antisuffragist, called for a roll call vote to table the amendment. Suffrage onlookers drew a sigh of relief when the move to table was stymied by a tie vote. One prosuffrage supporter had been brought from the hospital to cast his vote, and another legislator, Banks Turner, unexpectedly defected from the antisuffrage ranks. Refusing to accept the tie vote, Speaker Walker quickly called for reconsideration. As the names were called, suffragists watched in horrified silence as the speaker left his seat and approached Representative Turner. Throwing his arms about the startled legislator, Walker pleaded with him to vote against the amendment as the roll call proceeded. At last, Turner's name was called, and a tension-filled silence descended on the chamber; onlookers leaned forward in the gallery, all eyes were riveted on the scene below. Suddenly, Turner shook himself free of the speaker's embrace, rose from his seat, and shouted, "Nay!"[80]

Moments later, the vote to table stood tied; with no choice left but to decide the matter once and for all, the final vote was ordered. Would one representative change his vote to "aye" to break the deadlock? Or would some hesitant soul heed the antisuffragists' siren song and vote to defeat the federal amendment? To the crowds in the gallery, defeat seemed imminent; if victory was to be theirs, who would provide the one needed vote? Unobserved by the suffragists, first-term representative Harry Burn sat musing in his seat below. Minutes before, Burn had voted to table the amendment, and antisuffragists therefore felt confident of his negative vote. To symbolize his antisuffrage stand, the young politician sported a red rose — the antisuffragists' trade mark — in his lapel. But as Burn listened to the roll call, he recalled a promise he had made to his elderly suffragist mother. Although his constituency was strongly opposed to woman suffrage, Burn had vowed to his mother that he would cast his vote for suffrage under one condition: if, and only if, ratification hinged on one vote, he would provide that vote. Suddenly, Harry Burn was roused from his reverie: the speaker was calling his name to vote. Rising from his seat, he cast his rose to the floor and shouted out "Aye!" Suffragists in the gallery sat in stunned silence; the needed vote had miraculously appeared, the tie had been broken. Seconds later, deafening applause rained down on the young legislator as the speaker called in vain for order. Within minutes after the demonstration subsided, the federal woman suffrage amendment passed the house, and Tennessee became the thirty-sixth state to ratify.[81]

A week later the ratification certificate reached Washington, D.C., and was taken by special courier to the secretary of state for his signature. On August 26, 1920, when a weary but exultant Carrie Catt arrived in the city, she quickly placed a call to the secretary of state's office. Harriet Taylor Upton and Maud Wood Park stood beside her as she asked whether the certificate had been received. After a moment of silence, Catt turned to her friends and quietly said, "The Secretary has signed the proclamation." "So quietly as that," Park recounted years later, "we learned that the last step in the enfranchisement of women had been taken and the struggle of more than seventy years brought to a successful end."[82]

Although the struggle for the vote ended with the secretary of state's signature, the suffragists' celebration continued for several months. First there was a victory banquet at the Astor Hotel in New York City, where Catt, Upton, and other NAWSA leaders were toasted and cheered by the state's suffragists. "We are no longer petitioners, we are not wards of the nation but free and equal citizens," Catt told the assembly. Urging her audience to defeat any candidate who failed to represent the people, she concluded, "Let us do our part to keep [America] a true and triumphant democracy." Harriet Taylor Upton's remarks, although less serious than Catt's, were also appropriate: "The opponents [in Tennessee] accused me of being an Amazon. I didn't know what an Amazon was, except the river, so I looked it up, and I like it! I found that an Amazon is a strong, lithe woman who can put up a winning fight." Then, to the vast amusement of the crowd, Upton shook her corpulent body and shouted, "Also, I learned that she is THIN!"[83]

In Boston, too, suffragists celebrated the successful completion of their seventy-year crusade. Several weeks after the ratification proclamation was signed, the Massachusetts Woman Suffrage Association hosted their fellow activists in a victory rally at Faneuil Hall. After toasts and speeches, Mira Pittman, veteran suffragist and chairman of MWSA's finance committee, led the assembly in her own version of the Doxology:

> Praise God from whom all blessings flow,
> Praise Him all women here below.
> Now we can raise our voices high
> And shout hosannas to the sky.
> For we have won the mighty fight —
> Long did we labor for the right.
> And now in solemn thanks to Thee,
> We sing Thy praises. We are Free![84]

With victory came rejoicing, and the women who had served in the woman suffrage movement had good cause to celebrate. For not only had they achieved political equality, the suffragists had also created bonds of friendship and unity that would endure for the remainder of their lives. Not all of the nation's suffragists could experience the joys of freedom, however. Although all women were technically enfranchised by the Nineteenth Amendment, some, like southern black women, would wait for decades to enjoy their newly won right. Jim Crow laws were quickly rewritten to include black women, and on election day in Dixie, few black women would cast ballots. Southern white women had more cause to celebrate since they would be permitted to vote, but they were forced to live with the memory that most southern legislatures had refused to ratify the federal amendment.[85] Moreover, opposition to woman suffrage endured for decades in some states; in Mississippi the legislature did not endorse the Nineteenth Amendment until 1981.

Even without the South, NAWSA's strategy had proved successful. But the final steps in the crusade were not taken by suffragists alone. War work gave the movement an opportunity to publicize its power, and as the tide began to turn, the bandwagon effect helped to stimulate the political interest and powerful assistance of influential party leaders. Once the amendment passed through Congress, the growing belief in the inevitability of reform lent a momentum of its own. As the political parties grappled among themselves for credit for the amendment's ratification, party leaders pressured state representatives to act favorably in order to claim the allegiance of the new women voters. This dynamic, coupled with NAWSA's strong state-level organization, effective lobbying, and publicity techniques, propelled the federal amendment through the laborious process of ratification in record time. As a political pressure group, the suffrage machine had found a strategy that served the cause of votes for women well, and in the process it offered to other groups a way to sway the minds of the majority.

As for the suffragists themselves, they emerged from the decades-old struggle with a stronger sense of the American democratic tradition and a new feeling of self-esteem. Moreover, the movement had opened the door to limitless possibilities, both for women in the public realm and those in the private sphere. Perhaps Carrie Catt best expressed the sense of strength and confidence the cause created in its disciples. Recalling the women who had carried the banner of woman suffrage in the years since Seneca Falls, she reflected, "Ah, you were heroines all, — dear, blessed heroines all."[86] In the end, then, victory meant more than a ballot cast or a candidate elected. One veteran tried to put into words the meaning of their great accomplishment: "Throats choke, eyes shine, voices break . . . you can't feel enough. You can't let go enough. . . . We weren't a bit lady-like, we were boy-like, we were girl-like. We were like youth, like hope, like faith, — like victory."[87]

Conclusion: Woman Suffrage and the New Democracy

In assessing the accomplishments and limitations of the suffragists of NAWSA, an ambiguity exists that makes objective analysis difficult. Many years ago, when I described to historian Ellen DuBois my plans for a study highly critical of the suffragists, she cautioned that we must not forget the great thing they had done. For the suffragists *had* done a great thing: they had given America a model of a new democracy that not only enfranchised women but gave other groups the tools to protest their political and social exclusion in the years to come. As the feminist movement gained ground in the sixties and seventies, suffrage history was often the first women's history read by modern women, the suffragists their first heroes. It is therefore difficult to put these women under a sort of historical microscope, exposing their weaknesses as well as their strengths. To place both extremes in perspective, it makes sense to start with what the NAWSA suffragists accomplished and how they did it.

In the 1890s, NAWSA leaders took stock of their organization and found it wanting. Low membership, poor funding, ineffectual political strategy, unstable local and state associations, and virtually no public support for the cause all helped to explain the state of stagnation from which the movement suffered. By 1900, the suffragists also faced an organized, vocal, and well-financed opposition. A new strategy was needed to surmount these difficulties. Drawing inspiration from numerous sources — benevolent societies,

temperance, trade unions, popular politics, and urban political machines —
NAWSA leaders created a series of interconnected innovations that were of
crucial importance to the woman suffrage movement and to the future of
American politics.

An important innovation concerned the suffragists' public image, tarnished
by antisuffrage attacks and negative publicity. During the first decade of the
new century NAWSA leaders implemented a series of plans to cast the cause in a
more respectable light. The association drew on traditions, rituals, and history
to illuminate the ideals of female progress and self-fulfillment in a way that
proved highly attractive to young college-educated women. Such diverse resources as parlor meetings and popular sentimental fiction were exploited to
bring wealthy society matrons and eventually clubwomen into the suffrage
fold. With the creation of the "suffrage saint" through the elevation of Susan
B. Anthony to the status of a national heroic figure, patriotic and religious
overtones were added to the crusade. Lastly, as progressivism grew in strength
nationwide, woman suffrage gained a new cohort of both male and female
advocates who hoped that the vote would help to win a wide reform agenda.
Together with NAWSA's efforts to establish a new respectable image and to
enlarge its base of support through education and persuasion, public opinion
slowly turned from indifference to acceptance of the issue.

Historians of the suffrage movement have labeled the period 1896–1910
"the doldrums" because no states adopted woman suffrage amendments during that time. In light of NAWSA's image-building campaign, progressive impetus to reform, and the subsequent shift in public opinion, a better tag for these
years might be "the suffrage renaissance," for a definite rebirth of the movement took place. Without this turnabout in popular sentiment, the suffragists'
success would have been delayed, possibly for decades. The new positive image of NAWSA brought immediate benefits to the woman suffrage movement.
Membership totals and financial support soared, and by 1910 suffrage societies across the nation could look forward to more volunteers and better
funding. From this solid foundation, strategists implemented a new plan of
organization that capitalized on the movement's newfound momentum and
propelled the suffragists into the realm of practical politics.

For the suffrage movement, the period 1910–1915 was a time of transformation, as NAWSA evolved into an efficient political organization. The Woman
Suffrage Party plan and the political settlement idea meant not only more
converts to the cause but a trained staff of professional and volunteer organizers. Through their enrollment, canvassing, and publicity, organizers built a
stable network of local and state suffrage clubs. By 1915, NAWSA leaders had
hammered out an *outsider strategy* that could be called upon to exert home

pressure on reluctant politicians. Led by the NAWSA organizers, state and local activists forged a strong basis for constituency support bound together by a movement psychology that revitalized and sustained the crusade through its final years of struggle.

For the last stage of the campaign, NAWSA's system of political organization also relied on the development of an *insider strategy* composed of a professional lobby and modern publicity bureau.[1] Backed by home pressure, the lobby functioned as a nonpartisan task force to move the federal amendment through Congress. The publicity bureau disseminated news of tactical advances and kept the issue before the public through a barrage of press releases. During ratification, lobbyists besieged state legislatures and called forth the vast suffrage machine to assist them. By wielding pressure at all levels of the political spectrum through the appearance — if not the reality — of a massive prosuffrage constituency, ratification was accomplished in record time. Without this backup force, mere lobbying or political coercion would have proved ineffective, especially in the final stages of the crusade. Used together, NAWSA's insider and outsider strategies were highly successful in moving the federal amendment through Congress and the ratification process.

The pressure group created by NAWSA dramatically altered the course of the suffrage movement. Little attention has been paid, however, to the effect this new strategy had on NAWSA as an organization. Without doubt, the insider-outsider strategy, the standardization of propaganda and campaigns, the attention to image, and the centralization of control under Carrie Chapman Catt's leadership after 1915 greatly aided the federal amendment's progress through the Congress and the states. But often the gains made were matched by less obvious, though significant, losses. Standardization of all aspects of the association's propaganda and campaign procedures greatly increased efficiency, but spontaneity and democratic decision making at the state and local levels were lost. Concern for image won the NAWSA suffragists needed friends among conservative congressmen, but prompted association leaders to exaggerate membership totals, to distance themselves from controversial issues, and to engage in dirty tricks designed to discredit the militants. Furthermore, NAWSA's cultivation of the wealthy and prominent came too often at the expense of working women, who were sometimes seen by upper-class activists as little more than signatures on prosuffrage cards. Other groups, such as blacks, immigrants, pacifists, feminists, socialists and other radicals, were either excluded outright or marginalized.

Bureaucratic centralization also carried with it a troubling disregard for NAWSA's democratic heritage. One of the major effects of NAWSA's implementation of single-issue pressure group tactics was centralization of control within the top leadership and a concurrent loss of traditional democratic participation in policy making within the group. By 1916, policy for the entire organization was controlled almost exclusively by Catt's Executive Board, which decided what specific policy "decisions" would be shared with the NAWSA membership. The suffrage machine was designed to accomplish one goal: passage of the Nineteenth Amendment. As the new political strategy was put into action and NAWSA administration became more centralized, issues the organization had traditionally supported were pushed to the side in favor of the single goal of woman suffrage. By the second decade of the twentieth century, NAWSA leadership began to steer clear of such issues as equal pay for equal work, protective legislation for working women and children, and other reforms supported by large numbers of suffragists and other progressive women. The association's abandonment of class and gender issues came too easily in the absence of voices of protest, silenced by the Executive Board's seizure of all policy-making and planning authority for the association.

A friend of Catt's once described her as "an aristocrat with democratic tendencies," a fitting description of both the NAWSA president and many of its other leaders.[2] As the aristocratic edge of the NAWSA leadership gained ascendancy, the organization's growing disregard for internal democracy was extended to encompass a suspicion of democracy in practice. As president, Catt instituted a policy that virtually eliminated popular referenda as a backup to the federal route to suffrage. While some states were ill prepared for such contests, others were not, and they were deprived of the chance to wage campaigns by control from above. As political scientist Eileen McDonagh has demonstrated, growth in support for the federal amendment in the House of Representatives in the years 1915–19 directly correlates with the increase in the number of House members representing woman suffrage states.[3] Although it was clearly good strategy to prohibit futile state suffrage referenda, Catt's ban on all such efforts may have cost the movement a few needed votes in the House in the last years of the congressional fight.

With the erosion of NAWSA's democratic foundations, its leaders turned to accommodation, behind-the-scenes manipulations, and occasional deceit to press their case. The plan to substitute a watered-down compromise amendment for the original resolution was the last of many such betrayals of the movement's democratic heritage. In a sense, Catt's Winning Plan was at once responsible for the movement's triumph, and a symbol of the tainted dreams and empty rhetoric that replaced the suffragists' idealism of old. More than simply affecting NAWSA alone, the decision to move away from a democratic structure toward a centralized oligarchy would have important and long-lasting consequences for the women's movement after the Nineteenth Amendment was enacted.

Catt's redirection of the movement was a reflection of NAWSA leaders' heightened concern about the movement's image and public opinion, an innate consequence of pressure group politics. Two implications are worth noting. First, concern with image led NAWSA leaders to redefine the woman's movement as a suffrage movement, closing off the possibility of a broad-based feminist agenda both during and after the suffrage campaign. Indeed, *feminism* was a word suffragists rarely mentioned; to do so might taint the movement with the brush of extremism, socialism, or militancy.[4] Antisuffragists after 1910 often linked feminism with other radical causes or ideas, going so far in some cases as to proclaim feminism a Bolshevik plot. No matter how it was defined, feminism held the promise of role change for women, whereas votes for women offered only role equity without concomitant economic or societal transformation.[5] Catt and other NAWSA leaders correctly recognized the lack of a popular mandate for suffrage. To campaign for a full-fledged feminist agenda would open the movement to criticism from a variety of groups much larger and more powerful than the antisuffragists. A similar argument was made by NAWSA leaders whenever the question of allowing black participation in NAWSA was raised. Association members expressed a wide range of opinions — from support for political equality for blacks to virulent racism. But individual opinions aside, the association opted for a racist course of action, and NAWSA remained essentially a "whites only" organization. The goal of political equity for white women only was deemed safer and more attainable than role change or racial equity. Feminism, antiracism, and other related women's social issues were thus cast adrift in the name of NAWSA's public image.

Second, NAWSA leaders' concern for image also led them to shy away from any serious consideration of the National Woman's Party's militant tactics. Although neither organization made much effort to cooperate with the other, the duplication of effort and tactical blunders caused by this lack of cooperation stemmed in part from NAWSA's excessive concern with public image.[6] To associate with militants would lend credence to antisuffragists' claims of suffrage radicalism, a charge that Catt and other NAWSA officials wanted to avoid at all costs. At the same time, the militancy of the NWP, while embarrassing to the mainstream movement, also helped to confirm that NAWSA desired only moderate reform, not social revolution. By casting off all nonsuffrage issues and refusing to contemplate healing the split in the suffrage movement, NAWSA (and the NWP as well) not only limited the focus of the suffrage movement but also jeopardized the survival of a united women's movement after the vote was won. To play the game of pressure politics successfully, then, meant strict attention to image and public opinion at the expense of ideology, principles, and tactical alliances that might prove damaging to NAWSA's respectability. Pressure politics worked, but the suffragists of NAWSA would pay a price for their success that would be called to account after the passage of the Nineteenth Amendment.

The redefinition of the women's movement into a single-issue pressure group was strategically wise from the standpoint of the suffrage campaign, although not necessarily so for the postsuffrage women's movement. After ratification, expectations of a powerful women's movement ran high among both women's groups and politicians. Many believed that the new voters would organize into a gigantic gender-based pressure group, which would bloc vote to coerce politicians to endorse a woman's agenda. Those who had opposed woman suffrage shivered at the thought of a female vendetta that would sweep them out of office for their sins against organized womanhood. When a number of women's associations formed the Women's Joint Congressional Committee (WJCC) as a permanent lobby on Capitol Hill, many political observers assumed that women's interests would automatically be elevated to the status of policy and platform issues.[7]

By the end of the 1920s, however, all of these expectations had failed to materialize. Although a few pieces of legislation sponsored by the WJCC had been enacted, most notably the Sheppard-Towner Act for infant and maternal care, its overall success rate was poor compared to those of male-dominated economic lobbies. The expected female voting bloc had failed to form. Rather than a sudden increase in voter turnout brought about by women hastening to the polls for the first time, statistics showed the continuation of a steady decline in voter turnout begun in the 1890s. Critics were quick to explain this phenomenon by suggesting that women, having gained the ballot, were loath to use it. Indeed, the myth of the nonvoting woman provided one of the leading explanations for the decline in voter turnout that lasted for decades.[8] And as for politicians being forced to adopt a women's agenda or be voted out of office, nothing could have been further from reality. No women's agenda supported by a powerful prowoman constituency such as the one amassed by the suffragists made its presence felt in Washington.

Historians have attributed the gradual loss of the momentum built up by the suffrage movement to a variety of factors. Certainly the waning of progressive fervor after World War I, the first Red Scare, and the growth of a business-dominated consumer culture in the 1920s contributed to the women's movement's difficulties. The split between moderates and militants that originated in the suffrage campaign was never healed, leading to sharp internecine disagreements over tactics and goals that lasted for decades. Some women's organizations that participated in the WJCC found themselves on the decline and were consequently unable to contribute volunteers or money to support the lobby's efforts by the end of the decade.[9] And although some of the suffrage movement's most experienced lobbyists like Maud Wood Park continued to represent women's interests in Washington throughout the twenties, many left the fight for women's rights to a new generation of women — a cohort that some said was more interested in fast cars and spangled dresses than the causes of the past.

All of these factors played a part in what historian William O'Neill has called the "failure of feminism" in the 1920s, but the suffragists themselves have come in for a major share of the blame. The process of narrowing the women's movement to the single issue of woman suffrage resulted in a successful pressure group for votes for women, but it crippled the emerging women's movement after the vote was won. The NAWSA umbrella covered disparate groups, each with its own set of beliefs and goals. States' rights activists and civil egalitarians, preparedness advocates and pacifists, reactionaries and radicals formed an uneasy coalition under the NAWSA aegis, a coalition that did not remain intact despite the organization's efforts. It is not surprising, therefore, that this diverse constituency did not magically transform itself back into the women's movement of 1900 — a movement, it may be recalled, of many issues and perilously few members.[10]

The adherence to single-issue pressure tactics by NAWSA left the 1920s women's movement without a slate of issues or a broad-based constituency in support of a feminist agenda. Nonpartisanship — the mainstay of the NAWSA suffragists' strategy — was ill suited for the postsuffrage world of party politics. As with single-issue activism, nonpartisanship had served the suffragists well, but it did not provide voting women with an automatic entrée to political parties. Women's exclusion from party politics had been so complete that the vote alone was not sufficient to induct them into the party system. As we have seen, one branch of women's political culture evolved from such diverse sources as voluntary societies, literary clubs, parlor meetings and even sentimental fiction. This culture was nonpartisan, voluntaristic, and dependent on womanly influence rather than political power. By the 1910s, other influences, such as trade unionism, political machine organization, and popular politics, would mesh with women's traditional culture to help create a new political culture for women and NAWSA's suffrage machine. But even with these alternate sources of political inspiration, most women had no direct experience as actual participants in the party system when the Nineteenth Amendment was ratified.

Although NAWSA suffragists' nonpartisan tradition made amalgamation into the party structure difficult, the parties themselves made little effort to educate or include the new women voters. Only NAWSA took on the responsibility of educating women in the duties of citizenship through local citizenship schools and workshops held before the 1920 presidential election. There was no governmental and party involvement in educating the new voters on such things as how to cast a ballot, understanding party platforms, or the intricacies of delegate selection. Unlike the experience of black voters after the passage of the 1964 Voting Act, new female voters received no encouragement or support from the federal government. No federal pressure was applied to force the parties to extend equal representation to women, nor were the administrations of Harding, Coolidge, or Hoover inclined to welcome women's political participation.

Political participation has traditionally been measured not only through the vote but also by such factors as convention attendance, representation in national party committees and campaign activities, and running for office. In each of these areas, women remained second-class citizens despite their new designation as voters. Major party convention attendance by female delegates, for example, rose from 1 percent in 1916 to a mere 10 percent after the vote was won. Although the pattern from 1920 to 1940 showed occasional increases, the overall number of women delegates to party conventions remained very small until the 1940s. Moreover, those few women chosen as delegates usually served as alternates, a position defined by its junior status in keeping with women's presumed low political efficacy. Not until 1980 did the Democratic party have 50 percent female delegates; to date, the Republicans have never achieved delegate equity by gender.[11]

Female representation in party hierarchy was also a disappointment to women eager to participate fully in national level politics. Both the Democratic and Republican National Committees selected committeewomen from each state, but often these women were excluded from party inner councils.[12] Women's exclusion or possibly ineffectiveness within party platform committees is evident when one scans the platforms of the Democratic and Republican parties from 1924 onward. Not one plank dealing with women's movement issues appears in any of these platforms; only the 1920 platforms, written when the fear of a female bloc vote existed, contained any planks with direct relevancy to what might be termed a women's agenda.[13] As for women candidates for office, the parties neither encouraged women to run nor supported their campaigns with adequate funds and party pressure when they did seek election. The dearth of women in Congress and state legislatures that exists to this day was not merely a result of women's apathy toward politics or the suffragists' failure to sustain the women's movement after the vote was won. More important, the glaring lack of women in higher elected positions reflects both major political parties' apathy toward and rejection of women as political beings.[14]

One possible reason for party apathy toward women voters stemmed from the widespread belief that women were disinclined by nature or custom to involve themselves in politics. As early as 1924, two political scientists put forward the argument that the vote was insignificant to the postsuffrage women's movement because women refused to use their newly won privilege. Using a sample of about 1 percent of the voting population from a 1923 Chicago mayoral race, Charles E. Merriman and Harold F. Gosnell concluded that women were unlikely to vote because of such factors as apathy, disbelief in women voting, and objections from husbands.[15] By the 1940s, political scientists had honed this flimsy evidence into what one feminist scholar calls the "insufficient masculinization theory": women did not vote because they had little interest in politics, preferring to let their husbands express their political views for them at the polls.[16]

Political efficacy has traditionally been measured almost exclusively by an individual's activism in such party functions as conventions, rallies, and campaigning for party candidates. Before passage of the Nineteenth Amendment, women were either discouraged or barred from participating in these functions. After the early 1920s, when the new voters were briefly courted by nervous politicians, women were not encouraged to join parties, engage in party activities, or run for office. It is hardly surprising, then, that women scored low on measures of political efficacy well into the 1960s, as party activism was virtually the only standard used to measure political interest. This, in turn, was seen as evidence for women's presumed political apathy and consequent low voter turnout. As political scientist Marjorie Lansing notes, however, factors other than gender have been found to be far more important predictors of turnout. Education, age, region, race, and employment are variables of more significance than either gender or party activism in explaining voting patterns.[17] Neither gender nor political efficacy (when measured almost exclusively by party participation) are accurate predictors of turnout among women voters.[18]

Another factor that must be considered in measuring women's (and men's) political interest and subsequent voter turnout is referred to by political scientists as the "rational voter model." Political activism, whether by voting or other types of participation in the political process, also depends on the specific benefits that candidates and issues offer in return for voter support.[19] As we have seen, the political parties provided almost no incentives or issues to attract women voters through platform planks or support for women candidates. Moreover, male turnout also declined throughout the twentieth century. For example, during the 1920s, national voter turnout in presidential elections declined to just over 50 percent of the electorate, as opposed to an average of almost 80 percent before the 1890s.[20] Historian Paul Kleppner has demonstrated that although female voting patterns declined throughout much of the twentieth century, male voting turnout also suffered a similar decline.[21] These facts cast serious doubt on the argument that women merely lacked interest in politics and were content to allow men to guide their political destinies on their behalf.

For the better part of the twentieth century, however, many scholars continued to believe that political efficacy was a principal if not the primary factor in accounting for low female voter turnout. But one question remained unanswered: why did the woman suffrage movement generate massive demonstrations of political involvement — what modern historians might call "popular politics" — if women were devoid of political sentiment and tendencies toward activism? What has emerged in the decades since Gosnell's and Merriman's study are two types of responses formulated to reconcile the woman suffrage movement's outpouring of political activism with the received wisdom of the times that held (and to a certain extent still holds) women to be politically apathetic. The first and easiest response was to deny that women won the vote through their own efforts. For example, noted political scientist E. E. Schattschneider called the franchise expansion "one of the easiest victories of the democratic cause in American history." Warming to his theme, he continued: "Indeed the bulk of the newly enfranchised, including Negroes and nearly all women, won battles they never fought. The whole thing has been deceptively easy. . . . The newly enfranchised had about as much to do with the extension of the suffrage as the consuming public has had to do with the expanding market for toothpaste. The parties, assisted by some excited minorities, were the entrepreneurs, took the initiative and got the law of the franchise liberalized."[22] If the suffrage movement could be portrayed as insignificant and chivalrous parties, acting on behalf of "excited minorities," depicted as the true champions of democracy, the belief in women's lack of political activism could go unchallenged. A cursory survey of American history textbooks and political history monographs written before roughly 1970 reveals that this "denial theory" was widely accepted.[23]

The denial theory has not entirely faded away. It surfaced in a slightly altered form in historian Michael McGerr's 1986 monograph, *The Decline of Popular Politics*. McGerr explained the decline of voter turnout that took place at the end of the nineteenth century by what he defined as a corresponding death of popular politics — of torchlight parades and mass public demonstrations of political sentiment.[24] When one recalls the twentieth-century woman suffrage movement, McGerr's reports of the death of popular politics seem a bit premature. In this case, the denial theory takes the form of denying that women were politically active by simply ignoring the fact that they formed part of the populace that practiced what McGerr calls "popular politics."

In a 1990 article, McGerr amended his earlier thesis to include the political activism of the suffragists by attributing the origins of their publicity and propaganda tactics to the same nineteenth-century popular politics from which women were excluded. Women, claims McGerr, simply "borrowed" the male political style of a previous era, a political style, he maintains, that was rejected by the political parties twenty years earlier. The children's tale of *The Borrowers* comes to mind, with its tiny, dependent creatures who borrowed the flotsam and jetsam of the human race to eke out their existence. Were the suffragists simply pale shadows of the male-dominated political styles of bygone days, borrowing from a system already defunct? Why then were these styles or techniques so successful for the suffragists, yet barren of opportunity for the political parties? And if women were successfully participating in popular politics well into the second decade of the twentieth century, why were women not counted as part of the popular politics that McGerr claims died out a decade before women adopted them?[25]

A second type of response to the apparent contradiction between suffragists' political activism and female political apathy after 1920 denigrates the vote itself, rather than simply denying the significance of the suffrage movement. William O'Neill's now famous "suffrage as the failure of feminism" argument rests on the premise that the vote, once won, did women little good. The ballot, O'Neill argued, "did not materially help women to advance their most urgent causes; even worse, it did not help women to better themselves or improve their status. The struggle for women's rights ended during the 1920s, leaving men in clear possession of the commanding places in American life."[26] O'Neill explains that the lack of a sustaining feminist ideology during the heyday of the suffrage movement led to the failure of feminism after 1920.[27] Unlike those of the denial school, this argument credits the suffragists for winning the vote but questions the utility of the ballot without a sustaining feminist agenda and constituency. Certainly there is truth in the assertion that NAWSA failed to put forward a fully articulated feminist ideology; as we have seen, the association's leaders intentionally sought to divest the movement of any controversial issues that might detract from their sole objective of passing the federal suffrage amendment. In the decade after the passage of the Nineteenth Amendment, women's ballots did not bring a renewed women's movement to life, nor did they transform politics as many skeptics had predicted. The ballot seemed obsolete, like a buggy whip gathering dust next to a new Model T.[28]

In seeking an explanation for the falling voter turnout and, in particular, women's lack of political participation throughout much of the twentieth century, there is a direct link between the woman suffrage movement and the decline in the importance of the ballot. The existence of several mass movements in the early twentieth century demonstrates that the major political parties as traditionally conceived were not inclusive of the entire political nation. In addition to woman suffrage, the Anti-Saloon League and other Progressive Era reform organizations found their causes outside the parties' scope of interest and were forced to find new ways to engage in politics. Electoral politics and voting continued to be the province of the parties, and since party issues often were not those of greatest interest to individual citizens, it is not surprising that voter turnout declined. This is not to say that political interest or participation declined, but simply that it found other channels than the ballot box.

In an effort to rectify this division between traditionally defined "politics" and the new extra-party activism, historian Paula Baker has suggested a more general definition of politics, to include "any action, formal or informal, taken to affect the course or behavior of government or the community."[29] Certainly as the twentieth century unfolded, politics would come to be defined through both party and extra-party functions, and a broader definition of politics is in order. But even if we enlarge the definition of politics to take in extra-party activism, as Baker suggests, the period between the passage of the Nineteenth Amendment and World War II remains a dismal chasm into which the women's movement of old seems to have fallen. In the 1920s, women learned that the vote alone would not open doors to venues of political decision making long closed to them; despite early fears of retribution, party bosses quickly learned that women would not use the ballot to bloc vote, and thus they dropped any pretense of interest in the new citizens. The failure of the women's movement in the 1920s, however, has more significance than merely as an example of failed political strategy or of the vote's declining importance.

If we widen our focus to place the legacy of woman suffrage within the history of American politics as well as within the history of the women's movement, a different picture begins to emerge. As pioneers of pressure group politics, the suffragists understood better than many Americans that reform did not necessarily depend solely on party support nor political participation on party membership. The woman suffrage movement succeeded outside the party system as one of the first pressure groups, and it constituted one of the symptoms of a shift toward the relative irrelevance of the major parties as representative bodies. The move from a party-organized electorate to a modern electorate organized into a myriad of pressure groups could not be accomplished overnight, however. We need to see the decades of voter decline — and the decline in feminism — as a transition period, rather than simply as a time of flagging public interest in electoral politics in general or the failure of feminism in particular. In the 1920s and 1930s, individuals outside the party ranks adjusted slowly to the new system of pressure group politics, experimenting with new tactics and ideas over the course of several decades. With time, groups on the right and left of the political spectrum would develop pressure groups to represent their particular causes or interests, but during the transition period, few individuals felt themselves well represented either by parties or within pressure group politics.

Perhaps because this transition period has not been previously linked to the decline of the women's movement after the vote was won, some scholars have argued that depicting the suffrage movement as a benchmark for women in politics has "obscure[d] the similarities in women's political behavior before and after it." One historian argued that the suffrage movement disturbed the "smooth evolution" of voluntarism that characterized women's political activities before and after the suffrage campaign.[30] In my view, this argument rests on a confusion of nineteenth-century voluntarist persuasion with true pressure politics, and thus it does not clarify our vision of the twentieth-century women's movement.[31] Rather than viewing suffrage as an aberration, disrupting a mainly female voluntaristic system that would be readopted after the vote was won, I see the twentieth-century suffrage movement as marking an abrupt break with the older traditions of the nineteenth-century women's movement. It was both successful and dealt with power as much as persuasion — two attributes that the older movement did not possess. To disrupt the smooth evolution of a system that provided women no power does not seem much of a loss to me.

As the new political system matured, pressure groups increasingly usurped two of the parties' important functions: that of political education and socialization of voters and, more important, actual policy making.[32] For generations political scientists and to a lesser extent historians have debated the significance of this political transformation. The debate, framed as early as the 1930s, centered on the type and value of representation provided by pressure groups. On the positive side, V. O. Key portrayed pressure groups as beneficial to the workings of government.[33] They provided vital information to representatives on constituency issues and helped mobilize support for these issues by serving as a link between the parties and the home districts. Others, however, found the advent of pressure groups an alarming trend away from long-established principles of republican government and a counter-influence to the separation of powers. William Allen White called pressure groups "the invisible government," an adaptation of Elihu Root's term for the corrupt boss system.[34]

In many ways, pressure groups were — and are — a kind of invisible government. Although pressure group tactics were used by the suffragists of NAWSA to gain a sweeping democratic reform, one of the first serious attacks on the pressure system described it as "a method of short-circuiting the majority."[35] In one of the ironic twists that proves the axiom "politics makes strange bedfellows," both traditionalist and feminist scholars have faulted the system for its antidemocratic tendencies. "The flaw in the pluralist heaven," wrote one critic in 1960, "is that the heavenly chorus sings with a very strong upper class accent."[36] Feminists have also taken pressure groups to task for their "reliance on the most traditional kind of old-boy political network [and] the unabashed pursuit of narrow self-interest."[37]

Other characteristics of pressure group politics are cause for more serious concern. Most national-level groups claim to represent far more people than they actually do, often giving legislators a false picture of constituent opinion and support. Critics point out that despite the enormous power they wield, pressure groups are completely unregulated, their inner workings shrouded in secrecy. Members as well as the general public are often poorly informed about the financing, leadership, and decision-making process of these organizations.[38] Moreover, the structure of most pressure groups conforms to what one scholar labeled "the iron law of oligarchy," or the tendency of leaders of large organizations to consolidate power at the expense of democratic traditions.[39] Grassroots participation in such groups is usually confined to donating money and voting for preselected candidates or agendas.

Pressure groups have proliferated tremendously — by one 1987 estimate, there were more than 23,000 lobbyists in Washington alone — but they represent a relatively small segment of the population. For example, while only 16 percent of Americans hold managerial or professional level jobs, 88 percent of pressure group constituents belong to this group. Women comprise 51 percent of the nation's population, but women's organizations make up only a little over 1 percent of all pressure groups. In addition to the underrepresentation of gender, race, and age-defined cohorts, some groups — such as domestic servants, childcare workers, and housewives — have no pressure group representation at all. Not coincidentally, these three excluded constituencies are largely composed of women, racial minorities, and recent immigrants. Other interests are, if anything, overrepresented: corporations, for example, constitute more than 45 percent of all congressional pressure groups.[40]

We find confirmation of the undemocratic nature of pressure group politics as far back as its origins in the suffrage, temperance, and other Progressive Era reform movements. These organizations defined themselves as public interest groups, as opposed to narrowly conceived economic pressure groups that contain few actual constituents beyond paid lobbyists. One might expect to find a dearth of democratic decision making within private interest groups, for these groups generally serve only a narrow economic stratum of the population and make no claim to broad democratic representation. But what of public interest pressure politics, such as that which NAWSA helped create? We have seen how the adoption of pressure tactics led NAWSA leaders to put aside the democratic traditions of the nineteenth-century women's movement and cast out issues and factions they deemed extraneous to the single goal of woman suffrage. The association's obsession with respectability and public opinion more than any other cause led its leaders to disregard grassroots suffragists' opinions and wishes, downplay or ignore race and class issues, and thus confirm the validity of the "iron law of oligarchy."

The peculiar antidemocratic nature of pressure politics has had important consequences for the twentieth-century women's movement and American politics in general. The method developed by the NAWSA suffragists and adopted by scores of reform groups did introduce a new democracy that in time would give the vote to all Americans. Although this system was broadly inclusive in one sense — all Americans over eighteen enjoy the right to vote — it was not correspondingly participatory because effective political action has tended to move away from the ballot box and toward the mass suasion exerted by institutionalized pressure groups. This method altered not only the electorate but the parties as well. As political life increasingly became dominated by pressure groups, the parties assumed a "broker" role, doling out legislation and favors to competing interest groups, each with its own agenda, organization, and constituency. With this gradual alteration in function, the virtual representation of the past century — whether by family, by class, or by color — was replaced by representation mediated through pressure groups and coordinated by the parties.[41]

If we take NAWSA as an example, we see that the votes-for-women campaign assumed the functions of political parties by creating a political culture for women, an outlet for their personal and political energies, and an avenue for positive political change. The National American Woman Suffrage Association collected a constituency that had been excluded from party participation, trained it in modern political methodology, and used it as a battering ram to gain entrance into the political arena. Thus, the much-lamented demise of traditional party-dominated popular politics may arguably be seen as the just fate of a system that refused to include a majority of the population. The collective reform agendas of a dozen or more groups went unheeded by party leaders, and the inability of the party system to bend in accordance with the articulated will of the people brought it tumbling down.

With the rise of and competition from single-issue pressure groups the great parties eventually took what was left to them: the maintenance of the structure of government with limited ability to set its legislative agenda. Conservatives as well as reformers would have a hand in steering the ship of state, provided they could amass the image, constituency, and publicity required for successful single-issue campaigning. Because of its dependence on these requirements, the adoption of pressure politics mitigated the forces of radicalism at either end of the political spectrum and thus reinforced the traditional American tendency toward political compromise, gradualism, and moderation. Pressure groups ensure that whichever way the pendulum of politics swings, it will inevitably return to the center, as competing interests provide a sort of internal balance of power through counteraction and compromise.

In recent decades, pressure politics has often been wielded more effectively by the right than the left—the Equal Rights Amendment campaign of the 1970s and early 1980s provides one example. As the suffragists understood, the insider-outsider method is very much the key to success within this political system. To their misfortune, some of the suffragists' spiritual heirs seem to have missed crucial lessons of the suffrage campaign, choosing to favor ideological consistency over the cultivation of a respectable image and varied constituency. Few subsequent leftist movements have emulated the suffragists' single-mindedness, their willingness to suspend democratic principle, or their painstaking construction of an organization at all political levels.[42] Pressure politics offers success, but only at a considerable price. The price for the suffrage movement—a campaign for democracy—was the destruction of its democratic heritage and principles. Many modern feminists remain unwilling to discard ideology and principle for political expediency, one of several reasons that their cause has experienced limited success.

Much has been said about the failure of the woman suffrage movement to usher in a feminist millennium or to create a strong female presence in American politics. But were the suffragists themselves content with their own accomplishment? Some NAWSA veterans emerged from the suffrage campaign exhausted from reform work, and in the years afterward desired little more than to rest on their laurels. These women confined their political activism to casting a vote on election day and reading political columns in the local gazette. Others, like Ida Husted Harper, had believed that woman suffrage alone would bring about a perfect society; for Harper and those like her, the new democracy brought a sense of frustration with gradualism and political compromise. Suffragists like Maud Wood Park and Carrie Catt continued to look outside the party structure for the answers to societal problems, Park to the nonpartisan League of Women Voters and Catt to several citizen action and peace groups. For a minority of NAWSA leaders like Mary Garrett Hay and Minnie Fisher Cunningham, change could best be effected through the traditional party system. Although both women gained positions in the party hierarchy, neither were completely successful in integrating themselves into the male-dominated structure.[43]

More than thirty years after the suffrage crusade came to a close, Cunningham reflected on the spirit that carried the suffragists to victory in a letter to her old friend and fellow reformer Jane Y. McCallum:

> It was fun to go back and review the fight. . . . It was maddening to think that we somehow didn't carry on as vigorously as we could have done. It was puzzling to wonder why? Can you answer it? Did the League of Women Voters turn us away from fighting to studying? Something happened? What? . . . We should have gone on. Or should we? Perhaps it was better to simmer down. Only I don't believe it. But now, today, what of today? Will we go on shadow boxing for "reforms" we don't really care a whoop about — and could get directly if we really cared? Will we go on playing at being "busy," while the health department records people dying of starvation? Oh Jane darling, if only you and I were young and strong.[44]

At seventy-four, Jane McCallum was neither young nor strong. The aging activist read her friend's letter and penciled the following comment in the margin: "Her next to last paragraph [quoted above] made me heartsick. *Could* I have done a bit more? Sure I could have, with her faith in my ability. But there was always a lack of personal funds, and I was proud — Oh, an alibi, I guess." Others, like Laura Clay, were more philosophical. Writing to the elderly and blind Alice Stone Blackwell, Clay, too, pondered the meaning of the great suffrage campaign and the waning of progressivism in the years after suffrage: "I am not ever pained by the fact that the young accept it all as the course of nature, never knowing all it cost. But I had seen that with regard to the abolition of slavery. . . . I can remember in my young ignorance I supposed all social wrongs were redressed in the success of that Cause, and lo, as Womanhood dawned upon me I found another Cause awaiting all my zeal and devotion. And so it will ever be. All that those who wrought before need desire is that their spirit of love for the right and willingness to live for it should fall upon those who follow after."[45]

In the end, the woman suffrage movement did not bring forth a perfect society, nor had its leaders promised to do so. The "new democracy," like the old, did not establish that progressive and perfected order dreamed of by Americans since the eighteenth century; instead it was but one step toward their goal. The suffragists of NAWSA saw the future through the prism of their time, and their cause proved to be only one among many. It must be remembered that their vision of politics and society, flawed and narrow as it was, did in fact bring votes to women and thus achieved a significant expansion of American democracy. Sadly, their new democracy, like the old, was tainted and limited by racism and elitism, and their Winning Plan — the modern pressure group in embryo — compromised a larger progressive and feminist vision for America.

In moods of self-congratulation, Americans have been prone to envision their nation as a "city on a hill," a shining beacon of justice and democratic promise. It is worth remembering that this phrase is drawn from a warning, that "a city that is set on a hill cannot be hid" (Matthew 5:14). The contradictions within the woman suffrage campaign and inherent in the system of politics it helped originate — most strikingly the belief that democracy for some can be advanced by silencing the voices of others — continue to characterize politics today. The new democracy of 1920 must yet give way to another, more genuine system of representation so that Americans in some other time may call their nation a *true* democracy, with nothing to hide in that distant yet forbidding city upon the hill.

Notes

Introduction

1. *Washington Times*, March 22, 1914, clipping found in Doris Stevens Papers, box 8, Schlesinger Library, Radcliffe College, Cambridge, Mass. (hereafter cited as SL).

2. Among the many fine works on the woman suffrage movement in America, Flexner's *Century of Struggle* is the most comprehensive overview of the movement. Other landmark books are Scott and Scott, *One Half the People;* Kraditor, *Ideas of the Woman Suffrage Movement,* and DuBois, *Feminism and Suffrage.* Two good state studies (and there are others too numerous to mention) are Buechler, *Transformation of the Woman Suffrage Movement,* and Nichols, *Votes and More for Women.* For treatments of the militant Congressional Union/National Woman's Party, see Gluck, *From Parlor to Prison,* and Lunardini, *From Equal Suffrage to Equal Rights.* O'Neill's *Everyone Was Brave,* although flawed in many ways, offers a challenging thesis regarding the failure of feminism. Wheeler's *New Women of the New South* gives an overview of southern suffrage leaders. There are also countless articles, oral histories, contemporary sources, and biographies.

3. Odegard, *Pressure Politics,* was the first study to define the Anti-Saloon League as a pressure group. Other studies that treat the ASL as well as the entire temperance movement are Blocker, *Retreat from Reform,* and Blocker, *American Temperance Movements.* A perceptive account of the Anti-Saloon League itself is Kerr, *Organized for Prohibition.*

4. See, e.g., Claggett, "Life Cycle and Generational Models"; Kleppner, "Were Women to Blame"; Lazarsfeld, Berelson, and Gaudet, *People's Choice;* Merriman and Gosnell, *Non-Voting;* and Schattschneider, *Semisovereign People.*

5. One of the first efforts to rectify this oversight is a collection of essays edited by Tilly and Gurin, *Women, Politics and Change.* Although the contents of the volume are broader than woman suffrage alone, several essays address the issue. Other useful works on woman suffrage include Baxter and Lansing, *Women and Politics;* Katzenstein, "Feminism and the Meaning of the Vote"; McDonagh and Price, "Woman Suffrage in the Progressive Era"; and McDonagh, "Issues and Constituencies."

6. Burnham, "Party Systems and the Political Process."

7. The "failure of feminism" thesis was first introduced by O'Neill in *Everyone Was Brave.* A recent counterpoint to this theory can be found in Cott, "Across the Great Divide."

8. "A faction is a number of citizens," Madison wrote, "whether amounting to a minority of the whole, who are united and actuated by some common impulse of passion, or of interest, adverse to the rights of other citizens or to the permanent and aggregate interests of the community." James Madison, *The Federalist* No. 10 (New York: New American Library, 1961), 78.

9. Walt Whitman, "The Eighteenth Presidency" [1856], in *Walt Whitman: Complete Poetry and Selected Prose and Letters,* ed. Emory Halloway, 592; quoted in Thompson, *Spider Web,* 54.

10. Croly, *Progressive Democracy,* 317; quoted in Petracca, ed., *Politics of Interests,* 12.

11. Ginzberg, *Women and the Work of Benevolence,* gives the best overview of women's nineteenth-century voluntary organizations. Ginzberg points out the importance of indirect tactics, not only for such legislative favors as funding, but for the legal opportunities benevolent societies offered women. Although these tactics were definitely important to later pressure groups, I believe that it is incorrect to label these early efforts at political activism as pressure groups. See also Epstein, *Politics of Domesticity* for the political activities of women in benevolent causes.

12. Key, *Politics, Parties and Pressure Groups,* 23.

13. For more on "insider-outsider" strategies, see Ornstein and Elder, *Interest Groups, Lobbying and Policymaking.* For views of lobbyists, see Wilson, *Interest Groups in the United States,* and Berry, *Lobbying for the People.* Kay Schlozman offers an interesting discussion of the strengths and weaknesses of direct action for modern women's groups in "Representing Women in Washington."

14. Schlozman, "Representing Women in Washington," 341.

15. For a perceptive discussion of militancy and pressure politics, see Schlozman and Tierney, *Organized Interests and American Democracy.*

16. See Chambers, "Party Development," and Burnham, "Party Systems."

Chapter 1. Woman Suffrage in 1900

1. Maud Wood Park, "Clothes and a Cause," n.d., Maud Wood Park Papers, box 14, Library of Congress (hereafter cited as LC).

2. Harper, *Life and Work,* 1165–69.

3. *The History of Woman Suffrage* (hereafter cited as *HWS*) 4, 350–51, and *Proceedings of the Annual Convention of the National American Woman Suffrage Association* (hereafter cited as *Proceedings*), 1904, 3–9.

4. *HWS* 4, 396–404.

5. For a thorough discussion of Seneca Falls, see Flexner, *Century of Struggle*, chap. 5.

6. The best introduction to Stanton and Anthony is DuBois, ed., *Elizabeth Cady Stanton/Susan B. Anthony*. See also Stanton, *Eighty Years and More*, and Harper, *Life and Work*.

7. DuBois, *Feminism and Suffrage*, 96. DuBois's *Feminism and Suffrage* is the best treatment of the suffrage movement before 1870. See also Flexner, *Century of Struggle*, 145–56.

8. Wheeler, *New Women of the New South*, 113–16.

9. DuBois, ed., *Elizabeth Cady Stanton/Susan B. Anthony*, 226.

10. A good account of Catt's early involvement in the suffrage movement is Van Voris, *Carrie Chapman Catt*, esp. chaps. 2 and 3.

11. Catt's three-pronged plan of 1895 is quite similar to the organizational plan of the Anti-Saloon League, organized in 1893. See Kerr, *Organizing for Prohibition*, chap. 3.

12. Peck, *Carrie Chapman Catt*, 83–84.

13. Ibid., 85–86.

14. Noun, *Strong-Minded Women*, 236–44.

15. *HWS* 4, 387–88.

16. Susan B. Anthony to Catherine Waugh McCulloch, December 18, 1899, Dillon Collection, box 8, SL.

17. *HWS* 4, 365.

18. Although the quoted figure of 8,900 dues-paying suffragists is a very small enrollment for what was purported to be a national organization, many local suffrage societies accepted non-dues-paying members as well. These members, usually called "associate members," took little part in the day-to-day activities of the societies, but they contributed their support by signing prosuffrage petitions and attending mass rallies. There is no record of which clubs used the associate member affiliation, nor is there any indication of the numbers of non-dues-paying members. It is safe to say that their numbers grew by the tens of thousands as the twentieth century progressed, but in 1900 they were as few in number as their dues-paying cohorts.

19. *Proceedings, 1899*, 18–22.

20. *Proceedings, 1899*, 93–108 and 17–19.

21. Carrie Chapman Catt to Henry B. Blackwell, November 27, 1895, Carrie Chapman Catt Papers (hereafter cited as Catt Papers), reel 2, LC.

22. *HWS* 4, 365–66; Harper, *Life and Work*, 1167.

23. *HWS* 4, 381.

24. *Proceedings, 1899*, 23–24; *HWS* 4, 365.

25. The best accounts of black advocacy of woman suffrage are Aptheker, *Woman's Legacy*, chap. 3; and Higgenbotham, "In Politics to Stay." A fascinating new look at Alabama black women's clubs and their interest in the suffrage campaign can be found in Thomas, *New Woman in Alabama*, chap. 4. Terborg-Penn, "Afro-Americans in the Struggle," is also useful. Another perspective on black suffragism is provided by Alexander in "How I Discovered My Grandmother," and "Grandmother, Grandfather."

26. *HWS* 5, 366, 352.

27. Peck, *Carrie Chapman Catt*, 96–97.

28. Susan B. Anthony to Rachel Foster Avery, January 22, 1900, Susan B. Anthony Papers (microfilm edition), reel 1, LC.

Chapter 2. Anxiously Doubting Democracy

1. Although no book-length study of the antisuffrage movement has been published, there are several useful works on the subject. Kraditor, *Ideas of the Woman Suffrage Movement,* chap. 1, provides the best overview. See also Camhi, "Women against Women"; Marshall, "In Defense of Separate Spheres"; Stevenson, "Women Anti-Suffragists in the 1915 Massachusetts Campaign"; and Thurner, "Better Citizens without the Ballot."

2. Abbott, "Why Women Do Not Wish the Suffrage," 289–96.

3. Ibid.

4. "Woman's Progress versus Woman Suffrage," pamphlet issued by Massachusetts Association Opposed to the Further Extension of Suffrage to Women, n.d., National American Woman Suffrage Association Papers (microfilm edition; hereafter cited as NAWSA Papers), reel 27, LC; Chittenden, "Counter Influence to Woman Suffrage"; and Scott, "Woman's Relation to Government."

5. Married antisuffragists like Mrs. Schuyler Van Rensselaer commonly took their husbands' names and did not use their first names, even in correspondence to close friends. Some but not all suffragists also followed this practice. To cite one of many examples, after more than thirty years of working together, Carrie Catt and Harriet Upton continued to address each other in correspondence as "Mrs. Catt" and "Mrs. Upton." And whereas some, like Carrie Chapman Catt, retained their deceased husband's last name but not his full title, others chose to keep the "Mrs." but drop their husband's first name (e.g., Mrs. Harriet Laidlaw or simply Harriet Laidlaw). Although I did not keep a record of how many suffragists or their opponents used their husbands' full titles, my sense is that antisuffragists were more inclined to this practice; suffragists often retained the "Mrs." with their own first names, especially after they had worked in the movement for some years. The quotation is from Mrs. Schuyler Van Rensselaer, "Should We Ask for the Suffrage?" pamphlet issued by New York State Association Opposed to Woman Suffrage (hereafter cited as NYSAOWS), n.d., NAWSA Papers, reel 27, LC.

6. Speech by Supreme Court Justice Henry Billings Brown, April 1910, NAWSA Papers, reel 27, LC.

7. Leonard, "Ideal of Equality." For another example of the specialization of function argument, see "The Blank-Cartridge Ballot," pamphlet issued by the NYSAOESW, n.d., Broadside Collection, Virginia Historical Society, Richmond, Va. According to this pamphlet, the vote must be backed up by force, and "a ballot put into the box by a woman would be simply a blank cartridge."

8. Tarbell, "Woman's Power and Woman Suffrage," pamphlet issued by Massachusetts Association Opposed to Further Extension of the Suffrage to Women (hereafter cited as MAOFESW), 1911, NAWSA Papers, reel 27, LC.

9. Leonard, "Ideal of Equality."

10. Joe Gilpin Pyles, "Should Women Vote?" pamphlet issued by National Association

Opposed to Woman Suffrage (hereafter cited as NAOWS), 1913, NAWSA Papers, reel 27, LC.

11. Frothingham, "Real Case of the 'Remonstrants,' " 177.

12. John Dos Passos, "Equality of Suffrage Means the Debasement of Not Only Women but of Men," pamphlet issued by NAOWS, n.d., Suffrage Collection, box 17, Sophia Smith Collection, Smith College, Northampton, Mass.

13. Cleveland, "Would Woman Suffrage Be Unwise?"

14. Leonard, "Ladies' Battle."

15. Editorial, *Current Literature* 46 (April 1909): 372–74.

16. McCracken, *Women of America*, 97, 106.

17. "Household Hints," pamphlet issued by WASAM, n.d., NAWSA Papers, reel 12, LC.

18. Editorial, *Living Age* 272 (March 9, 1912): 587–92. For examples of antisuffrage articles that compare suffragists unfavorably, see "Feminine versus Feminist," *Living Age* 272 (March 9, 1912): 587–92; Abbott, "Profession of Motherhood"; and Goodwin, "Non-Militant Defenders of the Home."

19. Editorial, *Literary Digest* 34 (March 9, 1907): 374–75.

20. Cleveland, "Would Woman Suffrage Be Unwise?" Cleveland's article drew fire from numerous clubwomen and reformers, prompting one wit to predict that "the sage of Princeton would not be anxious to lay aside the rod and reel to discuss the subject again." See Editorial, *Literary Digest* 31 (October 7, 1905): 476.

21. Henry A. Stimson, "Is Woman's Suffrage an Enlightened and Justifiable Policy for the State?" pamphlet issued by MAOFESW, n.d., NAWSA Papers, reel 27, LC.

22. Abbott, "Assault on Womanhood." For another example of the "suffrage = divorce" equation favored by antisuffragists, see Seawell, *Ladies' Battle,* 110–14.

23. Editorial, *Outlook* 85 (April 6, 1907): 788.

24. *Trenton Evening Times,* January 28, 1914. Clipping found in Breckenridge Family Papers, box 702, LC.

25. Flier issued by Republican Section, NAOWS, n.d., NAWSA Papers, reel 27, LC.

26. Supreme Court Justice Walter Brown, speech to the Ladies Congressional Club, April 1910, NAWSA Papers, reel 27, LC.

27. Frothingham, "Real Case of the 'Remonstrants,' " 179.

28. Stimson, "Is Woman's Suffrage an Enlightened and Justifiable Policy?"

29. Mrs. William Forse Scott, "The Practical Limitations of Democracy," 1912, pamphlet issued by NAOWS, NAWSA Papers, reel 27, LC.

30. Goodwin, "Non-Militant Defenders of the Home."

31. Editorial, *Literary Digest* 18 (May 20, 1899): 572–74.

32. This sentiment was also expressed by Professor Edward D. Cope, author of the pamphlet "The Relation of the Sexes to Government," issued by NYSAOESW (n.d., Broadside Collection, Virginia Historical Society, Richmond, Va.): "What America needs is not an extension, but a restriction of the franchise."

33. Editorial, *North American Review* 190 (August 1909): 158–69. See also Helen Kendrick Johnson, "Woman's Progress versus Woman Suffrage," pamphlet issued by MAOFESW, n.d., NAWSA Papers, reel 27, LC.

34. "The Red behind the Yellow: Socialists Working for Suffrage," flier issued by NYSAOWS, 1915, Adele Clark Papers, box 130, Virginia Commonwealth University, Richmond, Virginia (hereafter cited as VCU). See also "Woman's Suffrage the Vanguard of Socialism," flier issued by the Virginia Association Opposed to Woman's Suffrage, Adele Clark Papers, box 130, VCU, which urges antisuffragists to "work with all your might against Socialism's vanguard — woman's suffrage."

35. Mary Dean Adams, "In Opposition to Woman Suffrage,' speech read before the joint senate and assembly of New York Judiciary Committee," February 24, 1909, and later published in pamphlet form by NAOWS, NAWSA Papers, reel 27, LC.

36. Ibid.

37. Deland, "Margaret versus Bridget"; for the entire Deland speech, see Deland, "Change in the Feminine Ideal."

38. Deland, "Change in the Feminine Ideal."

39. Van Rensselaer, "Should We Ask for the Suffrage?".

40. Poster, "Beware!" n.d., NAWSA Papers, reel 27, LC.

41. Publicity release sent to newspapers by American Constitutional League Field Secretary J. S. Eichelbarger, March 21, 1918, Adele Clark Papers, box 130, VCU. For other antisuffrage propaganda stressing the race question, see "That Deadly Parallel," flier, n.d.; "Virginia Warns Her People against Woman Suffrage," flier, n.d.; and "The People's Verdict on Woman Suffrage Is 'NO'!" flier issued by NAOWS, September 1919, all found in Adele Clark Papers, box 130, VCU.

42. "The Virginia Assembly and Woman Suffrage," pamphlet issued by the Virginia Advisory Committee Opposed to Woman Suffrage, n.d., Adele Clark Papers, box 130, VCU.

43. "Mr. Voter," n.d., flier in Woman's Rights Collection (hereafter cited as WRC), box 856, SL.

44. McCracken, "Woman Suffrage in the Tenements."

45. McCracken, "Women of America."

46. Meyer, "Woman's Assumption of Sex Superiority," 107.

47. See, e.g., Abbott, "Rights of Man"; and Van Rensselaer, "Should We Ask for the Suffrage?" pamphlet issued by NYSAOWS, n.d., NAWSA Papers, reel 27, LC.

48. Editorial, *North American Review* 178 (January 1904): 103–6.

49. Deland, "Change in the Feminine Ideal."

50. *HWS* 5, 6.

51. *HWS* 5, 32.

52. Shaw, *Story of a Pioneer,* 310–12.

53. *HWS* 5, 75–78. It should be noted, however, that despite the absence of a formal policy endorsing qualified suffrage, NAWSA affiliates in the South routinely included education qualifications in their publicity work for the ballot.

54. Ibid., 82–83 and 59–60.

55. Thomas, *New Woman in Alabama,* 70–72, chap. 4; and Terborg-Penn, "Afro-Americans in the Struggle," 313–18.

56. Logan, "Woman Suffrage," 487–89, quoted in Thomas, *New Woman in Alabama,* 87.

57. Terborg-Penn, "Afro-Americans in the Struggle," 318–19; Alexander, "Grandmother, Grandfather," 8–11; and Alexander, "How I Discovered My Grandmother."

58. The NAWSA policy on refusing to admit blacks was not a written policy as far as I have been able to tell. Indeed, what seems singular is the very absence from the NAWSA, Catt, and other suffrage papers of any reference to black suffragists. An occasional sentence might refer to a black club seeking admission to NAWSA, but the actual correspondence will be missing. As many of the suffrage collections were purged of sensitive matter before suffragists and their helpers turned the material over to archives, it is probable that material to and from black suffragists was destroyed in a belated effort to hide from history white suffragists' abandonment of black activists who shared their cause. According to Terborg-Penn, "Black women were nearly totally written out of the twentieth century state histories compiled for the *History of Woman Suffrage*" (281–82).

59. See Carrie Chapman Catt to Edith Hinkle League, July 17, 1918, Jane Y. McCallum Papers (hereafter cited as McCallum Papers), box 3, file 4, Austin History Center, Austin, Texas (hereafter cited as AHC).

60. Catt to League, July 17, 1918, McCallum Papers, box 3, file 4, AHC.

61. Wheeler, *New Women of the New South,* 116. Inviting black feminist Frances Ellen Harper to be one of the speakers at the International Council for Women, sponsored in 1888 by Anthony, Stanton, and other suffragists is an example of nineteenth-century efforts to include black activists in NAWSA functions. Except at the 1895 Atlanta convention, Anthony always invited Douglass or his son to appear on stage with other suffrage pioneers at the annual conventions until her death in 1906. According to both Rosalyn Terborg-Penn and Adele Logan Alexander, some individual black women like Adele Hunt Logan attained membership in NAWSA, and a few black suffrage clubs formed coalitions with white NAWSA affiliates. See Terborg-Penn, "Afro-Americans," 313, and Alexander, "How I Discovered My Grandmother," 30. For a description of the International Council for Women, see DuBois, ed., *Elizabeth Cady Stanton/Susan B. Anthony,* 176.

62. Anna Howard Shaw, "Our Ideal," speech to the NAWSA convention of 1905, Dillon Collection, box 22, SL.

63. *The Independent* 66 (May 20, 1909): 1056–69.

64. May Estelle Cook, "The New Day," in "Suffrage Songs," pamphlet issued by NAWSA, 1909, Dillon Collection, box 1, SL.

65. Charlotte Perkins Gilman, "Another Star," in "Suffrage Songs and Verses," 1911, WRC, box 856, SL.

66. Charlotte Perkins Gilman, "Song for Equal Suffrage," in "Suffrage Songs and Verses.".

67. Bowne, "Woman and Democracy."

68. Anna Howard Shaw, "Influence versus Power," speech, excerpts reprinted in pamphlet form by the Ohio WCTU, n.d., Dillon Collection, box 22, SL. For an example of WCTU literature featuring the suffrage argument, see also "Why Should I Vote?" pamphlet issued by the Western Washington WCTU, n.d., NAWSA Papers, reel 21, LC.

69. *Lexington (Ky.) Herald,* May 27, 1910. Clipping found in Breckenridge Family Papers, box 700, LC.

70. Abigail Scott Duniway to the Officers and Delegates of the National Equal Suffrage Convention, February 12, 1907, NAWSA Papers, reel 7, LC.; and Moynihan, *Rebel for Rights,* 207–13, chap. 12.

71. Although Anna Howard Shaw retained a lifelong sympathy with the prohibition movement, after the Oregon defeat in 1906 she was persuaded that the two crusades should go their separate ways. Several leading suffragists like Carolyn Bartlett Crane and Ella Stewart continued to be active in both reforms. Carrie Catt perhaps summed up the feeling of most suffragists in her 1923 account of the suffrage crusade. "Had there been no prohibition movement in the United States," Catt wrote, "the women would have been enfranchised two generations before they were." Catt and Shuler, *Woman Suffrage and Politics,* 279.

72. Editorial, *The Independent* 66 (May 20, 1909): 1056–67.

73. Max Eastman, speech to the 1910 NAWSA convention, quoted in *HWS* 5, 284–86.

74. Susan B. Anthony, "Woman's Half-Century of Evolution," 800–810; rpt. in Phelps, ed. *Debaters Handbook,* 15.

75. For more on the ERA Club and Kate Gordon, see Johnson, "Kate Gordon." See also Wheeler, *New Women of the New South,* 51–52; Loretta Zimmerman, "Jean Gordon," in James and James, eds., *Notable American Women* 2, 64–66; and Kemp, "Jean and Kate Gordon."

76. Jean Gordon, "Noblesse Oblige," speech to the NAWSA convention of 1908, quoted in *HWS* 5, 232.

77. Carrie Chapman Catt, "The Battle to the Strong," speech to the NAWSA convention of 1908, quoted in *HWS* 5, 241–42.

78. Kelley, "Home and the New Woman," 363.

79. Howe, "Case for Woman Suffrage."

80. Madeline McDowell Breckenridge, report to the National Federation of Women's Clubs, June 1908, in Breckenridge Family Papers, box 700, LC.

81. Anna Howard Shaw, "Tribute to William Lloyd Garrison," speech, n.d., Dillon Collection, box 22, SL.

82. There are two biographies of Kelley, but both are badly dated. See Goldmark, *Impatient Crusader,* and Blumberg, *Florence Kelley.* Jane Addams's work in the suffrage movement is discussed in Davis, *American Heroine,* 186–88.

83. Harper, "Why Women Cannot Vote."

84. The term *social feminist* was coined by William L. O'Neill in *Everyone Was Brave.* For O'Neill's definition of the term, see chap. 10. In a recent article, Nancy Cott has argued persuasively that the label is oversimplified and confusing. See Cott, "What's in a Name?"

85. What has come to be known as the "justice versus expediency argument" comes from a misreading of Kraditor, *Ideas of the Woman Suffrage Movement,* 43–44 and chap. 3. Kraditor in fact maintains that although expedient arguments for the vote appeared around the turn of the century and increased in number as the suffrage campaign progressed, the justice argument continued to be employed by suffragists until their victory in 1920.

86. Mrs. Arthur M. Dodge served as president of both NAOWS and the National Federation of Day Nurseries, vice president of the New York City Day Nursery Association, and was an active member of the Public Education Association. For examples of other leading antisuffragists who held positions of importance, see Martin, "Concerning Some of the Anti-Suffragist Leaders," 75–80; and Degler, *At Odds,* 350. Although there

has been no full-length study published on the American antisuffrage movement, a useful work is Camhi, "Women against Women." Camhi describes the majority of antisuffragists as "urban, wealthy, native-born, Republican and Protestant" and suggests that most were involved in at least one other activity besides antisuffragism. See Camhi, "Women against Women," 2–3 and chap. 1.

87. Camhi, "Women against Women," 2–3, 422–426. For a list of the national antisuffrage newspapers published by anti organizations, see Camhi, 153–56.

88. Editorial, "The Necessity of Woman Suffrage," *Harper's Bazaar* 41 (January 1907): 34–35.

89. Anna Howard Shaw, "Our Ideal," speech to the NAWSA convention of 1905, Dillon Collection, box 22, SL.

90. Frothingham, "Real Case of the 'Remonstrants,'" 179.

Chapter 3. The Suffrage Renaissance

1. Flexner, *Century of Struggle,* 256.
2. Ibid., 230.
3. Kenneally, "Woman Suffrage and the Massachusetts Referendum," 620–23. Prominent members of MAOFESW included Mary A. Dodge, Reverend O. B. Frothingham, Francis Parkman, Francis C. Lowell, and John Boyle O'Reilly. Such notable Bostonians as Charles Eliot, Charles Eliot Norton, John Fiske, Henry L. Higginson, and Charles Francis Adams were members of the MSA.
4. *HWS* 4, 735–37, and Kenneally, "Woman Suffrage and the Massachusetts Referendum," 625.
5. Kenneally, "Woman Suffrage and the Massachusetts Referendum," 630. In *HWS,* Alice Stone Blackwell's account of the 1895 referendum emphasizes the positive aspects of the contest. For example, Blackwell cites forty-eight towns that gave suffrage a majority and avoids mentioning the statistic included in Kenneally regarding the absence of female voters in forty-one towns. Poor preparation on the suffragists' part doubtless led to weak turnouts in some areas, as demonstrated by Blackwell's surprising admission that in most of the towns returning an adverse majority, no suffrage work had ever been attempted. *HWS* 4, 738.
6. Leonard, "Ladies' Battle," 386–89.
7. Minnie Reynolds to Alice Stone Blackwell, December 12, 1930, NAWSA Papers, reel 17, LC.
8. Susan B. Anthony to Rachel Foster Avery, January 22, 1900, Papers of Susan B. Anthony, reel 1, LC.
9. Carrie Chapman Catt to Catherine Waugh McCulloch, August 8, 1900, Dillon Collection, box 9, SL.
10. *Proceedings,* 1904, 14–15; Editorial, *Current Literature* 36 (April 1904): 386–89. In the *Proceedings,* corresponding secretary Kate Gordon directly addressed the so-called society plan, pointing out that many of America's most distinguished women were clubwomen or charity workers. Gordon saw a great opportunity for recruitment by working in other reform groups, and she urged suffragists to make their clubs "centers of power" by endorsing worthy causes and converting wealthy workers.

11. For more on NAWSA's treatment of black suffragists, see chap. 2.

12. Gluck, *From Parlor to Prison*, 45–46.

13. Monday Club of Richburg, New York, calendar for 1912, NAWSA Papers, reel 48, LC.

14. Quoted in Gluck, *From Parlor to Prison*, 12–13.

15. House Committee on the Judiciary, Hearing on Woman Suffrage, February 16, 1904, statement of Mary C. C. Bradford, WRC, folder 42, SL.

16. Carrie Chapman Catt to Mrs. Millicent Garrett Fawcett, October 19, 1909, Catt Papers, reel 3, LC.

17. See Dorothy Scura, "Ellen Glasgow." For more on the Virginia suffragists, see Graham, "Woman Suffrage in Virginia"; Coleman, "Penwoman of Virginia's Feminists"; and Wheeler, "Mary Johnston, Suffragist."

18. Margaret Campbell to Henry B. Blackwell, May 14, 1900, NAWSA Papers, reel 5, LC.

19. Blatch and Lutz, *Challenging Years*, 91–92; and DuBois, "Working Women."

20. *New York Call*, March 11, 1917. Quoted in Buhle, *Women and American Socialism*, 225.

21. *Literary Digest* 36 (February 29, 1908), 290–92.

22. For a detailed discussion of tradition and its uses, see Hobsbawm and Ranger, *Invention of Tradition*, 1–12.

23. *HWS* 5, 204–6. Anthony's interest in placing the work is well documented in Harper, *Life and Work*, 1278–79. Anthony stored the unsold volumes in the attic and basement of her Rochester, New York, home and enlisted the services of her sister, servant, and friends in the ongoing task of wrapping and mailing the books to libraries and individuals. In the nineteenth century, the history was occasionally returned by more conservative institutions. Harper reports that Harvard University returned the first three volumes, but by 1903 the university had recognized the validity of the movement to the extent of ordering volume 4 without prompting from the suffragists. Harper, *Life and Work*, 1279.

24. *HWS* 5, 60.

25. Carrie Chapman Catt to Alice Stone Blackwell, November 6, 1908, Catt Papers, reel 2, LC.

26. Anna Howard Shaw, "The Fate of the Republic," 1892 speech, Dillon Collection, folder 499, SL. Shaw continued, "That is where the weakness of every Republic lies, they have been fathered to death. The great need of our government today is a little mothering to undo the evil of too much fathering."

27. *HWS* 5, 263.

28. Phelps, ed., *Selected Articles on Woman Suffrage*.

29. Mary Gray Peck, report of the headquarters secretary, quoted in *HWS* 5, 266–68.

30. Press release, "Anti Suffrage News and Comment," n.d., issued by NYSAOWS, Dillon Collection, folder 2, SL.

31. Speech by Anna Howard Shaw to the NAWSA convention, April 14, 1910, WRC, folder 514, SL.

32. Harper, "Why Women Cannot Vote in the United States," 30–35.

33. M. Carey Thomas, "A New Fashioned Argument for Woman Suffrage," pamphlet dated October 17, 1908, WRC, folder 730, SL.

34. DuBois, ed., *Elizabeth Cady Stanton/Susan B. Anthony*, 226.

35. Ibid., 227.

36. Ibid., 244. For excerpts from *The Woman's Bible* and DuBois's commentary, see document 19, 228–45.

37. According to Ellen DuBois, although great efforts were made to preserve Anthony's memory, Stanton's papers were not collected and she found no biographer until 1940. DuBois, ed., *Elizabeth Cady Stanton/Susan B. Anthony*, 191–92.

38. The type of celebration orchestrated for the suffrage pioneers varied from year to year. There is ample coverage of the pioneers in the chapters on the annual conventions in *HWS* 5. See, e.g., the account of the 1902 convention, 31–34. For the quotation, see *HWS* 5, 123.

39. Anna Howard Shaw, letter to *Progress,* March 1910, Dillon Collection, box 22, SL. For examples of pioneer celebrations, see *HWS* 5, 30–31 and 219–20.

40. Maud Wood Park, "The College Equal Suffrage League: Introductory Notes," 1942, WRC, folder 696, SL; and *HWS* 5, 660–62.

41. *HWS* 5, 167; and Shaw, *Story of a Pioneer,* 221–23.

42. *HWS* 5, 170–71.

43. Maud Wood Park, "Address to the 28th Annual Convention of NAWSA, College Night," February 8, 1906, WRC, folder 855, SL.

44. Maud Wood Park, typescript of *Woman's Journal* article, "Debt to the Pioneers," March 30, 1907, WRC, folder 855, SL. For examples of this theme, see *HWS* 5, 173 and 226.

45. *HWS* 5, 1373; Harper, *Life and Work,* 1355.

46. Program, Kings County Political Equality League, Brooklyn, New York, February 14, 1903, NAWSA Papers, reel 26, LC.

47. Excerpts from this article appear in Harper, *Life and Work,* 1298–1304. See also *Pearson's Magazine,* March 1903. It is ironic that Stanton, a housewife and mother of a large family, was dropped from suffrage lore, while Anthony, who depended on her sister and niece for "wifely domestic duties," was the subject of Harper's recreation.

48. Harper, *Life and Work,* 1295–1304.

49. Ellen DuBois first used the term *suffrage saint* in a conversation with the author in 1986.

50. Shaw, *Story of a Pioneer,* 189–190.

51. Shaw maintained in her autobiography that she had received a subliminal message from the dying reformer bidding her to come to Rochester. Arriving unexpectedly, Shaw was reportedly told that Anthony had sent for her, but by the time the message reached her home, she was already en route to Rochester. Shaw, *Story of a Pioneer,* 228–30.

52. Shaw's account of the "shadowy review" gives a final and ironic testimony not only to the passing of Anthony but also to Stanton's removal from the suffrage pantheon. "Last of all," Shaw wrote, "[Anthony] spoke to the women who had been on her board and had stood by her loyally so long—Rachel Foster Avery, Alice Stone Blackwell, Carrie Chapman Catt, Mrs. Upton, Laura Clay, and others." Of Anthony's lifelong friend and

colleague Elizabeth Cady Stanton, Shaw, if not Anthony, said nothing. Shaw, *Story of a Pioneer,* 232–34.

53. Harper, *Life and Work,* 1604 and 1606–7.

54. Harper, *Life and Work,* 1607–10.

55. Anna Howard Shaw, "Address at Memorial Service for Susan B. Anthony," March 15, 1906, Dillon Collection, box 22, SL.

56. Accounts of the Anthony funeral are drawn from Shaw, *Story of a Pioneer,* 235–38; and Harper, *Life and Work,* 1429–44.

57. *New York Times,* March 18, 1906. Clipping may be found in the Breckenridge Family Papers, box 700, LC.

58. Notes from KERA memorial service for Susan B. Anthony by Mary Clay, March 22, 1906, NAWSA Papers, reel 5, LC. Some clubs issued memorial resolutions, such as the one sent to all NAWSA affiliates in Kentucky by Pauline H. Rosenberg, state president of KERA. See Notice to all Suffrage Organizations in Kentucky, March 13, 1906, NAWSA Papers, reel 26, LC.

59. See, e.g., program, ERA Club memorial service for Susan B. Anthony, May 8, 1906, NAWSA Papers, reel 26, LC.; and program, "A Meeting of Appreciation of the Life and Work of Susan B. Anthony," Interurban Political Equality Council of Greater New York, April 1, 1906, NAWSA Papers, reel 26, LC.

60. Harper notes that shortly before Anthony's death, NAWSA began to present large photographs of the reformer to public schools "in order that the children may become familiar with her face and interested in the work she represented." Harper, *Life and Work,* 1349.

61. Eugene V. Debs, "Susan B. Anthony: Pioneer of Freedom," *Pearson's Magazine* (July 1917). A copy of this article may be found in NAWSA Papers, reel 26, LC.

Chapter 4. Building a Constituency

1. Dunne, "Mr. Dooley on Woman's Suffrage." Dunne's commentary included a thinly veiled description of NAWSA president Anna Howard Shaw: "Doctor Arabella Miggs—as fine an' old gintleman as ye iver see in a plug hat, a long coat an' bloomers. She had ivvry argyment in favor iv female suffrage that ye iver heerd, an' years ago she made me as certain that women were entitled to a vote as that ye are entitled to my money. Ye are entitled to it if ye can get it."

2. Quoted in *Current Literature* 46 (April 1909): 371.

3. Abbott, "Assault on Womanhood," 780–88.

4. Anna Howard Shaw to Dear Co-Worker, 1910, Dillon Collection, folder 512, SL.

5. Inez H. Irwin to Maud Wood Park, March 29, 1910, NAWSA Papers, reel 11, LC.

6. Mary Hutchenson Page to Maud Wood Park, June 13, 1910, NAWSA Papers, reel 15, LC. Page had discussed the change in the movement in an earlier letter to Park as well. "Do you remember I used to say 'how strange it is! First you worry yourself to death trying to get a committee, and then you worry yourself to death trying to find something that they can and will do!' That phase has passed. We have 'At Homes' twice a month at headquarters. Last year we gave them civics subjects and the audiences were so small we were ashamed of them. This year we give them straight suffrage every time and although

we make much less effort to get the people, we are full to overflowing." Page to Park, March 23, 1910, Maud Wood Park Papers, box 5, LC.

7. Caroline Reilly to Catharine Waugh McCulloch, December 29, 1910, Dillon Collection, box 9, SL.

8. Catt refused to take credit for the idea of precinct organization, and she once credited Mary Garrett Hay with pioneering the plan in Colorado. Later, however, she wrote to a friend that "since the basis of all political work is the precinct, an organization along those lines cannot lay claim to much originality and doubtless the idea had occurred to many people." Catt to Mary Gray Peck, December 15, 1910, Catt Papers, reel 5, LC. For the best account of Catt's activities as an organizer in the 1890s, see Noun, *Strong-Minded Women,* 232–44.

9. Peck, *Carrie Chapman Catt,* 128–29.

10. Peck, *Rise of the Woman Suffrage Party.* Peck's article can be found in NAWSA Papers, reel 49, LC. It was reprinted in *Life and Labor,* June 1911, 166–69.

11. Peck, *Carrie Chapman Catt,* 169.

12. Some suffragists objected to the name on the grounds that NAWSA was a nonpartisan organization. These dissenters feared that the word *party* would suggest political affiliation. In a letter to Peck, Catt mentioned the long debate that had occurred over the new organization's name: "When nothing remained but the Woman Suffrage Party, that was adopted amid cool indifference of the majority, the positive disgust of the few, and the satisfaction of a half a dozen." Catt to Peck, November 8, 1910, Catt Papers, reel 5, LC.

13. Peck, *Rise of the Woman Suffrage Party.*

14. Ibid.

15. Ibid.

16. Carrie Chapman Catt to Mary Gray Peck, January 19, 1910, Catt Papers, reel 5, LC.

17. Shaw continued to object to the WSP, despite the endorsement of the NAWSA Advisory Committee, which recommended both the name and the use of the terms *leader* and *captain.* See Carrie Chapman Catt to Mary Gray Peck, January 29, 1911, Catt Papers, reel 5, LC.

18. Mary Gray Peck broached the subject of a national suffrage party to Catt in late 1910, but Catt refused to challenge NAWSA directly. Instead, she suggested a WSP conference on new methods to precede the NAWSA convention, followed by an adoption of the WSP method by the convention delegates. "If the Convention fails to take up the work," Catt wrote, "a national W.S.P. could then be talked of with reason." With the adoption of the WSP idea, plans for a rival association were laid to rest. Carrie Chapman Catt to Mary Gray Peck, December 15, 1910, Catt Papers, reel 5, LC.

19. Carrie Chapman Catt, quoted in Peck, *Rise of the Woman Suffrage Party.*

20. Speech to the NAWSA convention by Frances Squires Potter, July 2, 1909, quoted in Peck, *Rise of the Woman Suffrage Party.*

21. This is not to suggest that NAWSA abandoned its educational function, but rather that as membership totals grew, many suffrage societies focused on a more direct form of political activism. After 1910, education work took a secondary role to practical politics. This shift did not occur everywhere, however. In the South, where opposition to suffrage

remained strong throughout the second decade of the twentieth century, suffrage clubs continued to wage purely educational campaigns long after many organizations elsewhere had moved on to direct political involvement. See, e.g., Graham, "Woman Suffrage in Virginia."

22. Peck, *Rise of the Woman Suffrage Party.*

23. Ibid.

24. Socialist women were also prevented at times from cooperating with NAWSA by their own party. The question of whether the Socialists should work within or even in cooperation with the bourgeois suffrage crusade was debated on and off for years within the party. Outside the urban Northeast, the two groups collaborated frequently, but within New York City, the general rule was that each conducted its own campaign for votes for women. See Buhle, *Women and American Socialism,* 216–17 for the Socialist debate over suffrage, and chap. 6 on efforts at cooperation and obstacles that prevented it.

25. "Woman's Suffrage the Vanguard of Socialism," n.d., and "The Red behind the Yellow: Socialists Working for Suffrage," 1915, fliers issued by NYSAOWS, both in Adele Clark Papers, box 130, VCU.

26. Dye, *As Equals and As Sisters,* 122–24 and chap. 6. One clue to the WSP's interest in recruiting working and immigrant women can be found in the letterhead of the New York State Woman Suffrage Party as early as 1914. Listed as head of the Labor Committee is Mary Dreier, who was also an executive in the WTUL. As for the NAWSA affiliate—the New York State Woman Suffrage Association—no committee was designated for the recruitment of labor or labor reform. See letterhead for New York State Woman Suffrage Party in Harriet Laidlaw Papers, box 8, folder 134, SL; and annual report of the New York State Woman Suffrage Association, 1915, NAWSA Papers, reel 14, LC.

27. Harriet Laidlaw, "Organizing to Win by the Political District Plan," pamphlet, July 1914, NAWSA Papers, reel 12, LC.

28. Program, "Twenty Talks Presented by New York City WSP School for Suffrage Workers," September 15–27, 1911, NAWSA Papers, reel 48, LC.

29. As early as 1909, WSP organization had spread to Boston, Philadelphia, Chicago, Cleveland, Columbus, and Cincinnati, and suffrage schools were established in these localities in the next three years. "The Woman Voter," n.d., clipping found in Catt Papers, reel 8, LC.

30. Suffrage schools often charged one dollar for the entire course, or twenty-five cents per session. Although some were offered free of charge, most were too expensive for the average working-class woman to attend. See, e.g., Mary Hutchenson Page to Fellow Members of BESAGG, May 27, 1914, WRC, box 711, SL; and poster for "State Suffrage School," Madison, Wisc., June 18–24, 1914, in Breckenridge Family Papers, box 702, LC.

31. Working women had great difficulty attending weekly suffrage meetings. Even onetime events like parades caused considerable hardship. See, e.g., the correspondence of Abbie O'Connor, president of the Connecticut State Self-Supporting Woman's League, in which she futilely tried to arrange for members to attend a Connecticut Woman Suffrage Association parade. Despite her best efforts, the league's working women were unable to attend because of lack of funds and work conflicts. Abbie O'Connor to Emily

Pierson, August 28, 1916; and Abbie O'Connor to Rosmond Danielson, August 30, 1916; both in NAWSA Papers, reel 35, LC.

32. "State Suffrage School," Madison, Wisc., June 18–24, 1914, poster found in Breckenridge Family Papers, box 702, LC.

33. "Notes Taken on Organization" by Sara Algeo, NAWSA Papers, reel 25, LC. Algeo attended a lecture on organization given by Mary Garrett Hay, and she outlined Hay's remarks, with occasional direct quotes, such as the one cited here.

34. The distinction drawn by suffragists between "agitators" and "educators" is remarkably similar to that described by Georgi Valentinovich Plekhanov, theoretician of Russian Marxism. Lenin adopted Plekhanov's famous definition of the roles of the agitator and the propagandist in his 1902 tract *What Is to Be Done?* See Ulam, *Bolsheviks,* 121n, 181. Suffragists used the terms *agitator* and *educator* in an almost identical fashion, although they differed from Lenin on what they regarded as the true basis of reform. Lenin and Plekhanov stress the need to consider reform as a business, with set hours, paid workers, and the like. Suffragists went to great lengths to emphasize the voluntary nature of American reform, with "unpaid, patriotic, public service," despite the fact that suffrage organizers were in fact closer to the Lenin-Plekhanov definition. The voluntary definition of reform was doubtlessly thought to be more appealing to the majority of elite women, and thus the NAWSA leaders downplayed the more professional aspects of reform. The suffragist viewpoint and definition of terms is described in "Outline of Training for Suffrage Workers," n.d., Catt Papers, reel 8, LC.

35. Program, "Twenty Talks." For another view of suffrage school programs, see "Notes on Public Speaking" by Sara Algeo, NAWSA Papers, reel 25, LC.

36. For the suffrage speech brief, see Phelps, ed., *Selected Articles on Woman Suffrage,* xi–xiii.

37. Most professional organizers earned between $1,000 and $1,500 annually. For a discussion of one organizer's salary, see Louise Hall to Sara Algeo, August 12, 1912, NAWSA Papers, reel 1, LC. Occasionally a local club would acquire the financial backing of a prominent suffragist — or "angel" — who would pay the salary of a professional organizer. The Boston Equal Suffrage Association for Good Government, for example, relied on Mrs. Quincy Shaw's handsome donations to employ a professional organizer as the club's executive secretary. See Mary Hutchenson Page to Maud Wood Park, March 3, 1909, Maud Wood Park Papers, box 5, LC.

38. NAWSA and the WSP often hired part-time workers for specific speaking engagements with the understanding that the local suffrage club would pay part of the speaker's expenses. Clubs typically charged a small entrance fee in order to finance railroad fares, and hotel accommodations, while the national organization paid the speaker a flat weekly fee for compensation. See Carrie Chapman Catt to State Presidents, July 27, 1916, NAWSA Papers, reel 17, LC, for a discussion of financial arrangements for speakers sent to state and local clubs.

39. For a good description of the activities of part-time organizers, see Mary Hutchenson Page to Maud Wood Park, May 1, 1910, Maud Wood Park Papers, box 5, LC.

40. Report of Work for National College Equal Suffrage League, Maud Wood Park to M. Cary Thomas, April 18, 1912, NAWSA Papers, reel 5, LC. Park toured colleges in Ohio, Kansas, and Wisconsin in March and April 1910, holding conferences, business

meetings, and rallies. Speaking to more than seven thousand college women, Park reported a large number of converts to the cause as well as the creation of several new leagues.

41. There are almost no sources, either primary or secondary, dealing extensively with suffrage organizers as a group. I have been unable to locate any NAWSA records that indicate the numbers, names, pay, or other pertinent statistics of organizers in any given year. The following description of these important activists is thus necessarily impressionistic; the evidence to support my findings comes from a variety of sources, many of which touch only tangentially on the subject of organizers per se. I believe that the subject is one of crucial importance to the question of how the vote for women was won, and therefore it should not be neglected, despite the paucity of material dealing expressly with NAWSA organizers.

42. In the period 1910–14, state referenda campaigns were carried out by professional organizers, with varying degrees of support from local and state suffrage clubs. Often organizers traveled to an unorganized state to tackle both tasks simultaneously. One of the first reforms Catt put into effect when she assumed the presidency of NAWSA in 1915 was to restrict referenda campaigns to those states where organization had already been accomplished.

43. The term *flying squadron* appeared in suffrage rhetoric throughout the second decade of the twentieth century. During World War I, the suffragists probably used it to lend an air of patriotism to their cause as the term had wide usage during the war. It may have originated from Arthur Conan Doyle's Sherlock Holmes series, which featured Scotland Yard's famed "flying squad."

44. For a good description of the activities of a flying squadron at work, see clipping from the *Arkadelphia (Ark.) Gazette,* April 11, 1916, located in NAWSA Papers, reel 2, LC.

45. Florence Cotham to Miss Patterson, May 8, 1916, NAWSA Papers, reel 2, LC.

46. Zara Dupont was county chairman responsible for organization in Ohio in 1914. One of the wealthy DuPont family, Zara was called "Miss Kick" by family members, in reference to the numerous causes she espoused. Her activities as a NAWSA organizer are vividly detailed in the Memoirs of Zara Dupont, dictated to Edna Stantial, April 1943, NAWSA Papers, reel 7, LC.

47. Report of Auto Suffrage Campaign by Florence Luscomb, 1915, WRC, folder 637, SL.

48. The KERA suffrage library also included works by John Stuart Mill, Marietta Holley, Eliza Calvert Hall, Ida Husted Harper, Anna Howard Shaw, Carrie Chapman Catt, and a year's collection of the *Woman's Journal.* For a complete list of the library's holdings, see minutes, Kentucky Equal Rights Association, April 19, 1916, Breckenridge Family Papers, box 703, LC.

49. A copy of *Woman Suffrage: History, Arguments, Results,* 1915, written primarily by Alice Stone Blackwell, may be found in WRC, vol. 11, SL.

50. The Boston Equal Suffrage Association for Good Government undertook a massive membership drive in the years following 1909. One of the club's most successful activities was the suffrage study class, which met once a week to discuss such topics as "Woman Suffrage and Democracy" and "Objections to Woman Suffrage." The associa-

tion adapted the study class idea from the club's previous study group on municipal reform and used it successfully to forge a stronger bond between its members. Maud Wood Park, Report of the Executive Secretary, 6th Annual BESAGG Report, October 1910–October 1912, WRC, folder 716, SL.

51. Address by Maud Wood Park, in minutes of Boston's Ward 10 WSP meeting, October 23, 1911, WRC, vol. 48, SL.

52. Treasurer's report of canvass of ward 7, completed June 12-July 8, 1911 for the Cambridge Political Equality Association, WRC, folder 113, SL.

53. Memoirs of Zara Dupont.

54. Gertrude Halliday Leonard, MWSA quarterly report, June 1910, WRC, folder 671, SL.

55. Ibid.

56. Presidential report, Cambridge Political Equality Association, May 25, 1916, WRC, folder 114, SL.

57. *Lexington (Ky.) Herald,* December 13, 1914. Clipping found in the Breckenridge Family Papers, box 702, LC.

58. Breckenridge's policy regarding black suffrage support in Kentucky is described in Madeline McDowell Breckenridge to Mrs. John D. Hammond, May 28, 1915, Breckenridge Family Papers, box 685, LC.

59. Park, Report of the Executive Secretary, 6th Annual BESAGG Report, October 1910–October 1912, WRC, folder 716, SL.

60. Katzenstein, *Lifting the Curtain,* 44.

61. Ibid., 51–52.

62. MWSA Bi-Weekly Bulletin 9, October 1915, WRC, folder 671, SL.

63. Anonymous, notes on Columbus Day parade, Boston, October 12, 1913, WRC, folder 672, SL.

64. Order of parade, May 2, 1914, Boston, WRC, folder 672, SL.

65. "The 1914 Suffrage Parade," unsigned memoir (probably by Grace Johnson), WRC, folder 672, SL.

66. Clipping, "The Anti-Suffragists Are Also Well-Pleased," May 14, 1914, WRC, scrapbook, 25, SL.

67. For accounts of the Nashville fete, see program, May Day Demonstration, May 1, 1915, by the Nashville Equal Suffrage League; clipping, *Nashville Banner,* April 30, 1915; and clipping (probably from the *Lexington [Ky.] Herald*), May 7, 1915; all found in Breckenridge Family Papers, box 703, LC.

68. Clipping (probably from the *Lexington [Ky.] Herald*), May 7, 1915, found in Breckenridge Family Papers, box 703, LC.

69. A list of novelties for sale by the Massachusetts Woman Suffrage Association may be found in "Announcement of New Novelties," n.d., WRC, folder 663, SL.

70. Anna Snyder to Mrs. Henry Wade Rogers, December 10, 1915, NAWSA Papers, reel 11, LC.

71. MWSA quarterly letter, January 1913, WRC, folder 671, SL.

72. Madeline McDowell Breckenridge, Report of the Legislative Committee for 1911, Federation of Women's Clubs, Breckenridge Family Papers, box 701, LC.

73. Max Eastman to Sara Algeo, May 10, 1912, NAWSA Papers, reel 1, LC.

74. Although the historical record contains allusions to male suffrage clubs, I can find little evidence of activism undertaken by these groups. More often than not, the male clubs seemed to exist solely for the purpose of prosuffrage publicity and occasional financial support rather than to actively engage in the battle for the ballot. Most men's groups did not hold formal meetings beyond the initial organizational rally, and although their members were often listed as active supporters in suffrage propaganda, they took little part in the day-to-day campaign for the vote.

75. Mary Cushing Hall to Mrs. Whiting, September 30, 1918, NAWSA Papers, reel 13, LC; and Nichols, *Votes and More for Women,* 25–26.

76. For example, BESAGG hired male organizers and male translators to canvass the Italian wards of Boston. Male organizers were also used by BESAGG to canvass the area trade unions, although female workers also spoke to these groups on occasion. BESAGG executive board minutes, October 8, 1915, WRC, folder 713, SL.

77. Florence H. Luscomb to Dear Old Sport, June 24, 1917, WRC, folder 637, SL.

78. The NAWSA affiliates in New York and Boston spent time and money on organizing immigrant and, to a lesser degree, trade union constituencies, but in other regions little effort was attempted. In the South, suffragists made few sustained efforts to attract the workers in cotton mills and timber camps, miners, and white sharecroppers to the suffrage bandwagon. Instead, suffrage literature went out to the mill owners, timber barons, and other businessmen and industrialists.

79. Wyoming had been granted woman suffrage by an act of the legislature in 1869, and Utah women had been given the vote in 1896 when a suffrage provision had been inserted into the state constitution. The other suffrage states were Colorado (1893), Idaho (1896), and Washington (1910), all by referendum. For a complete list of the suffrage states, see NAWSA Papers, reel 32, LC.

80. For an excellent firsthand account of the California campaign of 1911, see Your Steady [Clara Hyde] to Carrie Chapman Catt, October 16, 1911, NAWSA Papers, reel 5, LC.

81. Shaw had at her disposal $30,000 donated by Mrs. Quincy A. Shaw of Boston to be used for state campaigns. Anna Howard Shaw to Julia [Caroline Bartlett Crane], April 3, 1912, Caroline Bartlett Crane Papers, box 40, Archives and Regional History Collections, Western Michigan University (hereafter cited as WMU), Kalamazoo, Mich.; Shaw, *Story of a Pioneer,* 296–97; and HWS 5, 337.

82. In Oregon, woman suffrage carried by a majority of only 4,161. Kansas and Arizona also narrowly passed the suffrage amendments, with a 10,787 majority in Kansas and a 7,240 majority in Arizona. Fact Sheet, n.d., NAWSA Papers, reel 11, LC.

83. For a discussion of the problems created for suffragists by the prohibition campaigns in Wisconsin and Ohio, see Catt and Shuler, *Woman Suffrage and Politics,* 186–88, 201.

84. Anna Howard Shaw to Julia [Caroline Bartlett Crane], April 18, 1912, Caroline Bartlett Crane Papers, box 40, WMU.

85. 6th Annual BESAGG Report, October 1910–October 1912, WRC, folder 716, SL.

86. Virginia Clark Abbott, "The History of Woman Suffrage and the League of Women Voters in Cuyahoga County [Ohio], 1911–1945," 1949, copy in NAWSA Papers, reel 49, LC.

87. Anna Howard Shaw to Julia [Caroline Bartlett Crane], n.d., Caroline Bartlett Crane Papers, box 40, WMU. Shaw wrote at length of her stormy interview with Mr. Mitchell, the MESA campaign director, and reported that both left the meeting "furiously mad."

88. Anna Howard Shaw to Julia [Caroline Bartlett Crane], n.d., Caroline Bartlett Crane Papers, box 40, WMU.

89. Mary Gray Peck, quoted in 6th Annual BESAGG Report, October 1910–October 1912, WRC, folder 716, SL.

90. Mary Gray Peck, typescript of a *New York Evening Post* article, October 4, 1912, NAWSA Papers, reel 49, LC.

91. The Wisconsin 1912 referendum is described in Catt and Shuler, *Woman Suffrage and Politics,* 186–88. The most common ploy used against the suffragists on election day was the failure to distribute the special pink suffrage ballots. In some areas, suffragists had mounted extensive publicity drives to familiarize voters with the pink ballot. On election day in Racine and the surrounding region, however, the suffrage ballots mysteriously appeared printed on white paper.

92. The various practices used to defraud suffragists of victory in the Michigan campaign of 1912 are described in Caruso, "History of Woman Suffrage in Michigan," 194–95; Flexner, *Century of Struggle,* 268; Catt and Shuler, *Woman Suffrage and Politics,* 181–84; and Shaw, *Story of a Pioneer,* 302.

93. The totals for the 1912 Michigan woman suffrage referendum were: 247,375 in favor, 248,135 opposed. Catt and Shuler, *Woman Suffrage and Politics,* 183.

94. Caruso, "History of Woman Suffrage in Michigan," 198–203 and 206–7.

95. Election returns are detailed in Catt and Shuler, *Woman Suffrage and Politics,* 185; and Caruso, "History of Woman Suffrage in Michigan," 209–11. Caruso places a share of the blame for the defeat on the suffragists' inability to get out the favorable vote, although she gives no analysis of why this failure occurred beyond the speculation that the MESA group was poorly financed. The antisuffragists, however, had large sums of money at their disposal and waged a heated campaign against the amendment.

96. Sylvia S. Videtto to Alice Stone Blackwell, September 28, 1913, NAWSA Papers, reel 13, LC. The assertion of a national vice trust was made repeatedly by suffragists throughout the twentieth century. In his fine book on the Anti-Saloon League's fight for prohibition, Austin Kerr maintains that in fact there was no conspiracy by the liquor industry to defeat woman suffrage. Brewers and distillers could rarely agree on tactics, or even on the necessity of organizing to defeat the prohibition forces. With this in mind, it seems improbable that the liquor industry, while doubtless not in favor of woman suffrage, spent more time and energy working to defeat woman suffrage than prohibition. States whose economies depended largely on distilling or brewing might mount onetime state or local campaigns against suffrage, but the concept of a national vice trust or liquor conspiracy must be viewed with skepticism. See Kerr, *Organized for Prohibition,* chaps. 1 and 7.

97. Carrie Chapman Catt to Mary Gray Peck, April 10, 1913, Catt Papers, reel 5, LC.

98. Anna Howard Shaw to Catharine Waugh McCulloch, April 25, 1913, Dillon Collection, folder 258, SL.

99. A good description of the "still hunt," or passive suffrage campaign, is found in Moynihan, *Rebel for Rights,* 207–9.

100. The *New York Sun,* for example, reported that between 1912 and 1915, ten states rejected woman suffrage by popular vote. See *New York Sun,* November 3, 1915, clipping found in NAWSA Papers, reel 49, LC.

101. The records of NAWSA for 1909 do not report the number of enrolled non-dues-paying suffragists. The figures cited here are taken from a collected volume of *Proceedings of the National American Woman Suffrage Association,* vols. 39–44, 1907–12, (n.p., n.d.). Data for 1909 comes from the 41st annual report of NAWSA, July 1–6, 1909, 38. Figures from 1912 are culled from the 44th annual report of NAWSA, November 21–26, 1912, 42.

102. For the 1909 figures, see *Proceedings,* 41st annual report of NAWSA, 117–21; and for 1912, see *Proceedings,* 44th annual report of NAWSA, 36–41.

103. On the variety of associations available to young women at the turn of the century, see Scott, *Natural Allies.*

104. National American Woman Suffrage Association, *Victory: How Women Won It,* 78.

105. Florence Luscomb to Dear Old Gussie, July 30, 1915, NAWSA Papers, reel 19, LC.

106. Anna Howard Shaw to Alice Stone Blackwell, n.d., NAWSA Papers, reel 18, LC.

107. Catharine Waugh McCulloch, "The 1910 Illinois Suffrage Auto Tours," Dillon Collection, box 4, SL.

108. Carrie Chapman Catt to Mary Gray Peck, April 16, 1916, Catt Papers, reel 5, LC.

109. Alice Duer Miller, "To the State Chairman," n.d., Vira Whitehouse Papers, box 1, folder 1, SL.

110. Florence Luscomb to Dear Old Gussie, July 30, 1915, NAWSA Papers, reel 19, LC.

111. Isobella Saunders to Catharine Waugh McCulloch, March 6, 1916, Dillon Collection, box 8, SL.

112. Madeline McDowell Breckenridge to Tevis Camden, November 4, 1914, Breckenridge Family Papers, box 683, LC.

113. Katzenstein, *Lifting the Curtain,* 39. Katzenstein later left the PWSA to join the National Woman's Party, but the above quote was taken from her report to the PWSA state convention, probably in 1910.

114. Excerpt from a letter from Florence Luscomb, October 1914, reprinted without salutation in NAWSA Papers, reel 14, LC.

115. Inez Haynes Irwin to Maud Wood Park, October 25, 1908, NAWSA Papers, reel 11, LC.

116. Elizabeth Hauser to Mary Gray Peck, November 14, 1910, NAWSA Papers, reel 9, LC.

117. Maud Wood Park to Mary Hutchenson Page, November 25, 1907, Maud Wood Park Papers, box 5, LC.

118. Excerpt from a letter by Florence Luscomb, November 1914, reprinted without salutation in NAWSA Papers, reel 14, LC.

119. A particularly poignant example of the efforts made by some suffragists to overcome their natural reserve concerns Carrie Catt. One young woman who sat behind Catt during one of the older woman's speeches observed that Catt constantly "was wringing her hands behind her when she was speaking." The young woman later commented on her observation and was astonished to discover that Catt suffered agonies of stage fright. When asked why she had chosen a career that was obviously so difficult for her, Catt replied, "I didn't choose it — it chose me and wouldn't let me go." Gluck, *From Parlor to Prison,* 94. See also Katzenstein, *Lifting the Curtain,* 50, for an account of one organizer's terror at public speaking and her battle to overcome her fright.

120. Laura Halsey to Maud Wood Park, August 9, 1918, NAWSA Papers, reel 15, LC.

121. Grace J. Clarke to Agnes Ryan, July 24, 1913, NAWSA Papers, reel 10, LC.

Chapter 5. The Front Door Lobby

1. Examples of Shaw's inefficiency are numerous, especially as NAWSA's membership grew and the association's finances became more complicated. Throughout 1910–12, letters of complaint flowed into NAWSA headquarters: organizers unpaid for months, suffrage literature unavailable for campaign states, serious bookkeeping errors, and cash flow problems that prohibited the Executive Board from meeting for two years. One disgruntled suffragist labeled Shaw "the Alpha and Omega of hot air." Mimmie Sheldon to Catharine Waugh McCulloch, August 9, 1910, Dillon Collection, box 7, folder 207, SL; Mary Gregg to Catharine Waugh McCulloch, July 1, 1910, Dillon Collection, box 7, folder 207, SL; Agnes Ryan to Members of the Official Board, December 24, 1910, Dillon Collection, box 25, folder 615, SL; and Ella Stewart to Jessie Ashley, August 29, 1911, Dillon Collection, box 25, folder 616, SL. Quote is from Abigail Scott Duniway to Catharine Waugh McCulloch, December 7, 1910, Dillon Collection, box 7, folder 208, SL.

2. The standard works on Paul and her suffrage organization, the National Woman's Party, are Stevens, *Jailed for Freedom;* Irwin, *Story of Alice Paul;* and, the most modern but overly partisan, Lunardini, *From Equal Suffrage to Equal Rights.* For the NWP's wartime militancy, see also Graham, "Woodrow Wilson, Alice Paul."

3. See, e.g., Anna Howard Shaw to Catharine Waugh McCulloch, February 19, 1914, Dillon Collection, folder 258, SL, in which Shaw writes: "I wish we could send the whole militant bunch back to Mrs. Pankhurst where they learned their absolutely idiotic methods." For an example of anti-Shaw sentiment, see Olive Mills Belches to Grace Johnson, February 2, 1916, WRC, box 134, SL.

4. Blatch and Lutz, *Challenging Years,* 93–94, 100–18. Among those belonging to Blatch's group who were strong supporters of working-class issues and who later left NAWSA in protest were Lavinia Dock, Charlotte Perkins Gilman, Florence Kelley, and Jessie Ashley.

5. Beard resigned from her place on the NAWSA Congressional Committee in 1914 and shortly afterward joined the CU as an officer. Kelley, the longtime chairman of NAWSA's Industrial Committee on Working Women and Children, resigned after pointing out to the NAWSA Executive Board that many suffragists held joint memberships in both organizations. Shaw's attacks, Kelley wrote, "certainly do not make for unity." Mary Beard to Mary Ware Dennett, 1914, NAWSA Papers, reel 32, LC; and Florence

Kelley to Madeline McDowell Breckenridge, September, 25, 1914, Breckenridge Family Papers, box 682, LC.

6. Throughout 1913 and 1914, NAWSA and Congressional Union leaders debated whether or not the CU should be accepted as an auxiliary of NAWSA, as well as whether NAWSA could accommodate Paul's conviction that militancy was the only way to win suffrage for women. The problems involved in this dispute are discussed from the NAWSA viewpoint in Anna Howard Shaw to the NAWSA president and Executive Council [probably 1913], Dillon Collection, box 7, folder 258, SL. See also a twenty-seven-page report of the NAWSA-CU split, December 5, 1913, NAWSA Papers, reel 32, LC, that contains the NAWSA Executive Council vote on the CU's admission as a NAWSA auxiliary. The final vote was fifty-four against admission, twenty-four in favor, and three blank ballots. Paul was informed of the decision February 19, 1914, by NAWSA Secretary Mary Ware Dennett.

7. Inez Hayes Irwin to Maud Wood Park, n.d., NAWSA Papers, reel 11, LC.

8. Little has been written on Gordon or her organization. Much of her correspondence concerning woman suffrage is preserved in the Laura Clay Papers, University of Kentucky Library, Lexington, Ky. See also Kenneth Johnson, "Kate Gordon"; and Wheeler, *New Women of the New South,* 140–58.

9. The exact number of marchers is a matter of dispute. Mary Grey Peck gives the number as six thousand, but Maud Wood Park puts the figure at ten thousand. I have used the more conservative estimate. See Peck, "Chicago — Where It Rained Planks," NAWSA Headquarters Newsletter, June 22, 1916, 4–7; and Park, *Front Door Lobby,* 12–15.

10. For accounts of the 1916 suffrage parade, see Peck, *Carrie Chapman Catt,* 245–48; and Park, *Front Door Lobby,* 12–15.

11. Peck, "Chicago — Where It Rained Planks."

12. The Democratic National Convention witnessed a "golden lane" of women clad in white and yellow who lined both sides of the street as the delegates walked to their meeting. See Peck, *Carrie Chapman Catt,* 248–52; and Park, *Front Door Lobby,* 12–15.

13. Park, *Front Door Lobby,* 15.

14. Quoted in Peck, *Carrie Chapman Catt,* 252.

15. Most of NAWSA's membership, including many white southerners, objected to the Shafroth-Palmer amendment, believing that it would direct attention away from the all-inclusive federal amendment and result in needless state referenda. The Shafroth-Palmer amendment drew most of its support from NAWSA's Congressional Committee, led by Ruth Hanna McCormick and Antoinette Funk, who ironically were northern Progressives and, for their time, liberal on the race issue. With the encouragement of some southern congressmen, however, the two women impetuously endorsed the amendment in 1914 without the approval of the NAWSA Executive Board, the Executive Council, or the annual convention. Thus the association found itself saddled with the substitute amendment until December 1915, when the delegates voted overwhelmingly to drop it from consideration. In a further ironic twist, Kate Gordon and her SSWSC refused to support the Shafroth-Palmer amendment because they believed McCormick and Funk were agents of the Republican Party. For more on this subject see Miller, *Ruth Hanna McCormick,* 89–99.

16. ERA Club minutes (microfilm edition), June 24, 1916, New Orleans Public Library (hereafter cited as NOPL).

17. Catt reported that "Everywhere people congratulate us upon the step forward and seem to feel that a new impetus has been given the movement." Carrie Chapman Catt to Anna Howard Shaw, June 28, 1916, Catt Papers, reel 6, LC. Mrs. Frank Roessing, however, expressed the opinion of NAWSA leaders: "We consider the Democratic plank weaker than the Republican plank because it definitely specifies action 'by states'." The Lodge rider appended to the GOP plank merely recognized the right of the states to act, but it did not make such action mandatory. Mrs. Frank Roessing to Mrs. Charles S. McClure, June 24, 1916, NAWSA Papers, reel 32, LC.

18. Park, *Front Door Lobby,* 15–16.

19. Quoted in Peck, *Carrie Chapman Catt,* 237.

20. First quote is from Carrie Chapman Catt to Ida Husted Harper, October 14, 1921, Catt Papers, reel 3, LC; second quote is from Peck, *Carrie Chapman Catt,* 257.

21. Kate Gordon to Catharine Waugh McCulloch, August 18, 1916, Dillon Collection, box 9, SL. See also Gordon to Laura Clay, July 27, 1916, Laura Clay Papers, box 10, University of Kentucky.

22. Catt's letter is quoted in part in minutes of the ERA Club, August 3, 1916, ERA Club Papers, NOPL.

23. Ibid.

24. *HWS,* 5, 492–93.

25. Speech by Woodrow Wilson to the forty-eighth annual convention of NAWSA, Atlantic City, N.J., September 8, 1916, rpt. from notes in NAWSA Papers, reel 32, LC. Charles Evans Hughes, the GOP candidate, declined to speak to the gathering, although he had won the support of many suffragists when he declared himself in favor of the federal suffrage amendment the previous July.

26. Catt had met in secret with the Executive Board and Executive Council shortly before the convention convened and had presented the three platforms. By the time of the convention, she had secured the backing of all NAWSA elected officers and most of the non-southern state association leaders. See Catt's discussion of this secret meeting in Catt to Maud Wood Park, April 18, 1933, Catt Papers, reel 5, LC.

27. Copies of the three platforms presented to the delegates at Atlantic City may be found in NAWSA, *The Woman Suffrage Year Book,* 1916, 85–86, WRC, folder 115, SL; and "The Three Platforms," NAWSA annual convention, 1916, NAWSA Papers, reel 32, LC.

28. Catt later inserted a resolution that permitted a state "not desiring to work for the federal amendment" to retain its membership in NAWSA, provided the state not work *against* the amendment. Although this was intended as a sop to the Gordons and their allies, the southerners' estrangement from NAWSA grew increasingly worse over time. A vivid account of the incident may be found in Peck, *Carrie Chapman Catt,* 257. For Catt's perspective, see Catt to Ida Husted Harper, October 14, 1921, Catt Papers, reel 3, LC.

29. Plan of work (also called the Winning Plan), *HWS,* 5, 510.

30. The "constructive policy" referred to is the Winning Plan sanctioned by the delegates at the Atlantic City convention. Note the key phrase "as though these details had

been agreed to." Carrie Chapman Catt to Presidents of State Auxiliaries, October 20, 1916, NAWSA Papers, reel 17, LC.

31. An account of Roessing's suggestion may be found in Mrs. Lewis Jerome Johnson, Continued Report of Progress of the Massachusetts Congressional Committee, October 30, 1916, NAWSA Papers, reel 32, LC.

32. Carrie Chapman Catt to Presidents of State Affiliates, September 20, 1916, NAWSA Papers, reel 17, LC.

33. Carrie Chapman Catt to Presidents of State Auxiliaries, September 18, 1916, NAWSA Papers, reel 17, LC.

34. Carrie Chapman Catt to Presidents of State Auxiliaries, October 20, 1916, NAWSA Papers, reel 17, LC.

35. Emma Gilette to Carrie Chapman Catt, August 5, 1916, NAWSA Papers, reel 33, LC.

36. For an excellent description of Ruth Hanna McCormick's lifelong career in politics, see Miller, *Ruth Hanna McCormick*. Chap. 3 details McCormick's suffrage work.

37. Carrie Chapman Catt to Maud Wood Park, January 18, 1916, NAWSA Papers, reel 15, LC; and Catt to Park, January 27, 1916, NAWSA Papers, reel 32, LC.

38. Park, *Front Door Lobby,* 14.

39. Gardener described her work with several prominent politicians in Helen Gardener to Ray Stannard Baker, June 11, 1925, NAWSA Papers, reel 8, LC. See also report of Helen Hamilton Gardener, vice chairman, Congressional Committee, April 13, 1919, NAWSA Papers, reel 32, LC.

40. There are many stories of Gardener's dealings with Champ Clark. One of the best may be found in Maud Wood Park to Inez Irwin, March 27, 1933, Maud Wood Park Papers, box 4, LC. The above strategy is detailed in Park, *Front Door Lobby,* 89–92.

41. Mabel Willard to Edna Stantial, March 1, 1930, Dillon Collection, folder 591, SL.

42. One good account of Gardener's thoughts on lobby conduct and strategy may be found in Helen Hamilton Gardener to Carrie Chapman Catt, August 18, 1916, WRC, folder 71, SL.

43. Park, *Front Door Lobby,* 1.

44. For a complete list of the fourteen committee members, see minutes of NAWSA Congressional Committee, April 11, 1917, WRC, folder 740, SL.

45. Ibid. McCormick was the wife of Illinois Progressive Medill McCormick and thus had many political and social contacts among the nation's Progressives. She was also the daughter of Mark Hanna and so was well connected to the Roosevelt family and other influential Republicans.

46. Maud Wood Park, congressional work for the Nineteenth Amendment, supplementary notes, February, 1943, WRC, folder 730, LC.

47. The best account of Suffrage House is in Park's humorous and informative *Front Door Lobby*. Unless otherwise noted, all descriptions come from this source.

48. Press release issued by NAWSA, November 30, 1916, Adele Clark Papers, box 150, VCU; and Helen Guthrie Miller to Mrs. B. B. [Lila] Valentine, December 2, 1916, Adele Clark Papers, box 150, VCU.

49. Park, *Front Door Lobby,* 33–35.

50. Ibid., 178–79.

51. For the year November 1, 1917–October 31, 1918, Park gives the figure

$17,964.59. See Park, *Front Door Lobby*, 32–33 for a description of how the committee met those expenses. Another source places the Congressional Committee yearly budget at $21,000. Included in this second budget are the Suffrage House rent and utilities, salaries for secretarial help, and so on. See Congressional Committee budget, March 21, 1917, WRC, box 730, SL.

52. Quotations are from Young, *Record of the Leslie Woman Suffrage Commission*, 13–16, 37–38. See also Peck, *Carrie Chapman Catt*, 224–25.

53. Young, *Record of the Leslie Woman Suffrage Commission*, 61–64, 85.

54. This figure represents the sum of the annual NAWSA budget and a portion of the Leslie fortune.

55. Young, *Record of the Leslie Woman Suffrage Commission*, 64–65.

56. Ibid., 67–79. See also Rose Young to Carrie Chapman Catt, November 14, 1916, NAWSA Papers, reel 24, LC.

57. Plate matter for Sunday supplements and suffrage special editions was routinely sent to state and local chapters during campaign drives. After purchasing the plate from NAWSA for a small fee, the local press chairman would offer the material free of charge to area newspapers. Plate matter was easy to insert and saved harried editors the trouble and expense of compiling their own stories. Thus editors who would have hesitated to include a small suffrage story often accepted a page or two of plate propaganda.

58. Young, *Record of the Leslie Woman Suffrage Commission*, 70–71.

59. Rose Young to Carrie Chapman Catt, November 14, 1916, NAWSA Papers, reel 24, LC.

60. Young, *Record of the Leslie Woman Suffrage Commission*, 71–73.

61. Park, *Front Door Lobby*, 28–29.

62. Ibid., 43.

63. Maud Wood Park to Inez Haynes Irwin, April 28, 1933, Maud Wood Park Papers, box 4, LC.

64. Lobby report (incomplete in original), January 4, 1917, NAWSA Papers, box 50, LC.

65. Lobby report, January 25, 1917, WRC, box 733, SL.

66. Lobby report, January 18, 1917, WRC, box 733, SL.

67. Quoted in Park, *Front Door Lobby*, 41.

68. Ibid., 44–45.

69. Maud Wood Park, Congressional Work for the Nineteenth Amendment: Supplementary Notes, February, 1943, WRC, folder 730, SL.

70. For Roessing's thoughts on the subject, see *HWS* 5, 509.

71. Carrie Chapman Catt to the state presidents and congressional chairmen, March 12, 1917, NAWSA Papers, reel 32, LC.

72. Ibid. See also Park, *Front Door Lobby*, 36–37.

Chapter 6. The Suffrage Machine

1. The February meeting is described at length in *HWS* 5, 721–22; and Peck, *Carrie Chapman Catt*, 267–68. For a discussion of pacifist sentiment within NAWSA, see Elizabeth Hauser to Mary Gray Peck, February 24, 1917, NAWSA Papers, reel 9, LC.

2. Quoted in Peck, *Carrie Chapman Catt*, 275.

3. Helen Guthrie Miller to Madam President [of state auxiliaries], March 16, 1917; and Nellie Shuler to My Dear President, May 22, 1917, NAWSA Papers, reel 17, LC. Part of the NAWSA war plan was the creation of several departments to oversee patriotic work, including food production, food consumption, Americanization, and protection of women's labor in time of war. See also Catt, "Ready for Citizenship," 816, clipping found in Catt Papers, reel 8, LC.

4. For NAWSA's war plans, see Carrie Chapman Catt to Our Presidents, April 2, 1917, NAWSA Papers, reel 17, LC; and minutes of NAWSA Congressional Committee, April 11, 1917, WRC, folder 740, SL. On the postponement of the amendment drive, see Carrie Chapman Catt to Presidents, April 13, 1917, NAWSA Papers, reel 17, LC.

5. For the Congressional Committee's debate on the issue of war work, see minutes of NAWSA Congressional Committee, April 19, 1917, WRC, folder 740, SL. Catt's and Park's scheme may be found in Carrie Chapman Catt to Maud Wood Park, April 13, 1917, NAWSA Papers, reel 15, LC.

6. Suffragists were linked not only to Schwimmer but also to the radical Industrial Workers of the World. See Clara Hyde to Mary Gray Peck, September 26, 1917, NAWSA Papers, reel 16, LC. More on Rosika Schwimmer may be found in Wiltsher, *Most Dangerous Women,* esp. chap. 1.

7. Radicals like Dorothy Day and Louise Bryant, for example, signed up with Alice Paul's organization, as did others from radical circles. On radicals and pacifism, see Jones, *Heretics and Hellraisers,* esp. 78–98 and chap. 4.

8. Sochen, *New Woman in Greenwich Village,* 105.

9. Colvin, *Rebel in Thought,* 144

10. Fishbein, *Rebels in Bohemia,* 156–57; and Jones, *Heretics and Hellraisers,* 106–9.

11. Wenona Pinkham to Miss Osgood, March 31, 1918, NAWSA Papers, reel 16, LC.

12. On the MWSA conflict, see Alice Stone Blackwell, Mary Livermore Barrows, and Louise Merritt Parker to Delegates and Alternates of MWSA, May 19, 1918, NAWSA Papers, reel 16, LC; Mira Pitman to Executive Board of MWSA, June 1, 1918, WRC, folder 667, SL; Mira Pitman to Mrs. Charles Sumner Bird, n.d., WRC, folder 665, SL; and Carrie Chapman Catt to Mrs. Charles Sumner Bird, May 31, 1918, WRC, folder 667, SL. For an example of pacifists' work in nonwar service, see minutes of the New York State WSP, April 17, 1917, Harriet Laidlaw Papers, box 8, SL.

13. *New York Tribune,* March 1, 1917.

14. One of the few secondary sources on the NLWS is Steinson, *American Women's Activism in World War I.* The WCCND is discussed at length in Breen, *Uncle Sam at Home,* esp. chap. 7.

15. Catt and Funk were also appointed to the executive board of the Women's Liberty Loan Committee.

16. *HWS* 5, 726–27 and chap. 7; and minutes of the New York State Woman Suffrage Party executive board meeting, April 17, 1917, Harriet Laidlaw Papers, box 8, SL.

17. Anna Howard Shaw to Harriet Laidlaw, August 16, 1917, Harriet Laidlaw Papers, box 8, SL. One of the tragedies of the suffrage movement was Shaw's appointment to the WCCND, a position she disliked intensely. Shaw found the lack of real authority frustrating, and she grew increasingly bitter over the treatment she received at the hands of male

bureaucrats and politicians. She wrote plaintively: "I have felt an outcast from my very own here in Washington all summer. It has not seemed like the old gripping work, and I cannot make it feel so." Nevertheless, the aging suffragist remained as the head of the WCCND until her death from influenza in 1919.

18. Many state suffrage societies volunteered for census taking, and all used their existing organizational structure for recruits. See, e.g., Mary Garrett Hay, report of the New York State WSP for 1918, NAWSA Papers, reel 38, LC; and Connecticut Woman Suffrage Association News Bulletin, February 8, 1917, NAWSA Papers, reel 35, LC. Quote is from the minutes of the New York State WSP, April 17, 1917, Harriet Laidlaw Papers, box 8, SL. For more on the New York census, see Vira Whitehouse to My Dear Ladies, February 9, 1917; resolution, New York State WSP executive committee, February 6, 1917; and Vira Whitehouse to George Glynn, executive auditor and chairman, Republican State Committee, March 31, 1917, all in Harriet Laidlaw Papers, box 8, SL.

19. Mrs. B. L. Robinson (president of the Women's Anti-Suffrage Association of Massachusetts) to Vilette Crosby, April 30, 1918, WRC, folder 711, SL.

20. The weighing-and-measuring campaign was but one of the many successful projects of the WCCND's Child Welfare Committee. For more on this subject, see Breen, *Uncle Sam at Home,* 127–29.

21. The above list of activities was taken from the letterhead of the BESAGG War Service Committee, n.d., WRC, folder 710, SL. For other activities of the War Service Committee, see war relief report, n.d., WRC, folder 710, SL; form letter from Wenona Pinkham, executive secretary of BESAGG, May 17, 1917, WRC, folder 711, SL; and clipping, *Boston Advertiser and American,* January 6, 1918, found in NAWSA Papers, reel 18, LC.

22. The survey of the foreign-born conducted by BESAGG is detailed in Report of the Americanization Committee, n.d., WRC, folder 710, SL.

23. Grace Bagley, BESAGG report on Americanization Committee, WRC, folder 714, SL. See also report of Special Committee on Americanization of Immigrants, April 17, 1919, WRC, folder 714, SL.

24. Clipping, *Lexington (Ky.) Herald,* June 22, 1918, found in Breckenridge Family Papers, box 704, LC.

25. Report of the 29th annual meeting of the Kentucky Equal Rights Association, March 11–12, 1919, Breckenridge Family Papers, box 704, LC.

26. Carrie Chapman Catt, Bulletin 3, February 15, 1918, Breckenridge Family Papers, box 703, LC; and Mrs. Raymond Brown, Bulletin 12, April 24, 1918, McCallum Papers, box 9, file 3, AHC. See also Sara Algeo to Comrades, April 26, 1918, NAWSA Papers, reel 1, LC; and *The Woman Citizen,* October 5, 1918, both found in Breckenridge Family Papers, box 704, LC.

27. The best source for the Women's Overseas Hospital is "Women's Overseas Hospitals, U.S.A., of the NAWSA," pamphlet, November 1919, copy found in McCallum Papers, box 20, AHC.

28. Ida Husted Harper, letter to the editor, *Dallas Evening Journal,* June 4, 1917, Catt Papers, reel 3, LC.

29. See, e.g., the form letter by Mrs. John Glover South, September 10, 1917, Breckenridge Family Papers, box 703, LC. South was both the president of the Kentucky Equal

Rights Association and a member of the state executive committee of the WCCND. The above letter, concerning the WCCND, is typed on NAWSA letterhead.

30. *Woman Citizen,* October 5, 1918, 375.

31. "As a War Measure," flier, n.d., NAWSA Papers, reel 39, LC. The listing of the jobs held by women during war included: mechanics, farmers, munition workers, mine workers, motor men, telegraphers, ambulance drivers, and bell "boys."

32. Vira Whitehouse, report of state chairman to the state conference, New York State WSP, August 29, 1917, Harriet Laidlaw Papers, box 8, folder 139, SL.

33. Maud Wood Park to State Congressional Chairmen, May 24, 1917, NAWSA Papers, reel 32, LC; and Park, *Front Door Lobby,* 89–92.

34. For Wilson's work for the new committee, see Woodrow Wilson to the Honorable Edward W. Pou, May 14, 1917, WRC, folder 735, SL. The petition is described in Maud Wood Park to State Congressional Chairmen, May 24, 1917, NAWSA Papers, reel 32, LC.

35. Stevens, *Jailed for Freedom,* 66; and *New York Times,* January 12, 1917.

36. Quoted in Irwin, *Story of Alice Paul,* 202.

37. Quoted in Maud Wood Park to State Congressional Chairmen, May 24, 1917, NAWSA Papers, reel 32, LC.

38. Carrie Chapman Catt to Alice Paul, May 24, 1917, NAWSA Papers, reel 8, LC.

39. Carrie Chapman Catt to James P. Hornaday, May 24, 1917, NAWSA Papers, reel 33, LC. Marked in the margin of this letter is a handwritten note: "Sent to all press correspondents." See also Carrie Chapman Catt to T. E. Spencer, May 24, 1917, National Woman's Party Papers (microfilm edition), reel 43.

40. David Lawrence to Carrie Chapman Catt, May 25, 1917; and Thomas Logan to Catt, May 25, 1917; both in NAWSA Papers, reel 33, LC.

41. Mrs. John Glover South, president of the Kentucky Equal Rights Association, to Kentucky newspapers, March 28, 1917, Breckenridge Family Papers, box 703, LC.

42. *The Suffragist,* June 30, 1917, 6–8.

43. *Washington Times,* June 21, 1917.

44. *Washington Times,* June 22, 1917. For photographs of the incident, see, e.g., *Philadelphia Inquirer,* June 23, 1917.

45. National Woman's Party press release, June 22, 1917, Woodrow Wilson Papers (microfilm edition), reel 209, LC.

46. Helen Gardener to Harriet Laidlaw, June 27, 1917, Harriet Laidlaw Papers, box 8, folder 137, SL.

47. Maud Wood Park, Helen Gardener, and Ethel Smith, report of special interview with Speaker Champ Clark, June 23, 1917, NAWSA Papers, reel 32, LC.

48. Senator A. A. Jones to Maud Wood Park, June 30, 1917, NAWSA Papers, reel 32, LC. See also Special Interview with Jones conducted by Park, Gardener, and Smith, June 26, 1917, NAWSA Papers, reel 32, LC; and Maud Wood Park to State Congressional Chairmen and State Presidents, July 7, 1917, NAWSA Papers, reel 32, LC.

49. Ethel M. Smith to Carrie Chapman Catt, June 26, 1917, WRC, folder 735, SL. The letter is marked "confidential." Smith also suggested to the journalist that "this suggestion should be his own, and should in no way seem to come from us." A duplicate of this letter may be found in NAWSA Papers, reel 19, LC.

50. Maud Wood Park, report on press situation, July 5, 1917, NAWSA Papers, reel 32, LC.

51. Committee on Public Information, *Official Bulletin* 1, no. 46 (July 3, 1917): 2, Doris Stevens Papers, box 8, folder 229, SL.

52. The lobbyists contacted correspondents with the United Press, Associated Press, and the International News, in addition to journalists with the *New York Evening Post, Washington Times, Washington Star,* and *Washington Evening Star.* Maud Wood Park to J. P. Yoder, July 3, 1917, NAWSA Papers, reel 32, LC; and Park, report on press situation, July 5, 1917, NAWSA Papers, reel 32, LC. Park's report may also be found in WRC, folder 730, SL. The scheme to deprive the NWP of publicity was still in effect in February 1918 when a Suffrage House lobbyist wrote the following to Texas Equal Suffrage Association president Minnie Fisher Cunningham: "Some of the papers have done one thing and its the best that can be done—only you have to manage it with a man whom you can trust and who trusts you—keep them [the NWP] out of the Press. Even adverse publicity suits them—any sort, and absolute silence as to discussion, and as to their existence, is the only way. However we can't be put in the position of opposing them." "B" to Minnie Fisher Cunningham, February 25, 1918, McCallum Papers, box 3, file 5, AHC.

53. Memorandum by Woodrow Wilson to Joseph P. Tumulty, n.d., Woodrow Wilson Papers, reel 209, LC.

54. For an example of compliance with Wilson's suggestion of a "bare colorless chronicle," see Arthur Brisbane to Joseph P. Tumulty, November 9, 1917, Woodrow Wilson Papers (microfilm edition), case file 1215, LC. The following newspapers were checked for their coverage of significant militant activity on June 20–23, 1917 (White House riots), July 18–20, 1917 (arrests and riots), and August 14–18, 1917 (arrests and riots): *Washington Evening Star, Washington Times, Washington Post, New York Times, New York World, New York Tribune, New York Herald, Baltimore Sun, Chicago Tribune, Philadelphia Inquirer,* and *Cleveland Plain Dealer.* None of these newspapers refrained from front page coverage of these events, despite the efforts of NAWSA, Creel, and the Wilson administration.

55. Creel's Committee on Public Information fell prey to this tendency. The CPI was founded by Wilson to enlist public opinion behind the war effort, but its propagandists went far beyond simple publicity to whip up a furor of hatred for all things German. The Red Scare of 1919–20 can be attributed in part to the committee's overzealous work.

56. For a good treatment of *The Masses* and its advocacy of suffrage see Jones, *Heretics and Hellraisers,* 95–105 and chap. 4.

57. Under the aegis of the Industrial Protection Committee, many local and state associations endorsed protective legislation for women and children. For example, in 1918 BESAGG endorsed bills pending before the state legislature that included a forty-eight-hour work restriction for women and minors, housing legislation, and a resolution providing for weekly payment of wages. The Boston group also worked to convince legislators to create a minimum wage board. In light of the successful reform work by BESAGG and other suffrage societies, Catt's objections seem all the more narrow and unreasonable. Report of BESAGG, January 28, 1919, WRC, folder 716, SL.

58. "When those who read the public press learn that we are interested in the women

carrying their own packages, women [workers] in the Fire Department, which was one of the things turned in on a clipping, and every other sort of thing in Washington, and yet nothing goes out to indicate that we are even aware that there is a Federal Amendment, I do not consider it valuable press work," Catt angrily wrote to Smith. Catt concluded her letter by saying, "I would rather that one little paragraph [about woman suffrage] of four lines would get into the press over the country, than columns and columns about carrying our own packages." Carrie Chapman Catt to Ethel Smith, August 3, 1917, Catt Papers, reel 6, LC. For Smith's response, see Ethel Smith to Carrie Chapman Catt, August 20, 1917, NAWSA Papers, reel 19, LC.

59. Maud Wood Park to State Congressional Chairmen and State Presidents, July 7, 1917, NAWSA Papers, reel 32, LC.

60. Quoted in Morgan, *Suffragists and Democrats,* 118–19.

61. NAWSA press release, September 24, 1917, Harriet Laidlaw Papers, box 8, SL.

62. See *HWS* 5, 577; and Park, *Front Door Lobby,* 117–18.

63. Carrie Chapman Catt to Mary Gray Peck, October 23, 1917, Catt Papers, reel 5, LC.

64. Mary Garrett Hay, Report of the New York State Woman Suffrage Party, 1915, NAWSA Papers, reel 38, LC; Mary Garrett Hay, report of the campaign activities in the five boroughs of Manhattan, Brooklyn, Bronx, Richmond and Queens, 1915, NAWSA Papers, reel 38, LC; and Annual Report of the New York State Woman Suffrage Party, November 30–December 2, 1915, NAWSA Papers, reel 14, LC. See also "Organization in New York" by Sara L. G. Fritz, 1915, NAWSA Papers, reel 25, LC.

65. Mary Garrett Hay, first campaign district report, December 1916, NAWSA Papers, reel 38, LC; and Annual Report, New York State WSP, November 30–December 2, 1915, NAWSA Papers, reel 14, LC.

66. "Suffrage Training School," flier, January and February 1917, New York State WSP, NAWSA Papers, reel 48, LC; program for suffrage training school, New York State WSP, found in Harriet Laidlaw Papers, box 8, SL; form letter by Vira Whitehouse for New York State WSP, June 22, 1916, Harriet Laidlaw Papers, box 8, SL; and James Laidlaw to Dear Sir, May 3, 1916, Harriet Laidlaw Papers box 8, SL.

67. Report of Mrs. Norman Whitehouse, chairman, New York State WSP, 1917, NAWSA Papers, reel 48, LC.

68. For an account of Hay's work with Tammany Hall, see Peck, *Carrie Chapman Catt,* 277–78; and Maud Wood Park, Supplementary Notes on Mary Garrett Hay, March 1943, NAWSA Papers, reel 38, LC.

69. Peck, *Carrie Chapman Catt,* 277; and Park, *Front Door Lobby,* 119–20.

70. The Socialists, pacifists, and first generation German Americans were united in their desire for peace and believed that enfranchised women would provide additional pressure against America's entry into World War I. Therefore, the WSP suffrage forces in New York City gained a new constituency crucial to the success of their reform. For the radical coalition, see Clara Hyde to Mary Gray Peck, December 5, 1917, NAWSA Papers, reel 16, LC. The Socialist women's part in the New York campaign is described in Buhle, *Women and American Socialism,* 233–39. See also Dye, *As Equals and As Sisters,* 129–30, 137. The *New York Times* quote is cited in Buhle, *Women and American Socialism,*

237. For the vote totals, see Mary Garrett Hay, "To Members of Congress," December 14, 1917, NAWSA Papers, reel 48, LC.

71. The scene at New York headquarters is described in Carrie Chapman Catt to Lucy Anthony, April 30, 1943, NAWSA Papers, reel 15, LC.

72. Anna Howard Shaw to Ella Stewart, November 30, 1917, Dillon Collection, box 22, SL.

73. Mary Hutchenson Page to Maud Wood Park, February 20, 1918, Maud Wood Park Papers, box 5, LC.

74. Carrie Chapman Catt, "Address to the Legislatures of the United States," 1919, Dillon Collection, box 1, SL.

75. Park, *Front Door Lobby*, 120–21.

76. Ibid., 123–25.

77. Of the numerous examples of Gardener's contacts with the president, see Helen Hamilton Gardener to Woodrow Wilson, August 16, 1918, WRC, folder 71, SL, in which she asked the president for suggestions on the Senate vote scheduled in October 1918. In her dealings with Wilson, Gardener was not above flattery: "Your vision on this, as in other great questions, is so clear and so comprehensive — so inclusive of its future bearings on world, as well as national politics — that if you once made the people see what it means for America's Senate to go wrong on this great principle at this time, it seems to me the reaction from 'back home' could hardly fail to be great enough to push some of the men . . . over the fence." Wilson responded with a promise to "keep my eye open for suitable occasions when I may, either in the way you suggest or in some other way, be influential in bringing about the result we both desire." Wilson to Gardener, August 24, 1918, WRC, folder 71, SL.

78. Park, *Front Door Lobby*, 135; and Flexner, *Century of Struggle*, 301.

79. Park, *Front Door Lobby*, 137.

80. Ibid. See also Mabel Willard to Mary Hutchenson Page, January 12, 1918, WRC, folder 736, SL.

81. Park, *Front Door Lobby*, 158–60.

82. Hay's strategy is discussed in Clara Hyde to Mary Gray Peck, March 17, 1918, NAWSA Papers, reel 16, LC.

83. Carrie Chapman Catt to State Presidents and Congressional Chairmen, May 23, 1918, NAWSA Papers, reel 32, LC.

84. Carrie Chapman Catt to Presidents and Congressional Chairmen, September 18, 1918, NAWSA Papers, reel 17, LC.

85. Carrie Chapman Catt, Bulletin 23, August 20, 1918, Breckenridge Family Papers, box 703, LC.

86. Carrie Chapman Catt, Bulletin 9, March 21, 1918, Breckenridge Family Papers, box 703, LC.

87. Mrs. James W. Wadsworth to Carrie Chapman Catt, February 12, 1918, NAWSA Papers, reel 48, LC. An ongoing theme the antisuffragists returned to frequently in the years after 1916 was that of woman suffrage as a political machine. See, e.g., "The Woman Bosses," *The Woman Patriot* 3 (April 26, 1919): 4.

88. Quoted in Park, *Front Door Lobby*, 205–6.

89. The initial vote on October 1, 1918, stood at sixty-two for and thirty-four against the measure, including pairs, fifty-four for and thirty against, excluding pairs. Thirty-four Democrats and thirty-two Republicans favored the resolution, while twenty-two Democrats and twelve Republicans voted nay. Senate Woman Suffrage Committee Chairman A. A. Jones changed his vote to nay in order to allow the resolution to be reconsidered, giving a final total, excluding pairs, of fifty-three ayes and thirty-one nays. Park, *Front Door Lobby*, 211–12.

90. Clipping entitled "Federal Law Called Useless by the ERA Club," *New Orleans Times-Picayune*, n.d., found in minutes of the ERA Club, January 12, 1918, ERA Club Papers, NOPL.

91. Laura Clay to Kate Gordon, March 18, 1918, Laura Clay Papers, box 11, University of Kentucky Library.

92. For the attack on the amendment, see "An Open Letter to U.S. Senator Ramsdell Opposing the Federal Amendment for Woman Suffrage," by Harry Gamble, January 26, 1918, NAWSA Papers, reel 27, LC. Gamble's letter discussed at length the race question in the South and argued that "black women are far more fearless than their men, and will not be deterred by either opinions or intimidation from pursuing their ends." Gordon's reprimand may be located in Justina L. Wilson to Jean Gordon, April 29, 1918, Harriet Laidlaw Papers, box 9, SL.

93. Kate Gordon to Justina Wilson, May 7, 1918, Harriet Laidlaw Papers, box 9, SL.

94. Justina Wilson to Kate Gordon, May 17, 1918, NAWSA Papers, reel 9, LC.

95. Kate Gordon to Alice Stone Blackwell, July 18, [1918?], NAWSA Papers, reel 9, LC.

96. For a good example of the Louisiana appeal, see "Joint Campaign Committee for Ratification of State Amendment for Woman Suffrage," flier, found in minutes of the ERA Club, November, 1918, ERA Club Papers, NOPL.

97. Laura Clay resigned from the NAWSA affiliate, KERA, in October 1918, and the Gordons and their ERA Club withdrew in November of the same year. Laura Clay to Christine South, October 8, 1918, Laura Clay Papers, University of Kentucky Library; and ERA Club Minutes, November 17, 1918, ERA Club Papers, NOPL. It should be noted that NAWSA never debated the value of the federal amendment on racial grounds even when responding to states' rights suffragists' arguments concerning white supremacy. Clearly the federal amendment offered at least a faint hope of political equality to black women, but NAWSA leaders never appealed to that constituency, even after the departure of the Gordons and Clay from the association.

98. Carrie Chapman Catt, Bulletin 20, July 6, 1918, Breckenridge Family Papers, box 703, LC. See also Mrs. Frank J. Shuler, Bulletin 39, November 26, 1918, Breckenridge Family Papers, box 703, LC.

99. Carrie Chapman Catt, Bulletin 32, November 18, 1918, Breckenridge Family Papers, box 703, LC. See also Catt, Bulletin 41, November 25, 1918, Breckenridge Family Papers, box 704, LC.

100. Carrie Chapman Catt, Bulletin 44, January 2, 1919, Breckenridge Family Papers, box 704, LC.

101. Park, *Front Door Lobby*, 239–40.

102. The four targeted Senators were John W. Weeks (R-Mass.), Willard Saulsbury (D-

Del.), David Baird (D-N.J.), and George W. Moses (R-N.H.). The plan to defeat the opposition senators standing for reelection was based on an effort by the Massachusetts Woman Suffrage Association in 1912 when MWSA campaigned against Republican senatorial candidate Roger Wolcott. Massachusetts suffragists circulated Wolcott's negative voting record on such issues as fair labor standards, woman suffrage, child labor, and prohibition. Influential in the Wolcott campaign was MWSA organizer Margaret Foley, who also served with distinction in the anti-Weeks campaign. As a result of the suffragists' efforts, Wolcott was replaced by a prosuffrage senator. See MWSA Quarterly Letter, January, 1913, WRC, folder 671, SL.

103. Members of the nonpartisan committee included MWSA president Alice Stone Blackwell (R); Esther Andrews, organizer for the Jewish Council of Women (R); Blanche Ames, chair of MWSA's Congressional Committee and daughter-in-law of Governor Oliver Ames (R); Theresa Crowley, lawyer and member of BESAGG (D); Mabel Gillespie, secretary of the Women's Trade Union League (D); Grace Johnson, president of BESAGG (Prog.); Florence Perkins, past-president of the Massachusetts Federation of Women's Clubs (R); Mary Mahan, active in Catholic affairs (D); and Wenona O. Pinkham, executive secretary of BESAGG (R). Personnel of the Non-Partisan Campaign Committee, WRC, folder 664, SL.

104. For a list of the bills Weeks voted against, see "Defeat John Weeks," flier, NAWSA Papers, reel 13, LC. The list includes Weeks's votes against a federal income tax, the creation of the Federal Trade Commission, and a rural credits measure.

105. Preparation of the flier is described in Park, *Front Door Lobby*, 214–15. A copy of the flier may be found in WRC, folder 663, SL.

106. For the committee's work with organized labor see Maud Wood Park, Summary of Congressional Work, NAWSA Papers, reel 32, LC; and Grace Johnson to Mary Sleeper, October 23, 1918, NAWSA Papers, reel 13, LC.

107. For a discussion of Jewish support for the anti-Weeks campaign, see Maud Wood Park, Summary of Congressional Work, n.d., NAWSA Papers, reel 32, LC; and Park, *Front Door Lobby*, 229.

108. Grace Allen Johnson to Mary Sleeper, October 23, 1918, NAWSA Papers, reel 13,LC; and circular, "The Murder of McCall," n.d., found in NAWSA Papers, reel 13, LC.

109. Carrie Chapman Catt to Mrs. Charles Sumner Bird, May 31, 1918, WRC, folder 667, SL; Catt to Mrs. Bird, October 1918, WRC, folder 667, SL; and Mrs. Charles Sumner Bird to My Dear Chairman, June 24, 1918, NAWSA Papers, reel 3, LC.

110. Grace Johnson to Mary Sleeper, October 23, 1918, NAWSA Papers, reel 13, LC; and Carrie Chapman Catt to Mrs. Oakes Ames, October 14, 1918, WRC, folder 667, SL.

111. Teresa Crowley to Maud Wood Park, November 6, 1918, WRC, folder 49, SL.

112. Congressional Committee, "Anti-Weeks Campaign," August 14, 1918, WRC, folder 668, SL; "Do You Want to Give Senator Weeks Another Opportunity to Repudiate the Women of Your State?" leaflet, October 16, 1918, NAWSA Papers, reel 13, LC; and Blanche Ames to Maud Wood Park, November 5, 1918, WRC, folder 667, SL.

113. See, e.g., Carrie Chapman Catt to Grace Johnson, November 8, 1918, WRC, folder 667, SL; and Clara Hyde to Mary Gray Peck, November 6, 1918, NAWSA Papers, reel 16, LC.

114. Another factor in Weeks's defeat was the presence of a third contestant in the election, who drew votes away from the Republican senator. The negative publicity generated by the Non-Partisan Committee certainly influenced voters as well, and it was partially responsible for the defeat.

115. Teresa Crowley to Maud Wood Park, November 6, 1918, WRC, folder 49, SL.

116. Park, *Front Door Lobby,* 215–16.

117. Carrie Chapman Catt to Maud Wood Park, April 18, 1933, Catt Papers, reel 5, LC.

118. Carrie Chapman Catt to Maud Wood Park, November 23, 1918, Catt Papers, reel 5, LC.

119. Flexner, *Century of Struggle,* 326–27. The "Unholy Alliance" is discussed in Maud Wood Park to Congressional Chairmen, October 5, 1918, NAWSA Papers, reel 49,LC.

120. Carrie Chapman Catt to Maud Wood Park, February 9, 1919, WRC, folder 737, SL.

121. "It will not be difficult for the Devil with pockets lined to pick off a couple or three men in the Senate," Catt confided to Park, "and that would block the procedure for two years more." Catt to Park, February 1, 1919, Catt Papers, reel 5, LC.

122. Ibid.

123. See, e.g., report of the 28th and 29th annual convention of the Kentucky Equal Rights Association, November 30–December 1, 1919, Breckenridge Family Papers, box 704, LC; report of the KERA Congressional Committee, March 11–12, 1919, Breckenridge Family Papers, box 704, LC; and Carrie Chapman Catt to Maud Wood Park, January 15, 1919, Catt Papers, reel 5, LC

124. Press release, Kentucky Equal Rights Association, January 16, 1919, Breckenridge Family Papers, box 704, LC.

125. Catt and Shuler, *Woman Suffrage and Politics,* 339.

126. Carrie Chapman Catt to Maud Wood Park, November, 1918, Catt Papers, reel 5, LC.

127. Carrie Chapman Catt to Maud Wood Park, [no month or day] 1918, Catt Papers, reel 5, LC.

128. For the entire text of this amendment (SJ Res. 223), see *Congressional Record,* 65th Cong., 3d sess., February 12–24, 1919, vol. 57, pt. 4, p. 3542.

129. Gay's amendment, SJ Res 224, was introduced on February 18, 1919, and referred to the Committee on Woman Suffrage. For a copy of this amendment, see *Congressional Record,* 65th Cong., 3d sess., February 12–24, 1919, vol. 57., pt. 4, p. 3636. See also Catt and Shuler, *Woman Suffrage and Politics,* 335–37.

130. The second resolution (SJ Res. 226), introduced by Senator Kenneth McKellar on February 20, 1919, may be found in the *Congressional Record,* 65th Cong., 3d sess., February 12–24, 1919, vol. 57, pt. 4, p. 3823. For the failure of the Front Door Lobby to endorse these measures, see Carrie Chapman Catt to Maud Wood Park, March 1, 1919, Catt Papers, reel 5, LC, in which Catt states: "I think it was right for you to turn down the offer of further concessions. Gay's promise to vote for a new measure was altogether too small a concession to give us much encouragement that any kind of concession can meet the demands of the south. The whole incident seems to indicate that the attitude of the

South is not states' rights, or negroes, or anything else, but shere [*sic*] opposition to woman suffrage."

131. Carrie Chapman Catt to Ruth White, July 11, 1918, Suffrage Collection, box 4, folder 29, SS.

132. Since the measure was never reported out of committee, the text of the resolution was not recorded in the *Congressional Record, Senate Documents,* or various Woman Suffrage Committee reports and publications.

133. Carrie Chapman Catt to Maud Wood Park, March 1, 1919, Catt Papers, reel 5, LC.

134. *Woman Citizen,* April 5, 1919, 940.

135. Ibid.

136. See Catt and Shuler, *Woman Suffrage and Politics,* 335.

137. The House vote of May 21, 1919, was 304 to 89. Two hundred Republicans supported the measure, with 19 voting against it; 102 Democrats favored it with 70 opposed. Additionally, one Prohibitionist and one Independent voted aye. See Carrie Chapman Catt to Congressional Chairmen, NAWSA Papers, reel 49, LC, for a breakdown of the House vote. For a brief description of the event, see also Catt and Shuler, *Woman Suffrage and Politics,* 340–41.

138. Park, *Front Door Lobby,* 259.

139. One Democratic leader was disgusted at the Democrats who objected in debate to the federal amendment, stating to Mary Garrett Hay that "the party had buried itself by the actions of the 65th Congress and that its representatives dug a deeper grave for it today by their speeches." Clara Hyde to Mary Gray Peck, June 5, 1919, NAWSA Papers, reel 16, LC.

140. Park, *Front Door Lobby,* 212.

141. Ibid., 266–67.

142. Clara Hyde to Mary Gray Peck, June 5, 1919, NAWSA Papers, reel 16, LC.

Chapter 7. Ratification

1. Carrie Chapman Catt, Bulletin 10, April 3, 1918; and tentative agenda of the Executive Council, Indianapolis, April 18–19, 1918, McCallum Papers, box 9, file 3, AHC.

2. Carrie Chapman Catt, Bulletin 13, May 22, 1918; and Mrs. Henry Wade Rogers, Bulletin 15, June 3, 1918, both in Breckenridge Family Papers, box 703, LC.

3. Carrie Chapman Catt, Bulletin 27, October 8, 1918, Breckenridge Family Papers, box 703, LC.

4. Carrie Chapman Catt, Bulletin 11, April 3, 1918, Breckenridge Family Papers, box 704, LC. See also plans for ratification, n.d., Breckenridge Family Papers, box 703, LC.

5. Mrs. Henry Wade Rogers, Bulletin 15, June 3, 1918, Breckenridge Family Papers, box 703, LC.

6. Carrie Chapman Catt to Maud Wood Park, June 17, 1919, NAWSA Papers, reel 15, LC.

7. Carrie Chapman Catt to Maud Wood Park, June 24, 1919, Catt Papers, reel 5, LC.

8. Carrie Chapman Catt, Bulletin 33, November 18, 1918, Breckenridge Family

Papers, box 703, LC. Among the ten states that would require strenuous efforts, Catt listed Connecticut and Tennessee. Both of these states failed to ratify in 1919; Tennessee was the last state to approve the amendment, and Connecticut did not ratify it until after the federal amendment had been signed by the secretary of state in August 1920.

9. Nettie Rogers Shuler to State Presidents, October 4, 1919, Breckenridge Family Papers, box 690, LC. The states that comprised the delegation to NAWSA in March 1919, were: Georgia, Texas, Alabama, Florida, South Carolina, Virginia, North Carolina, Maryland, Mississippi, Kentucky, Louisiana, Tennessee, and West Virginia. Of these, only Tennessee, Texas, Kentucky, and West Virginia eventually ratified the federal amendment.

10. Nettie Rogers Shuler to State Presidents, October 4, 1919, Breckenridge Family Papers, box 690, LC. The NAWSA Executive Board clearly had little hope of southern ratification. In Virginia and Texas, however, where state leaders had maintained close contact with the parent organization, NAWSA leaders hoped for a last-minute miracle; consequently, NAWSA continued to send these two state associations money, organizers, and support during their bids for ratification.

11. Members of the two commissions were chosen for their political affiliations and influence. Mrs. John Glover Smith and Marjorie Shuler, Republicans, were sent to the Northwest to visit GOP governors, while Minnie Fisher Cunningham and Mrs. Ben Hooper, Democrats, visited the southwestern states that voted that ticket. Carrie Chapman Catt, Bulletin 78, September 10, 1919, Breckenridge Family Papers, box 704, LC; and Carrie Chapman Catt to Katharine Ludington (confidential), August 5, 1919, NAWSA Papers, reel 32, LC.

12. Carrie Chapman Catt, Bulletin 78, September 10, 1919, Breckenridge Family Papers, box 704, LC. See also Peck, *Carrie Chapman Catt,* 317; and Carrie Chapman Catt to Katharine Ludington, August 5, 1919, NAWSA Papers, reel 32, LC. Catt's letter to Ludington continues: "The situation of each of these is pretty bad, but I believe that when we get up to the point where we need only two more ratifications, the legislatures of Connecticut and Vermont can be asked to petition the Governors and that if they hesitate now, they will not do so then."

13. Massachusetts, the eighth state to ratify, passed the amendment on June 25, 1919. Members of the Cambridge Council of 100 may be found on the MWSA letterhead, May 1919, WRC, folder 112, SL.

14. Peck, *Carrie Chapman Catt,* 317.

15. State referenda were a constant problem for NAWSA executives. As early as November 1917, when Massachusetts asked for assistance in a campaign for presidential suffrage, Catt convinced state activists to redirect their efforts to the federal amendment. See Carrie Chapman Catt to Grace Johnson, November 19, 1917, Catt Papers, reel 4, LC.

16. Carrie Chapman Catt to Congressional District Chairmen of the Arkansas Equal Suffrage Central Committee, January 9, 1919, NAWSA Papers, reel 2, LC.

17. Carrie Chapman Catt to State Presidents, January 11, 1919, NAWSA Papers, reel 17, LC. See also Carrie Chapman Catt to Maud Wood Park, January 16, 1919, NAWSA Papers, reel 15, LC.

18. See, e.g., Carrie Chapman Catt to Madeline McDowell Breckenridge, December 15, 1919, and Breckenridge to Catt, December 20, 1919, Breckenridge Family Papers, box 691, LC.

19. Carrie Chapman Catt to Minnie Fisher Cunningham, January 23, 1919, McCallum Papers, box 9, file 1, AHC. See also Emma Winner Rogers to Jessie Daniel Ames, January 28, 1919, McCallum Papers, box 19, file 4, AHC.

20. Nettie R. Shuler to Mrs. Nonnie B. Mahoney, January 23, 1919; and Carrie Chapman Catt to Minnie Fisher Cunningham, January 23, 1919, both in McCallum Papers, box 9, file 1, AHC.

21. Carrie Chapman Catt to Minnie Fisher Cunningham, January 23, 1919; and report of Finance Committee, TESA, submission campaign fund, March 1–June 12, 1919, both in McCallum Papers, box 9, file 1, AHC. According to the Finance Committee's calculations, Texas suffragists spent in excess of $9,000 on the May referendum and the ratification campaign together. Given that Catt had estimated that $40,000 was needed for "difficult states," one of which was Texas, the Texas activists fell some $31,000 short of Catt's goal. That the women managed to ratify the federal amendment in June 1919 was therefore an extraordinary accomplishment.

22. Minnie Fisher Cunningham to Dear Suffragist, May 5, 1919; and Cunningham to Carrie Chapman Catt, May 5, 1919, both in McCallum Papers, box 3, files 1 and 2, AHC. See also "Outline of Campaign for Carrying the Suffrage Amendment at the Special Election on May 24, 1919," pamphlet, McCallum Papers, box 3, file 2, AHC.

23. Oscar A. Seward to Jessie Daniel Ames, May 10, 1919, McCallum Papers, box 19, file 4, AHC.

24. Minnie Fisher Cunningham to Dear Suffragist, May 17, 1919, McCallum Papers, box 3, file 1, AHC.

25. Plan of organization, Texas Association Opposed to Woman Suffrage, April 1916, McCallum Papers, box 20, file 3, AHC.

26. Wells's letter is quoted at length in Minnie Fisher Cunningham to County Chairmen of the Democratic Party in Texas, May 17, 1919, McCallum Papers, box 3, file 1, AHC.

27. Flier sent to Senator R. W. Dudley, March 26, 1919, found in McCallum Papers, box 9, file 4, AHC. The envelope that brought the material to Senator Dudley bore the return address of Mrs. Martin Lee Calhoun, Selma, Alabama, but upon investigation TESA members discovered that no such person existed. Similar material from the mysterious Mrs. Calhoun can be found in the Adele Clark Papers, VCU, and in the Breckenridge Family Papers, LC.

28. Circular, no title or date, found in McCallum Papers, box 9, file 4, AHC.

29. The totals were: 141,773 for and 166,893 votes against the state amendment.

30. Cunningham to Dear Suffragist, June 5, 1919, McCallum Papers, box 3, file 1, AHC.

31. Mrs. M. Lee Adams to Jessie D. Ames, May 31, 1919; and Jessie D. Ames to Miss Eleanor Brackenridge, June 7, 1919, both in McCallum Papers, box 19, file 2, AHC.

32. Rose Young, press release, July 31, 1919, McCallum Papers, box 9, file 3, AHC. Young quotes University of Texas professor Caswell Ellis on the German opposition: "Comal and Gillespie Counties, composed practically entirely of Germans, gave only 128 votes for the Suffrage-Alien Amendment and 1,3396 [*sic*] against it; that is over ten to one against. If we would see how the German vote went, take a box which is all German; for

instance, in Travis County the voting box at Germania Hall stood 41 against and 1 for the Amendment."

33. Carrie Chapman Catt to Minnie Fisher Cunningham, June 9, 1919; and Cunningham to Catt, June 14, 1919, McCallum Papers, box 3, file 2, AHC.

34. For an excellent description of the impeachment of Ferguson and its ramifications in regard to the suffrage movement, see Gould, *Progressives and Prohibitionists*, chaps. 7 and 8, and 254–57.

35. Texas Legislature, *Texas House Journal*, 36th Legislature, Second Called Session, June 24, 1919.

36. Mrs. E. B. (Vernice) Reppert to Minnie Fisher Cunningham, June 7, 1919; and Cunningham to Reppert, June 17, 1919, both in McCallum Papers, box 3, file 4, AHC.

37. Jane Y. McCallum, untitled notes on the Ratification Campaign, n.d., found in McCallum Papers, box 3, file 7, AHC; and Minnie Fisher Cunningham to Carrie Chapman Catt, July 2, 1919, McCallum Papers, box 3, file 9, AHC.

38. Ibid. For a discussion of Ferguson's efforts to attack the primary law, see Carrie Chapman Catt to Presidents of States Which Have Ratified the Federal Suffrage Amendment, October 8, 1919, NAWSA Papers, reel 49, LC.

39. For more detail on the Texas suffrage movement, see Taylor, "Woman Suffrage Movement in Texas."

40. See *HWS* 6, 15.

41. Ibid., 144.

42. The best account of the KERA's activities may be found in last annual report of the KERA, March 11, 1919, Breckenridge Family Papers, box 704, LC. Good descriptions of the work done by the three-woman ratification committee are contained in Madeline McDowell Breckenridge to Carrie Chapman Catt, December 31, 1919; Breckenridge to Mrs. Samuel Castleman, December 15, 1919; and Breckenridge to Catt, December 15, 1919, all in Breckenridge Family Papers, box 691, LC. For Laura Clay's work see KERA last annual report, cited above, and Fuller, *Laura Clay*, 153–61.

43. "1918 Oklahoma," anonymous report of the Oklahoma campaign, NAWSA Papers, reel 49, LC.

44. Aloysius Larch-Miller to Dear One, n.d., NAWSA Papers, reel 14, LC. Larch-Miller, one of the few advocates of the federal amendment, expressed her anguish tersely: "I am sick — heart sick."

45. Marjorie Shuler, report on the Oklahoma Special Session, n.d., NAWSA Papers, reel 14, LC; and NAWSA press release, September 8, 1919, NAWSA Papers, reel 49, LC.

46. Marjorie Shuler, report on the Oklahoma Special Session, NAWSA Papers, reel 14, LC; and Marjorie Shuler to Carrie Chapman Catt, October 13, 1919, NAWSA Papers, reel 14, LC.

47. Aloysius Larch-Miller to Dear One, n.d., NAWSA Papers, reel 14, LC.

48. Clipping from the *Shawnee (Okla.) Daily News*, January 17, 1920, found in Aloysius Larch-Miller to Nettie Shuler, January 18, 1920, NAWSA Papers, reel 14, LC.

49. "Capitol Flag at Half Mast for Girl Suffragist," clipping, *Oklahoma City Times*, February 2, 1920, found in NAWSA Papers, reel 14, LC. Among the other suffrage casualties of the deadly influenza epidemic of 1918–19 that took thousands of lives nationwide was NAWSA pioneer Anna Howard Shaw. Shaw's war work took her to

crowded troop trains and other sites; disregarding the government warnings to avoid crowded areas, she contracted the virus and died at her home in New York, attended by her lifelong companion Lucy Anthony.

50. Minnie Fisher Cunningham to Senator Robert L. Owen, February 2, 1920, NAWSA Papers, reel 14, LC.

51. In truth, Robertson's conversion had another, less altruistic, source. Rumors circulated that U.S. Indian commissioner and influential Democrat Cato Sells had informed Robertson that "the candidacy of Senator Owen for the Democratic nomination for president would fall upon cold ears in the national committee until the governor did something for the women of Oklahoma." Robertson and Owen were political allies, and Sells's threat apparently moved the reluctant governor to action. The rumor concerning Cato Sells was reported in a political column by "W.M.H." in the *Daily Oklahoman,* January 11, 1920, clipping found in NAWSA Papers, reel 49, LC.

52. Catt sent telegrams to Senator Thomas P. Gore, Senator Robert Owen, and Representative Scott Ferris on February 25, 1920. Copies may be found in NAWSA Papers, reel 14, LC. In a telegram to Helen Gardener on February 26, 1920, Catt mentioned that Wilson had wired the two Oklahoma legislative leaders, and that Gore and Ferris were in the state as well. Telegram, Catt to Gardener, February 26, 1920, NAWSA Papers, reel 14, LC.

53. Telegrams from Carrie Chapman Catt were sent to these men on February 25, 1920. Copies may be found in NAWSA Papers, reel 14, LC. See also Catt to Mrs. Desha Breckenridge (Ky.), Mrs. Percy Pennybacker (Tex.), Edna Breckenridge (Md.), Mrs. Jessie Daniel Ames (Tex.), and Mrs. George Gellhorn (Mo.), all found in NAWSA Papers, reel 14, LC, asking for home pressure from these states to be directed toward Governor Robertson.

54. Telegram, Katharine Pierce to Nettie Shuler, February 25, 1920, NAWSA Papers, reel 14, LC.

55. One account of the Oklahoma legislative battle may be found in the *St. Louis Post-Dispatch,* February 28, 1920, clipping found in NAWSA Papers, reel 48, LC. The quote is from the *Daily Oklahoman,* January 11, 1920, clipping found in NAWSA Papers, reel 49, LC.

56. Katharine Ludington to Katharine Hepburn, January 21, 1918, NAWSA Papers, reel 34, LC. See also Daphne Selden to Rosamond Danielson, January 8, 1918, NAWSA Papers, reel 35, LC.

57. Instructions for political workers, adopted by the Connecticut Joint Legislative Committee, January 20, 1918, NAWSA Papers, reel 35, LC.

58. Minutes of the CWSA executive board, March 5, 1919, NAWSA Papers, reel 35, LC; and Nichols, *Votes and More for Women,* 18–21. The Connecticut experiment at cooperation was the only such effort made by NAWSA and the NWP. Unfortunately, in most states, longtime NAWSA state societies found themselves confronted by newly established NWP associations that put forward different strategies during the ratification campaign. This led not just to duplication of effort, as is so often cited in histories of the period, but to mass confusion at the legislative level, to wasted time and funds, and, ultimately, to defeat for both groups.

59. Plans for ratification campaign, enclosed in a letter from Daphne Selden to Blanche

Stoutendurgh, May 31, 1919, NAWSA Papers, reel 34, LC. See also Katharine Ludington to Connecticut Suffragists, May 26, 1919; and Mrs. Samuel Russell and Katharine Ludington to Fellow Workers, June 14, 1919, both in NAWSA Papers, reel 35, LC. The efforts of the CWSA to lobby legislators is detailed in Report of the CWSA, 1919–20, by executive secretary Ruth Dadourian, NAWSA Papers, reel 34, LC.

60. The machine controlled the Connecticut senate, and it maintained an influential minority in the house. In 1919, for example, it defeated bills to protect women and children, to shorten the work week, to restrict child labor, and to create a minimum wage commission. Moreover, the machine voted favorably on legislation that enlarged the powers of the Connecticut Light and Power Company, a company in which machine boss Roraback held a financial interest. "The Republican Machine in 1919–1920," compiled by CWSA, n.d., NAWSA Papers, reel 34, LC. See also Nichols, *Votes and More for Women,* 30–31.

61. Nichols, *Votes and More for Women,* 32–33.

62. Plans for campaign, included in Mary Elizabeth Hutt to Rosamond Danielson, April 20, 1920, NAWSA Papers, reel 34, LC.

63. Report of CWSA, 1919–1920, by executive secretary Ruth Dadourian, NAWSA Papers, reel 34, LC; statement of Republican suffragists, n.d., signed by Mrs. Willis Austin and ten others, NAWSA Papers, reel 34, LC; and Ruth Dadourian to Rosamond Danielson, July 1, 1920, NAWSA Papers, reel 35, LC.

64. In spite of the exertions of the CWSA, Connecticut did not ratify the federal amendment until September 14, 1920, almost a month after the amendment was ratified by Tennessee.

65. Carrie Chapman Catt to Mary Gray Peck, March 28, 1920, Catt Papers, reel 5, LC

66. For a good discussion of the Republican Party's efforts to capitalize on the woman suffrage amendment to the discomfort of the Democrats, see Morgan, *Suffragists and Democrats,* 148–49.

67. Quoted in Peck, *Carrie Chapman Catt,* 328–29.

68. Ibid., 331.

69. For a good discussion of the difficulties facing suffragists in Tennessee, see Peck, *Carrie Chapman Catt,* 329–31; and Park, *Front Door Lobby,* 275–76.

70. Sue Sheldon White to Alice Paul, July 3, 1920, NAWSA Papers, reel 35, LC. Sue Sheldon White was one of the few suffragists who had maintained contact with NAWSA after joining the National Woman's Party. Although she tried to remain on friendly terms with NAWSA officials, Catt and others refused to trust her completely.

71. See Flexner, *Century of Struggle,* 334, for a clear discussion of the Justice Department decision. Gardener's and Wilson's actions are recounted in Park, *Front Door Lobby,* 275–76.

72. In addition to NAWSA and the antisuffragist organizations, the National Woman's Party sent lobbyists to Nashville for ratification. For a description of NWP activity, see Louis, "Sue Shelton White."

73. Peck, *Carrie Chapman Catt,* 331. For a good description of Laura Clay's activities and perspective, see Fuller, *Laura Clay,* 160–61.

74. Speech by Mrs. Guilford Dudley, May 16, 1941, Catt Papers, reel 9, LC.

75. Peck, *Carrie Chapman Catt,* 334–36.

76. Carrie Chapman Catt to Mary Gray Peck, August 15, 1920, Catt Papers, reel 5, LC.

77. Mrs. James Pinckard to Carrie Chapman Catt, July 23, 1920, NAWSA Papers, reel 16, LC.

78. Peck, *Carrie Chapman Catt,* 332. See also handbill, printed by the Selma, Alabama, United Daughters of the Confederacy, Chapter 53, July 7, 1919, found in Laura Clay Papers, box 11, University of Kentucky Library. In *The History of Woman Suffrage,* Ida Husted Harper had mentioned that Lee's daughter, Annie Custis Lee, had died homeless because of her love for the Union. The UDC regarded this statement as a "most unwarranted, false and malicious attack [on] the character of Robert E. Lee, the sacredness and sanctity of his home invaded, and his family maligned." The offending passage is found in *HWS* 2, 23.

79. Peck, *Carrie Chapman Catt,* 332.

80. The best account of the dramatic contest in the Tennessee House of Representatives is found in Catt and Shuler, *Woman Suffrage and Politics,* 444–49. See also Flexner, *Century of Struggle,* 336–37; and Morgan, *Suffragists and Democrats,* 148–51.

81. Speaker Walker inadvertently aided the suffragists by changing his vote to aye to permit reconsideration. The Tennessee legislature traditionally considered a majority of the house to be fifty, since the total membership stood at ninety-nine. Because the suffrage amendment passed by a technical majority of forty-nine out of the ninety-six members present, Walker's vote made the final count fifty in favor of ratification. House rules provided that an amendment must be reconsidered within three days, and thanks to Walker's ill-considered vote, antisuffragists were unable to secure a majority for reconsideration. In desperation, Walker led a band of thirty-eight representatives on a flight out of state to prevent a quorum, but suffragists managed to collect a quorum and quash a vote to reconsider. Next the antisuffragists brought an injunction against the governor to prohibit him from forwarding the amendment to Washington for signing by the secretary of state; within days the injunction was also thrown out, and the amendment was rushed to the Capitol, much to the chagrin of the antisuffragists. Morgan, *Suffragists and Democrats,* 151. As for Harry Burn, antisuffragists filed charges of bribery against the young legislator, but he was cleared of any wrongdoing. *Richmond Times-Dispatch,* August 20, 1920, p. 1.

82. Park, *Front Door Lobby,* 276.

83. Peck, *Carrie Chapman Catt,* 341–42.

84. Mira Pittman, "The Woman's Doxology," September 1920, NAWSA Papers, reel 16, LC.

85. Of the ten states that failed to ratify, none was above the Mason-Dixon line. The states that refused to comply were Louisiana, Alabama, Mississippi, Georgia, Florida, North Carolina, South Carolina, Virginia, Delaware, and Maryland.

86. Carrie Chapman Catt to Our Ex-Field Workers, Thanksgiving Day, 1920, Catt Papers, reel 4, LC.

87. Report by Harriet Taylor Upton presented at NAWSA's final convention, n.d., NAWSA Papers, reel 20, LC.

Conclusion

1. NAWSA was not the only suffrage association with a professional lobby and publicity bureau. These innovations had been introduced by Alice Paul as early as 1913, when she served as chairman of NAWSA's Congressional Committee, and they continued to form the backbone of National Woman's Party strategy throughout the last years of the suffrage campaign. Paul's genius for publicity is well documented throughout Lunardini, *From Equal Suffrage to Equal Rights.*

2. Carrie Chapman Catt to Mary Gray Peck, October 23, 1912, Catt Papers, reel 5, LC. The quoted phrase reads in its entirety: "Dear Pan [Catt's nickname for Peck], I am an aristocrat with democratic tendencies, you say, and you regret that I am not a Socialist! Aha, why? The Socialists are too tame and gentle. I'm for Pandemonium let loose! You don't know me. I am only restrained and walking the chalkline to get the vote, and it now looks as if it might be so long deferred that I shall die respectable and my descendants think of me as conservative." In light of Catt's current reputation among some suffrage historians, her words assume a decidedly prophetic connotation.

3. McDonagh, "Issues and Constituencies." McDonagh also makes the point that state-level suffrage was more important than party identification or region in determining whether a House member voted for the woman suffrage amendment.

4. For a thorough discussion of the uses and abuses of the word *feminism,* see Cott, *Grounding of Modern Feminism,* chap. 1. As Cott notes, the word was not used in America until the second decade of the twentieth century, and then only very rarely by NAWSA.

5. The National American Woman Suffrage Association was not the only organization that argued for role equity instead of role change. According to historian Nancy Schrom Dye, the WTUL campaigned for the vote on the basis of role equity and supported such issues as protective legislation, fair wages, and better bargaining power for working women. By the 1920s, the issue of equity versus societal change split what was left of the woman's movement into fragments that would persist for over thirty years. See Dye, *As Equals and As Sisters,* and Cott, *Groundings of Modern Feminism,* chap. 4.

6. There were many other causes for the split between NAWSA and the NWP. One major reason for the lack of cooperation between the two groups lay with leadership: both Paul and Catt were unwilling to share command. The tactical differences over coercion versus persuasion were also important, as were differences in definitions of partisanship. For a clear, if overly favorable, explication of the National Woman's Party's ideology and strategy, see Lunardini, *From Equal Suffrage to Equal Rights,* and Irwin, *Story of Alice Paul.*

7. The Women's Joint Congressional Committee is described in Lemon's excellent book, *Woman Citizen,* 55–57. See also Cott, *Grounding of Modern Feminism,* chap. 3; and Dorothy Johnson, "Organized Women as Lobbyists."

8. Historian Paul Kleppner was the first to explode this myth by demonstrating that turnout declines for women were only slightly greater than for men. See Kleppner, "Were Women to Blame?"

9. A good brief discussion of these and other contributing factors to the decline of the

woman's movement as a political force in the 1920s is Dorothy Johnson, "Organized Women as Lobbyists."

10. It is worth noting that the National Woman's Party, also constructed as a single-issue organization, failed to sustain its pre-1920 membership. When the NWP decided to pursue yet another single issue—the Equal Rights Amendment—to the exclusion of all others, the group's membership fell to an all-time low of about 150 by the mid-twenties. See Cott, *Grounding of Modern Feminism,* 72, for membership statistics, and chap. 2 for discussion of the NWP's strategy in pursuing a legal route to equality and its consequences.

11. Jennings, "Women in Party Politics."

12. Anderson, "Women's Citizenship in the 1920s."

13. See Donald Bruce Johnson, ed., *National Party Platforms,* 213–355, for the national platforms of the two major parties for the elections of 1920–32.

14. Recently, one historian has argued that there was a "domestication of politics" in the late nineteenth and early twentieth century, as women voters entered the male-dominated field of party politics and men took up the female-inspired tactics of pressure politics. When one looks at the near absence of women in party politics and in elected or appointed positions from 1920 until the present day, however, it is difficult to conclude that party politics became "domesticated" or that women took up political roles previously defined as masculine. The exact opposite might be said to have occurred. Party politics remained male dominated, and the suffragists' political innovations were adopted not just by men, but by antireform conservative groups inimical to feminist concerns. For more on the domestication of politics argument, see Baker, "Domestication of Politics," and Baker, *Moral Framework of Public Life.*

15. Merriman and Gosnell, *Non-Voting.*

16. The idea of women's dependency on their husbands for political decision making first appeared in Lazarfeld, Berelson, and Gaudet, *People's Choice,* 48–49, and 141. Jane Jaquette coined the phrase "insufficient masculinization theory," also called the "why can't a woman be more like a man" argument, in her excellent overview of the literature on female voter turnout. See Jaquette, ed. *Women in Politics,* xviii.

17. In the 1960s, for example, when the gap between the numbers of men and women in college narrowed and as women continued to enter the workforce, the gap between men's and women's turnout statistics narrowed proportionately. For a discussion of the effects on turnout by education, age, race, employment, and other factors, see Baxter and Lansing, *Women and Politics,* chap. 6.

18. Lansing, "American Woman," and Baxter and Lansing, *Women and Politics,* chaps. 2 and 3.

19. Baxter and Lansing, *Women and Politics,* 111.

20. Statistics are quoted in Cott, *Grounding of Modern Feminism,* 101.

21. Kleppner, "Were Women to Blame," 621–43.

22. Schattschneider, *Semisovereign People,* 98–99.

23. On the rare occasions when a scholar noted the expansion of the franchise as an important political movement, too often the account took the form of, for example, David Morgan's 1972 book, *Suffragists and Democrats,* which focused primarily on the

political parties' response to woman suffrage. Although Morgan does include some material on NAWSA and the NWP, his perspective is definitely one of the parties' involvement and their eventual success in passing the Nineteenth Amendment.

24. McGerr dates the decline of popular politics from the 1890s, in accordance with what Walter Dean Burnham and others have found to be the beginning of the "fourth party period." Set in motion by the sectional realignment that occurred in 1896, the fourth party period is characterized by a dramatic decline of voter turnout that lasts throughout much of the twentieth century. When one considers the obvious display of popular politics during the suffrage campaign after 1910, however, McGerr's correlation between the supposed death of such political expression and twentieth-century voter decline lacks substance. For a good overview of the party periods, see Chambers, "Party Development," and Burnham, *Current Crisis in American Politics*, 25–57.

25. See McGerr, "Political Style and Women's Power."

26. O'Neill, *Everyone Was Brave*, 269. Also quoted and discussed in Baxter and Lansing, eds. *Women and Politics*, 20.

27. Michael McGerr expands O'Neill's argument to include the suffragists' failure to overcome the tensions between the classes and the races or to continue to experiment with popular politics. Characterizing the suffragists as "victims of their own success," McGerr charitably urges readers to keep the "disappointing outcome of the Nineteenth Amendment" from obscuring the crucial role of the suffrage movement in women's political history. McGerr, "Political Style and Women's Power," 882–85.

28. Feminist scholars, too, have wondered why the ballot seemed to decline in importance just as women gained the franchise. See, e.g., Lebsock, "Women and American Politics."

29. Baker, "Domestication of Politics," 622.

30. See Cott, "Across the Great Divide," 151–54; and McGerr, "Political Style and Women's Power," 855.

31. As I have suggested in the Introduction, the pressure system NAWSA created had the female voluntaristic and benevolent societies of the nineteenth century as one of its many roots, but other influences were equally involved. And although voluntarism was an important influence on the formation of pressure politics, it was a very distant relative to the twentieth-century political system.

32. Historians of the American party system point out that the nineteenth-century parties had four major functions: political education and socialization of voters; policy making; electing candidates and filling offices; and "nation-building" (the amalgamation of regional, ethnocultural, or class interests). A good depiction of the major party functions is Burnham, "Party Systems." For more on the declining power of parties, see Walker, *Mobilizing Interest Groups in America*.

33. Key defined pressure groups as "private associations [which] promote their interests by attempting to influence government rather than by nominating candidates and seeking responsibility for the management of the government." Key, *Politics, Parties and Pressure Groups*, 23. According to Graham K. Wilson, Key's benign views of pressure groups and their lobbyists, who were more helpful than coercive, was shared by many scholars well into the 1950s. Wilson, *Interest Groups in the United States*, 111.

34. Quoted in McKean, *Party and Pressure Politics*, 431.

35. Schattschneider, *Party Government,* 189.

36. Schattschneider, *Semisovereign People,* 35.

37. Schlozman, "Representing Women in Washington," 337.

38. McKean, *Party and Pressure Politics,* 626–28.

39. For more on "the iron law of oligarchy," see Michels, *Political Parties,* chap. 2; Schlozman and Tierney, *Organized Interests and American Democracy,* 133–35; and Kerr, *Organized for Prohibition,* 6–7.

40. Hedrick Smith speculates on the number of congressional lobbyists in *The Power Game,* quoted in Petracca, ed., *Politics of Interests,* 13. For statistics on the composition of pressure groups, see Schlozman and Tierney, *Organized Interests and American Democracy,* 65–68.

41. The repercussions of the rise of pressure groups over the course of the twentieth century is discussed in Hays, "Political Parties and the Community-Society Continuum." Hays describes the parties' loss of vitality and a consequent alienation of their traditional grassroots constituency. Parties slowly began to rely on pressure groups to serve as links between constituents and party officials, defining issues and suggesting policy.

42. For a particularly lucid dissection of the errors of the Equal Rights Amendment (ERA) campaign, see Mansbridge, *Why We Lost the ERA;* and Boles, *Politics of the Equal Rights Amendment.*

43. Hay, for example, was appointed chairman of the New York Republican Party's Women's Division, and although she exerted some influence on party leaders in the period immediately after the suffrage victory, her power waned as her male colleagues learned that women failed to vote in proportion to their numbers. Cunningham continued to be active in the Texas Democratic Party until her death in the 1970s, but aside from an unsuccessful 1944 bid for governor of Texas, she, too, was never granted a position of real authority in party leadership. Cunningham's fifty years of political work remains a fascinating subject; a full-length study of her career would be a vital contribution to the subject of women in twentieth-century politics.

44. Minnie Fisher Cunningham to Jane Y. McCallum, n.d. [probably 1953], McCallum Papers, AHC.

45. Laura Clay to Alice Stone Blackwell, June 9, 1931, NAWSA Papers, reel 5, LC. It is ironic that Clay, a southerner and, by the ratification period, an antisuffragist, corresponded with the New Englander Blackwell until Blackwell's death. This is a good example of the lasting friendships forged within the suffrage movement, despite disagreements over tactics.

Bibliography

Manuscript and Archival Collections

LIBRARY OF CONGRESS, WASHINGTON, D.C.

Susan B. Anthony Papers
Alice Stone Blackwell Papers (microfilm edition)
Madeline McDowell Breckenridge Papers
Sophonisba Breckenridge Papers
Carrie Chapman Catt Papers (microfilm edition)
William Gibbs McAdoo Papers
National American Woman Suffrage Association Papers (microfilm edition)
Maud Wood Park Papers
Joseph P. Tumulty Papers
Woodrow Wilson Papers (microfilm edition)

NATIONAL ARCHIVES, WASHINGTON, D.C.

George Creel Papers

NEW ORLEANS PUBLIC LIBRARY, NEW ORLEANS, LA.

ERA Club Papers (microfilm edition)

AUSTIN TEXAS HISTORY CENTER, AUSTIN

Jane Y. McCallum Papers

KING LIBRARY, UNIVERSITY OF KENTUCKY, LEXINGTON

Laura Clay Papers

TEXAS WOMEN'S UNIVERSITY, DENTON

National Woman's Party Papers (microfilm edition)

SCHLESINGER LIBRARY, RADCLIFFE COLLEGE, CAMBRIDGE, MASS.

Blanche Ames Papers
Lucy Anthony Papers
Caroline Lexow Babcock Papers
Boston Equal Suffrage Association for Good Government Papers
Cambridge Political Equality League Papers
Teresa Crowley Papers
Dillon Collection
Margaret Foley Papers
Helen Hamilton Gardener Papers
Edna Gellhorn Papers
Alice Hamilton Papers
Ida Husted Harper Papers
Inez Haynes Irwin Papers
Grace Johnson Papers
Florence Kitchelt Papers
Harriet Laidlaw Papers
Gertrude Leonard Papers
Florence Luscomb Papers
Alma Lutz Papers
Catharine Waugh McCulloch Papers
Massachusetts Woman Suffrage Association Papers
NAWSA Congressional Committee Papers
New York State Association Opposed to Woman Suffrage Papers
Agnes Ryan Papers
Anna Howard Shaw Papers
Jane Norman Smith Papers
Nellie Nugent Sommerville Papers
Edna Stantial Papers
Doris Stevens Papers
Ella Stewart Papers
Anna Churchill Tillinghast Papers
Harriet Taylor Upton Papers
Sue Sheldon White Papers
Vira Whitehouse Papers
Women's Rights Collection

SOPHIA SMITH LIBRARY, NORTHAMPTON, MASS.

Suffrage Collection

VIRGINIA COMMONWEALTH UNIVERSITY LIBRARY, RICHMOND
Papers of Adele Clark

VIRGINIA HISTORICAL SOCIETY, RICHMOND
Broadside Collection
Adele Clark Papers
Nora Houston Papers
Lila Valentine Papers

VIRGINIA STATE LIBRARY AND ARCHIVES, RICHMOND
Ida Thompson Collection (also called the Suffrage Collection)

Contemporary Sources

Abbott, Lyman. "The Assault on Womanhood." *Outlook* 91 (April 3, 1909): 780–88.
——. "The Profession of Motherhood." *Outlook* 91 (April 10, 1909): 836–40.
——. "The Rights of Man: A Study in Twentieth-Century Problems." *Outlook* 68 (June 8, 1901): 353–55.
——. "Why Women Do Not Wish the Suffrage." *Atlantic Monthly* 92 (September 1903): 289–96.
Anthony, Susan B. "Woman's Half-Century of Evolution." *North American Review* 175 (December 1902): 800–810.
Bax, Emily. *Miss Bax of the Embassy.* Boston: Houghton Mifflin, 1939.
Bernbaum, Ernest, ed. *Anti-Suffrage Essays by Massachusetts Women.* Boston: Forum, 1916.
Blatch, Harriet Stanton, and Alma Lutz. *Challenging Years: The Memoirs of Harriet Stanton Blatch.* New York: G. P. Putnam, 1940.
Bowne, Borden Parker. "Women and Democracy." *North American Review* 191 (April 1910): 527–36.
Brownlow, Louis. *A Passion for Anonymity: The Autobiography of Louis Brownlow.* Chicago: University of Chicago Press, 1958.
Caffey, Francis B. "Suffrage Limitations in the South." *Political Science Quarterly* 20 (March 1905): 52–67.
Catt, Carrie Chapman, and Nettie Rogers Shuler. *Woman Suffrage and Politics.* Seattle: University of Washington Press, 1969.
Chittenden, Alice Hill. "The Counter Influence to Woman Suffrage." *The Independent* 67 (July 29, 1908): 248–49.
Cleveland, Grover. "Would Woman Suffrage Be Unwise?" *Ladies Home Journal* 22 (October 1905): 7–8.
Colvin, Sarah T. *A Rebel in Thought.* New York: Island, 1944.
Congressional Record. 65th Cong., 3d sess., 1919. Vol. 57, pt. 4.
Creel, George. *Rebel at Large: Recollections of Fifty Crowded Years.* New York: G. P. Putnam, 1947.
Croly, Herbert. *Progressive Democracy.* New York: Macmillan, 1915.

Daniels, Josephus. *The Wilson Era: Years of War and After, 1917–1923*. Chapel Hill: University of North Carolina Press, 1946.

Deland, Margaret. "The Change in the Feminine Ideal." *Atlantic Monthly* 105 (March 1910): 297–302.

——. "Margaret versus Bridget." *The Independent* 67 (December 16, 1909): 1394–95.

DuBois, Ellen, ed. *Elizabeth Cady Stanton/Susan B. Anthony Correspondence, Writings and Speeches*. New York: Schocken, 1981.

Duniway, Abigail. *Pathbreaking: An Autobiographical History of the Equal Suffrage Movement in the Pacific Coast States*. Portland: James, Kerns and Abbot, 1914.

Dunne, F. P. "Mr. Dooley on Woman's Suffrage." *American Magazine* 68 (June 1909): 198–200.

Eastman, Crystal. *On Women and Revolution*. Oxford: Oxford University Press, 1978.

Frothingham, O. B. "The Real Case of the 'Remonstrants' against Woman Suffrage." *Arena* 2 (July 1890): 177.

Fry, Amelia. "Conversations with Alice Paul." Transcript of interview conducted by Fry. Berkeley, Calif.: Regional Oral History Office, 1976.

Goodwin, Grace. "The Non-Militant Defenders of the Home." *Good Housekeeping* 55 (July 1912): 75–80.

Harper, Ida Husted. *The Life and Work of Susan B. Anthony*. 3 vols. Indianapolis: Hollenbeck, 1908.

——. "Why Women Cannot Vote in the United States." *North American Review* 179 (July 1904): 30–41.

The History of Woman Suffrage, vol. 1, ed. Elizabeth Cady Stanton, Susan B. Anthony, and Matilda Joselyn Gage, 1881; vol. 2, ed. Stanton, Anthony, and Gage, 1882; vol. 3, ed. Stanton, Anthony, and Gage, 1886; vol. 4, ed. Anthony and Ida Husted Harper, 1902; vol. 5, ed. Harper, 1922; vol. 6, ed. Harper, 1922. Rpt. New York: Arno, 1969.

Houston, David. *Eight Years with Wilson's Cabinet, 1913–1920*. 2 vols. Garden City, N.Y.: Doubleday, Page, 1926.

Howe, Julia Ward. "The Case for Woman Suffrage." *Outlook* 91 (April 3, 1909): 780–88.

Irwin, Inez Haynes. *Angels and Amazons: A Hundred Years of American Women*. Garden City, N.Y.: Doubleday, Doran, 1933.

——. *The Story of Alice Paul and the National Woman's Party*. Fairfax, Va.: Denlinger's, 1977.

James, Edward T., and Janet W. James, eds. *Notable American Women*, vol. 2. Cambridge: Harvard University Press, 1971.

Johnson, Donald Bruce, ed. *National Party Platforms*, vol. 1. Rev. ed. Urbana: University of Illinois Press, 1978.

Katzenstein, Caroline. *Lifting the Curtain: The State and National Woman Suffrage Campaigns in Pennsylvania as I Saw Them*. Philadelphia: Dorrance, 1955.

Kelley, Florence. "The Home and the New Woman." *Outlook* 93 (October 16, 1909): 363.

Lawrence, David. *The True Story of Woodrow Wilson*. New York: George H. Doran, 1924.

Leonard, Priscilla. "The Idea of Equality for Men and Women." *Harper's Bazaar* 43 (May 1909): 525–26.

———. "The Ladies' Battle." *Current Literature* 36 (April 1904): 386–89.

McAdoo, William Gibbs. *Crowded Years*. Boston: Houghton Mifflin, 1931.

McCracken, Elizabeth. "Woman Suffrage in the Tenements." *Atlantic Monthly* 96 (December 1905): 750–59.

———. *The Women of America*. New York: Macmillan, 1903.

———. "The Women of America: Woman Suffrage in Colorado." *Outlook* 75 (November 28, 1903): 737–44.

Marden, Orison Swett. *Woman and Home*. New York: Thomas Y. Crowell, 1915.

Martin, I. T. "Concerning Some Anti-Suffragist Leaders." *Good Housekeeping* 55 (July 1912): 75–80.

Meyer, Annie Nathan. "Women's Assumption of Sex Superiority." *North Atlantic Review* 178 (January 1904): 107–10.

National American Woman Suffrage Association. *Victory: How Women Won It*. New York: H. W. Wilson, 1940.

Owen, Harold. *Woman Adrift*. New York: Dutton, n.d.

Pankhurst, E. Sylvia. *The Suffragette: The History of the Women's Militant' Suffrage Movement, 1905–1910*. New York: Sturgis and Walton, 1912.

Park, Maud Wood. *Front Door Lobby*. Boston: Beacon, 1960.

Peck, Mary Gray. *Carrie Chapman Catt, A Biography*. New York: H. W. Wilson, 1944.

———. *The Rise of the Woman Suffrage Party*. Woman and Government Series, ed. Myra Hartshorn, ser. V-H. Chicago: Saul Brothers, 1911.

Phelps, Edith M., ed. *Selected Articles on Woman Suffrage*. Debaters Handbook Series. Minneapolis: H. W. Wilson, 1912.

Scott, Mrs. William Forse. "Women's Relation to Government." *North American Review* 19 (April 1910): 549–58.

Seawell, Molly E. *The Ladies Battle*. New York: Macmillan, 1911.

Senate Committee on the District of Columbia. *Women's Suffrage and the Police: Three Senate Documents*. New York: Arno Press and the *New York Times*, 1971.

Shaw, Anna Howard. *The Story of a Pioneer*. New York: Harper and Brothers, 1928.

Stanton, Elizabeth Cady. *Eighty Years and More: Reminiscences, 1813–1897*. New York: Schocken, 1988.

Stevens, Doris. *Jailed for Freedom*. New York: Boni and Liveright, 1920.

Texas Legislature. *Texas House Journal*. 36th Legislature, Second Called Session, June 24, 1919.

Tibbles, C. E. *Book of Letters: How to Make the Best of Life vs. Woman Suffrage*. Published privately by the author, 1912.

Tucker, Henry St. George. *Woman Suffrage by Constitutional Amendment*. William L. Storrs Lecture Series. New Haven: Yale University Press, 1916.

Young, Rose. *The Record of the Leslie Woman Suffrage Commission, Inc., 1917–1929*. New York: Leslie Woman Suffrage Commission, 1929.

Secondary Sources

Adams, Mildred. *The Right to Be People*. Philadelphia: J. B. Lippincott, 1967.

Alexander, Adele Logan. "Grandmother, Grandfather, W. E. B. Du Bois and Booker T. Washington." *The Crisis* (February 1983), 8–11.

———. "How I Discovered My Grandmother and the Truth about Black Women and the Suffrage Movement." *MS Magazine* (November 1983), 29–35.

Altheide, David L., and John M. Johnson. *Bureaucratic Propaganda.* Boston: Allyn and Bacon, 1980.

Alpern, Sara, and Dale Baum. "Female Ballots: The Impact of the Nineteenth Amendment." *Journal of Interdisciplinary History* 16 (summer 1985): 43–67.

Andersen, Kristi. "Women and Citizenship in the 1920s." Pages 177–98 in *Women, Politics and Change,* ed. Louise Tilly and Patricia Gurin. New York: Russell Sage Foundation, 1990.

Anderson, Katharyn L. "Practical Political Equality for Women: Anne Martin's Campaigns for the U.S. Senate in Nevada in 1918 and 1920." Ph.D. diss., University of Washington, 1978.

Aptheker, Bettina. *Woman's Legacy: Essays on Race, Sex, and Class in American History.* Amherst: University of Massachusetts Press, 1982.

Arendale, Marirose. "Tennessee and Women's Rights." *Tennessee Historical Quarterly* 39 (spring 1980): 62–78.

Aronoff, Craig E., and Otis W. Baskin. *Public Relations: The Profession and the Practice.* New York: West Publishing, 1983.

Baker, Paula. "The Domestication of Politics: Women and American Political Society, 1780–1920." *American Historical Review* 89 (June 1984): 620–47.

———. *The Moral Frameworks of Public Life: Gender, Politics, and the State in Rural New York, 1870–1930.* New York: Oxford University Press, 1991.

Baxter, Sandra, and Marjorie Lansing. *Women and Politics: The Visible Majority.* Rev. ed. Ann Arbor: University of Michigan Press, 1983.

Becker, Susan. *The Origins of the ERA: American Feminism between the Wars.* Westport, Conn.: Greenwood, 1981.

Bernays, Edward L. *Crystallizing Public Opinion.* New York: Boni and Liveright, 1923.

Berry, Jeffery M. *Lobbying for the People: The Political Behavior of Public Interest Groups.* Princeton: Princeton University Press, 1977.

Bland, Sidney R. "Fighting the Odds: Militant Suffragists in South Carolina." *South Carolina Historical Magazine* 82 (January 1981): 32–43.

———. "New Life in an Old Movement: Alice Paul and the Great Suffrage Parade in 1913 in Washington, D.C." *Records of the Columbia Historical Society* 48 (1971–72): 657–78.

Blocker, Jack S. *American Temperance Movements: Cycles of Reform.* Boston: Twayne, 1989.

———. *Retreat from Reform: The Prohibition Movement in the United States, 1890–1913.* Westport, Conn.: Greenwood, 1976.

Blum, John Morton. *Joe Tumulty and the Wilson Era.* Boston: Houghton Mifflin, 1951.

Breen, J. William. *Uncle Sam at Home: Civilian Mobilization, Wartime Federalism and the Council of National Defense, 1917–1919.* Westport, Conn.: Greenwood, 1984.

Buechler, Steven M. *The Transformation of the Woman Suffrage Movement: The Case of Illinois, 1850–1920.* New Brunswick, N.J.: Rutgers University Press, 1986.

Buhle, Mary Jo. *Women and American Socialism, 1870–1920.* Urbana: University of Illinois Press, 1983.

Buhle, Mary Jo, and Paul Buhle. *The Concise History of Woman Suffrage.* Urbana: University of Illinois Press, 1978.

Burnham, Walter Dean. *The Current Crisis in American Politics.* New York: Oxford University Press, 1982.

———. "Party Systems and the Political Process." Pages 277–307 in *The American Party Systems: Stages in Political Development,* ed. William Chambers and Walter Dean Burnham.. New York: Oxford University Press, 1967.

Camhi, Jane Jerome. "Women against Women: American Anti-Suffragism, 1880–1920." Ph.D. diss., Tufts University, 1973.

Campbell, Barbara Kuhn. *The Liberated Woman of 1914: Prominent Women in the Progressive Era.* Studies in American History and Culture, no. 6. New York: UMI Research, 1979.

Caruso, Virginia Ann P. "A History of Woman Suffrage in Michigan." Ph.D. diss., Michigan State University, 1986.

Chambers, William. "Party Development and the American Mainstream." Pages 3–32 in *The American Party Systems: Stages in Political Development,* ed. William Chambers and Walter Dean Burnham. New York: Oxford University Press, 1967.

Chambers, William, and Walter Dean Burnham, eds. *The American Party Systems: Stages in Political Development.* New York: Oxford University Press, 1967.

Claggett, William. "The Life Cycle and Generational Models of Development of Partisanship: A Test Based on the Delayed Enfranchisement of Women." *Social Science Quarterly* 60 (March 1980): 643–50.

Claus, Ruth Freeman. "Militancy in the English and American Woman Suffrage Movements." Ph.D. diss., Yale University, 1975.

Coleman, Elizabeth D. "Penwoman of Virginia's Feminists." *Virginia Cavalcade* 6 (winter 1956): 8–11.

Coleman, Willie. "Keeping the Faith and Disturbing the Peace: Black Women from Anti-Slavery to Women Suffrage." Ph.D. diss., University of California at Irvine, 1982.

Costain, Anne. "Social Movements as Interest Groups: The Case of the Woman's Movement." Pages 285–307 in *The Politics of Interest: Interest Groups Transformed,* ed. Mark P. Petracca. Boulder, Colo.: Westview, 1992.

Cott, Nancy F. "Across the Great Divide: Women in Politics before and after 1920." Pages 153–77 in *Women, Politics and Change,* ed. Louise Tilly and Patricia Gurin. New York: Russell Sage Foundation, 1990.

———. "Feminist Politics in the 1920s: The National Woman's Party." *Journal of American History* 71 (June 1984): 43–68.

———. *The Grounding of Modern Feminism.* New Haven: Yale University Press, 1987.

———. "What's in a Name? The Limits of 'Social Feminism': or, Expanding the Vocabulary of Women's History." *Journal of American History* 76 (December 1989): 809–29.

Davis, Allen F. *American Heroine: The Life and Legend of Jane Addams.* London: Oxford University Press, 1973.

Degler, Carl. *At Odds: Women and the Family in America from the Revolution to the Present.* Oxford: Oxford University Press, 1980.

DuBois, Ellen. *Feminism and Suffrage: The Emergence of an Independent Women's Movement in America, 1848–1869.* Ithaca: Cornell University Press, 1978.

———. "Making Women's History: Activist Historians of Women's Rights, 1880–1940. *Radical History Review* 49 (winter 1991): 61–84.

———. "Working Women, Class Relations, and Suffrage Militance: Harriet Stanton Blatch and the New York Woman Suffrage Movement, 1894–1909." *Journal of American History* 74 (June 1987): 34–58.

Dye, Nancy Schrom. *As Equals and as Sisters: Feminism, the Labor Movement, and the Women's Trade Union League.* Columbia: University of Missouri Press, 1980.

Earhart, Mary. *Frances Willard: From Prayers to Politics.* Chicago: University of Chicago Press, 1944.

Epstein, Barbara Leslie. *The Politics of Domesticity: Women, Evangelism and Temperance in Nineteenth-Century America.* Middletown, Conn.: Wesleyan University Press, 1981.

Evans, Richard J. *The Feminists: Women's Emancipation Movements in Europe, America and Australia, 1840–1920.* Totowa, N.J.: Barnes and Noble, 1977.

Faber, Doris. *Petticoat Politics: How American Women Won the Right to Vote.* New York: Lothrop, Lee and Shepard, 1967.

Filene, Peter. "An Obituary for 'The Progressive Movement.'" *American Quarterly* (spring 1970): 20–34.

Fishbein, Leslie. *Rebels in Bohemia: The Radicals of The Masses, 1911–1917.* Chapel Hill: University of North Carolina Press, 1982.

Flexner, Eleanor. *Century of Struggle: The Woman's Rights Movement in the United States.* Cambridge: Harvard University Press, 1959.

Fowler, Robert Booth. *Carrie Catt: Feminist Politician.* Boston: Northeastern University Press, 1986.

Frankel, Noralee, and Nancy S. Dye, eds. *Gender, Class, Race and Reform in the Progressive Era.* Lexington: University of Kentucky Press, 1991.

Friedl, Bettina. *On to Victory: Propaganda Plays of the Woman Suffrage Movement.* Boston: Northeastern University Press, 1987.

Fuller, Paul. *Laura Clay and the Woman's Rights Movement.* Lexington: University Press of Kentucky, 1975.

Gallagher, Robert. "The Fight for Women's Suffrage: An Interview with Alice Paul," Pages 182–201 in *Historical Viewpoints,* vol. 3, ed. John Garraty. 3d ed. New York: Harper and Row, 1978.

———. "I Was Arrested, of Course . . . ." *American Heritage* 25 (February 1974): 16–24.

Gammage, Judie W. "Quest for Equality: An Historical Overview of Women's Rights in Texas, 1890–1975." Ph.D. diss., North Texas State University, 1982.

Ginzberg, Lori D. *Women and the Work of Benevolence: Morality, Politics, and Class in the Nineteenth-Century United States.* New Haven: Yale University Press, 1990.

Gluck, Sherna. *From Parlor to Prison: Five American Suffragists Talk about Their Lives.* New York: Vintage Books, 1976.

Goldmark, Josephine. *Impatient Crusader: Florence Kelley's Life Story.* Urbana: University of Illinois Press, 1953.

Gordon, Felice. *After Winning: The Legacy of the New Jersey Suffragists, 1920–1947.* New Brunswick, N.J.: Rutgers University Press, 1986.

Gould, Lewis L. *Progressives and Prohibitionists: Texas Democrats in the Wilson Era.* Austin: University of Texas Press, 1973.

Graham, Sara Hunter. "Woman Suffrage in Virginia: The Equal Suffrage League and Pressure Group Politics, 1909–1920." *Virginia Magazine of History and Biography* 101 (April 1993): 227–50.

———. "Woodrow Wilson, Alice Paul and the Woman Suffrage Movement." *Political Science Quarterly* 98 (Winter 1983–1984): 665–79.

Greenstone, J. David, ed. *Public Values and Private Power in American Politics.* Chicago: University of Chicago Press, 1982.

Grimes, Alan P. *The Puritan Ethic and Woman Suffrage.* New York: Oxford University Press, 1967.

Hall, Jacquelyn Dowd. *Revolt against Chivalry: Jessie Daniel Ames and the Women's Campaign against Lynching.* New York: Columbia University Press, 1979.

Hay, Melba. "Madeline McDowell Breckenridge: Kentucky Suffragist and Progressive Reformer." Ph.D. diss., University of Kentucky, 1980.

Hays, Samuel P. "Political Parties and the Community-Society Continuum." Pages 152–81 in *The American Party System,* ed. William Chambers and Walter Dean Burnham. New York: Oxford University Press, 1967.

Higginbotham, Evelyn B. "In Politics to Stay: Black Women Leaders and Party Politics in the 1920s." Pages 199–220 in *Women, Politics and Change,* ed. Louise Tilly and Patricia Gurin. New York: Russell Sage Foundation, 1990.

Hobsbawm, Eric and Terence Ranger, eds. *The Invention of Tradition.* Cambridge: Cambridge University Press, 1983.

Howard, Anne Bail. *The Long Campaign: A Biography of Anne Martin.* Reno: University of Nevada Press, 1985.

Jaquette, Jane, ed. *Women in Politics.* New York: John Wiley, 1974.

Jennings, Kent M. "Women in Party Politics." Pages 221–48 in *Women, Politics and Change,* ed. Louise Tilly and Patricia Gurin. New York: Russell Sage Foundation, 1990.

Johnson, Dorothy. "Organized Women as Lobbyists in the 1920s." *Capitol Studies* 1 (spring 1972): 41–58.

Johnson, Kenneth. "Kate Gordon and the Woman Suffrage Movement in the South." *Journal of Southern History* 38 (August 1972): 365–92.

Jones, C. Margaret. *Heretics and Hellraisers: Women Contributors to the Masses, 1911–1917.* Austin: University of Texas Press, 1991.

Katzenstein, Mary F. "Feminism and the Meaning of the Vote." *Signs* 10 (autumn 1984): 4–26.

Kemp, Kathryn W. "Jean and Kate Gordon: New Orleans Reformers, 1898–1933." *Louisiana History* 24 (1983): 389–401.

Kenneally, James J. "Woman Suffrage and the Massachusetts Referendum of 1895." *The Historian* 30 (August 1968): 620–38.

Kerr, K. Austin *Organized for Prohibition: A New History of the Anti-Saloon League.* New Haven: Yale University Press, 1985.

Key, V. O. *Politics, Parties and Pressure Groups.* 4th ed. New York: Thomas Y. Crowell Company, 1958.

Kleppner, Paul. "Were Women to Blame? Female Suffrage and Voter Turnout." *Journal of Interdisciplinary History* 12 (spring 1982): 621–43.

Kraditor, Aileen. *The Ideas of the Woman Suffrage Movement, 1890–1920.* New York: Doubleday, 1971.

Lagemann, Ellen C. *A Generation of Women: Education in the Lives of Progressive Reformers.* Cambridge: Harvard University Press, 1979.

Lansing, Marjorie. "The American Woman: Voter and Activist." Pages 5–24 in *Women in Politics,* ed. Jane Jaquette. New York, John Wiley, 1964.

Lazarsfeld, Paul, Bernard Berelson, and Hazel Gaudet. *The People's Choice: How the Voter Makes Up His Mind in a Presidential Campaign.* New York: Duell, Sloan and Pearce, 1944.

Lebsock, Suzanne. "Women and American Politics, 1880–1920." Pages 35–62 in *Woman, Politics and Change,* ed. Louise Tilly and Patricia Gurin. New York: Russell Sage Foundation, 1990.

Lemons, Stanley J. *The Woman Citizen: Social Feminism in the 1920s.* Urbana: University of Illinois Press, 1973.

Liddington, Jill, and Jill Norris. *One Hand Tied behind Us: The Rise of the Women's Suffrage Movement.* London: Virago Limited, 1978.

Link, Arthur. *Wilson: Campaigns for Progressivism and Peace, 1916–1917.* Princeton: Princeton University Press, 1965.

——. *Woodrow Wilson and the Progressive Era, 1910–1917.* New York: Harper and Row, 1954.

Louis, James P. "Sue Shelton White and the Woman Suffrage Movement in Tennessee, 1913–1920." *Tennessee Historical Quarterly* 22 (June 1963): 170–90.

Lunardini, Christine. *From Equal Suffrage to Equal Rights: Alice Paul and the National Woman's Party, 1910–1928.* New York: New York University Press, 1986.

McCormick, Richard L. *The Party Period and Public Policy: American Politics from the Age of Jackson to the Progressive Era.* New York: Oxford University Press, 1986.

McDonagh, Eileen L. "Issues and Constituencies in the Progressive Era: House Roll Call Voting on the Nineteenth Amendment, 1913–1919." *Journal of Politics* 51 (February 1989): 119–36.

McDonagh, Eileen L., and Douglas H. Price. "Woman Suffrage in the Progressive Era: Patterns of Opposition and Support in Referenda Voting, 1910–1918." *American Political Science Review* 79 (June 1985): 415–35.

McGerr, Michael E. *The Decline of Popular Politics: The American North, 1865–1928.* New York: Oxford University Press, 1986.

——. "Political Style and Women's Power, 1830–1930." *Journal of American History* 77 (December 1990): 864–85.

McGovern, James R. "Anna Howard Shaw: New Approaches to Feminism." *Journal of Social History* 2 (winter 1969): 135–53.

McKean, Dayton David. *Party and Pressure Politics.* Boston: Houghton Mifflin, 1949.

Mansbridge, Jane. *Why We Lost the ERA.* Chicago: University of Chicago Press, 1986.

Marshall, Susan. "In Defense of Separate Spheres: Class and Status Politics in the Antisuffrage Movement." *Social Forces* 65 (December 1986): 327–51.

Merriman, Charles E. and Harold F. Gosnell. *Non-Voting: Causes and Methods of Control.* Chicago: University of Chicago Press, 1924.

Michels, Robert. *Political Parties,* trans. Eden and Cedar Paul. New York: Free Press, 1958.

Miller, Kristie. *Ruth Hanna McCormick: A Life in Politics, 1880–1944.* Albuquerque: University of New Mexico Press, 1992.

Mitchell, David. *The Fighting Pankhursts.* New York: Macmillan, 1967.

Morgan, David. *Suffragists and Democrats.* East Lansing: Michigan State University Press, 1972.

Moynihan, Ruth Barnes. *Rebel for Rights: Abigail Scott Duniway.* New Haven: Yale University Press, 1983.

Nichols, Carole. *Votes and More for Women: Suffrage and After in Connecticut.* New York: Institute for Research in History/Haworth, 1983.

Nie, Norman H., Sidney Verba, and John R. Petrocik. *The Changing Shape of the American Voter.* Cambridge: Harvard University Press, 1976.

Noun, Louise R. *Strong-Minded Women: The Emergence of the Woman Suffrage Movement in Iowa.* Ames: Iowa State University Press, 1969.

Odegard, Peter. *Pressure Politics: The Story of the Anti-Saloon League.* New York: Columbia University Press, 1926.

O'Neill, William. *Everyone Was Brave.* New York: Quadrangle, 1969.

Ornstein, Norman, and Shirley Elder. *Interest Groups, Lobbying and Policymaking.* Washington, D.C.: Congressional Quarterly Press, 1978.

Paulson, Ross Evans. *Women's Suffrage and Prohibition: A Comparative Study of Equality and Social Control.* Glenview, Ill.: Scott, Foresman, 1973.

Petracca, Mark P., ed. *The Politics of Interests: Interest Groups Transformed.* Boulder, Colo.: Westview, 1992.

Raeburn, Antonia. *The Militant Suffragists.* London: Michael Joseph, 1973.

——. *The Suffragette View.* New York: St. Martin's, 1976.

Rosen, Andrew. *Rise Up, Women.* London: Routledge and Kegan Paul, 1974.

Sapiro, Virginia. "The Gender Basis of American Social Policy." *Political Science Quarterly* 101 (1986): 221–38.

Schattschneider, E. E. *Party Government.* New York: Holt, Rinehart, Winston, 1943.

——. *The Semisovereign People: A Realist's View of Democracy in America.* Hinsdale, Ill.: Dryden, 1960, 1975.

Schlozman, Kay L. "Representing Women in Washington: Sisterhood and Pressure Politics." Pages 339–82 in Tilly, Louise and Patricia Gurin, eds. *Women, Politics and Change.* New York: Russell Sage Foundation, 1990.

Schlozman, Kay L., and John T. Tierney. *Organized Interests and American Democracy.* New York: Harper and Row, 1986.

Schmidt, Cynthia A. B. "Socialist-Feminism: Max Eastman, Floyd Dell, and Crystal Eastman." Ph.D. diss., Marquette University, 1983.

Scott, Anne Firor. *Natural Allies: Women's Associations in American History.* Urbana: University of Illinois Press, 1991.

Scott, Anne F., and Andrew M. Scott *One Half the People: The Fight for Woman Suffrage.* Philadelphia: J. B. Lippincott, 1975.

Scura, Dorothy. "Ellen Glasgow and Women's Suffrage." *Research in Action* 6 (spring 1982): 12–15.

Sears, David O., and Leonie Huddy. "On the Origins of Political Disunity among

Women." Pages 249–77 in *Women, Politics and Change,* ed. Louise Tilly and Patricia Gurin. New York: Russell Sage Foundation, 1990.

Smith, Ann W. "Anne Martin and a History of Woman Suffrage in Nevada, 1869–1914." Ph.D. diss., University of Nevada, Reno, 1976.

Sochen, June. *The New Woman in Greenwich Village, 1910–1920.* New York: Quadrangle/New York Times Book Company, 1972.

Springer, Barbara Anne. "Ladylike Reformers: Indiana Women and Progressive Reform, 1900–1920." Ph.D. diss., Indiana University, 1985.

Steinberg, Charles S. *The Creation of Consent: Public Relations in Practice.* New York: Hastings House, 1975.

Steinson, Barbara J. *American Women's Activism in World War I.* New York: Garland, 1982.

Stevenson, Louise. "Woman Antisuffragists in the 1915 Massachusetts Campaign." *New England Quarterly* 52 (March 1979): 80–93.

Tax, Meredith. *The Rising of the Women.* New York: Monthly Review Press, 1980.

Taylor, A. Elizabeth. "The Last Phase of the Woman Suffrage Movement in Georgia." *Georgia Historical Quarterly* 43 (March 1959): 11–28.

———. "The Origin of the Woman Suffrage Movement in Georgia." *Georgia Historical Quarterly* 28 (June 1944): 63–80.

———. "Revival and Development of the Woman Suffrage Movement in Georgia." *Georgia Historical Quarterly* 42 (December 1958): 339–54.

———. "The Woman Suffrage Movement in North Carolina." *North Carolina Historical Review* 38 (January and April 1961): 45–62 and 173–89.

———. *The Woman Suffrage Movement in Tennessee.* New York: Bookman Associates, 1957.

———. "The Woman Suffrage Movement in Texas." *Journal of Southern History* 17 (May 1951): 194–215.

Terborg-Penn, Rosalyn. "Afro-Americans in the Struggle for Woman Suffrage." Ph.D. diss., Howard University, 1977.

Thomas, Mary Martha. *The New Woman in Alabama: Social Reforms and Suffrage, 1890–1920.* Tuscaloosa: University of Alabama Press, 1992.

Thompson, Margaret Susan. *"The Spider Web:" Congress and Lobbying in the Age of Grant.* Ithaca: Cornell University Press, 1985.

Thurner, Manuela. "Better Citizens without the Ballot: American Antisuffrage Women and Their Rationale during the Progressive Era." *Journal of Women's History* 5 (spring 1993): 33–60.

Tilly, Louise, and Patricia Gurin, eds. *Women, Politics and Change.* New York: Russell Sage Foundation, 1990.

Tracker, Janice Law. "The Suffrage Prisoners." *American Scholar* 41 (summer 1972): 409–23.

Ulam, Adam. *The Bolsheviks: The Intellectual and Political History of the Triumph of Communism in Russia.* New York: Collier Books, 1965.

Van Voris, Jacqueline. *Carrie Chapman Catt: A Public Life.* New York: Feminist Press, 1987.

Walker, Jack L., Jr. *Mobilizing Interest Groups in America: Patrons, Professionals and Social Movements.* Ann Arbor: University of Michigan Press, 1991.

Wheeler, Marjorie Spruill. "Mary Johnston, Suffragist." *Virginia Magazine of History and Biography* 100 (January 1992): 99–118.

———. *New Women of the New South: The Leaders of the Woman Suffrage Movement in the Southern States.* New York: Oxford University Press, 1993.

Wiebe, Robert. *The Search for Order, 1877–1920.* New York: Hill and Wang, 1967.

Wilson, Graham K. *Interest Groups in the United States.* Oxford: Clarendon, 1981.

Wiltsher, Anne. *Most Dangerous Women: Feminist Peace Campaigners of the Great War.* London: Pandora, 1985.

Zimmerman, Loretta E. "Alice Paul and the National Woman's Party, 1912–1920." Ph.D. diss., Tulane University, 1964.

———. "Jean Gordon." Pages 64–66 in *Notable American Women,* vol. 2, ed. Edward T. James and Janet Wilson James. Cambridge: Harvard University Press, 1971.

Index

91; and Congressional Committee,
91–92, 94, 95; and passage of federal
amendment, 100–101, 108–9, 114–
15, 119, 123, 125, 126
parlor meetings, 37–38, 50–52, 78, 148,
153
Paul, Alice, 64, 142; and Congressional
Committee, 81–82, 90; and CU, 82–
83, 90; and NWP, 102, 106–7
Peabody, George Foster, 67
Peck, Mary Gray, 56
Pennsylvania, 59, 131
Pennsylvania Limited Suffrage League,
31
Pennsylvania Woman Suffrage Association (PWSA), 64–65, 100
Pinchot, Mrs. Gifford (Cornelia Bryce),
84
Pinckard, Mrs. James, 143
Pinkham, Wenona, 102
pioneers, suffrage, 3, 34, 36, 42–52, 113;
veneration of, 4, 33, 45, 51
Pittman, Mira, 145
political organization of NAWSA, xv, 7–
8, 72–73, 81, 83–90; model of WSP,
54–62; and political campaigns, 68–
73, 111–13, 119–22; centralization
of, 81, 83–84, 86–89, 109–10, 113,
132, 149–51; and partisan politics,
89–90, 112, 115, 122. *See also* Congressional Committee (NAWSA);
Woman Suffrage Party; state-level organization of NAWSA
political parties: and pressure groups, xi,
xv–xvi, 161–62; and participation of
women, xii, 51–52, 152–59, 162–63;
Democratic, xvi, 84–85, 94, 106,
112, 118, 127, 137, 139, 154; and
1916 and *1920* party platforms, 84–
85, 141; Republican, 84, 94, 115,
119–21, 127; 137; 140–41, 154;
southern Democrats, 114–15, 119.
See also National Woman's Party;
Progressive Party; Socialist Party;
Woman Suffrage Party

political settlements, 56–57, 58, 148
Potter, Frances Squires, 56–57, 58
Pou, Edward, 111
press: and press work of NAWSA, 9–10,
59, 73, 87–88, 90, 94–95, 117, 149;
hostile, 43; and image of S. B. Anthony, 47–50; manipulation of, 107–
9, 111
pressure groups: NAWSA's emergence as,
xi–xviii, 52, 83, 113, 122, 146, 149–
50; undemocratic nature of, 126,
149–50, 160–61, 164; and fracturing
of women's movement, 151–53; and
politics, 158–62. *See also* Congressional Committee (NAWSA); Front Door
Lobby
Progressive Party, 71, 92, 120, 135,
140
prohibition, 27, 69–72, 114, 120, 135
propaganda, xv, 26, 36, 37, 40, 56, 60,
105, 157; of antisuffragists, 11, 15–
19, 34, 52; anti-liquor, 27; standard-
ized, 90, 94, 113, 149
public image, of NAWSA, 151–52, 161;
poor, 10, 14–16, 20–21; attempts to
improve, 24, 26–27, 36–39, 45–46,
47, 52, 54, 148–49
public opinion, 36, 105, 148, 151–52,
161; manipulation of, 26, 108–10,
119
public speaking, 61, 64–65, 67–68;
training in, 4, 57, 59–60, 112
publicity, created by NAWSA, 41, 59, 73,
81, 87–88, 94, 104–5, 117, 133, 146,
147–48, 157
publicity stunts, xv, 65–66, 68, 72, 90,
105

racism: of NAWSA, 5, 21–25, 110, 149,
151, 164; of antisuffragists, 17–21; in
southern states, 18, 22–23, 83, 85,
124, 134, 137, 139, 143, 145; and
egalitarian suffrage, 22, 25, 29–31,
43, 134. *See also* blacks; states' rights
Radcliffe College, 45, 65, 91

nation of Gordon and Clay, 117–18, 136

Steinem, Pauline, 41

Stone, Lucy, 6, 36, 43, 50, 65

street meetings, 64–65, 68, 105

Suffrage House, 92–95, 98, 123, 130

Suffrage Referendum State Committee (Mass.), 34

suffrage saint, 47–51, 52, 148

Taft, William Howard, xvii

Tammany Hall, 55, 112

Tarbell, Ida, 13

temperance movement, xiv, 49, 51, 52, 69–72, 148. *See also* prohibition; Woman's Christian Temperance Union (WCTU)

Tennessee, 139, 141–44

Terrell, Mary Church, 23, 24

Texas, 132–36, 139

Texas Equal Suffrage Association (TESA), 85, 132–36

Thomas, M. Carey, 42, 45

tradition, establishing suffrage, 39–40, 44–47, 51

Tumulty, Joseph P., 108–10, 114

Turner, Banks, 143–44

United Daughters of the Confederacy, 143

Universal Peace Union, 9

upper-class women: and indirect influence, xiii-xiv, 19–20, 28, 31; recruitment of, 6, 29, 36–39, 51, 59, 63, 68, 149; limited opportunities for, 12, 74

Upton, Harriet Taylor, 69–70, 127, 142–43, 145–46

Utah, 131, 139

Vassar College, 46

Vermont, 131

Villard, Oswald Garrison, 67

Virginia, 58

Virginia Equal Suffrage League, 39

virtual representation, 16, 18–21, 31, 161

voluntarism, xiii–xv, 12, 19–20, 28, 31, 37, 74, 153, 159

Wadsworth, James, 84, 122–23

Wadsworth, Mrs. James D., 117

Wage Earners Suffrage League, 113

Walker, Seth, 143–44

Washington (state), 139

Weeks, John W., 119–21, 122

Wells, Ida B., 24

Wells, Mrs. James B., 133–34

West Virginia, 139

White, Ruth, 91, 124

White, William Allen, 160

Whitehouse, Vira, 76, 103, 112

Whitman, Walt, xiii

Willard, Mabel, 93, 121

Wilson, Woodrow, xvii, 82, 85, 87; and World War I, 98, 123; and Russian banner incident, 106, 108–9; and federal amendment, 111, 112, 114, 138–39, 142

Winning Plan, 88–90, 151, 164

Wisconsin, 59, 69–71

Woman Citizen, 95, 105

Woman Suffrage: History, Arguments, Results, 62

Woman Suffrage Party (WSP), 55–62, 73; organizational scheme, 55, 97, 103, 148; Industrial Section, 58, 112–13; and N.Y. referendum, 112–13

Woman's Bible, The, 44

Woman's Christian Temperance Union (WCTU), xiv-xv, 9, 27, 57, 71

Woman's Committee of the Council of National Defense (WCCND), 103, 105

women: in politics, xii, 51–52, 152–59, 162–63; professional, 4, 6, 12, 42, 45–47, 52, 65, 74–75, 148; and charity work, 12, 19–20, 28, 31; opportunities for, 12, 74; 19th-century ideal of, 12–16, 19–20; in workforce, 12–13, 42, 74; as a class apart, 13, 15, 17, 19, 20; husbands represent,

A Note on the Type

The text of this book was set in a digitized

version of Sabon, a typeface originally designed

by well-known typographer Jan Tschichold. It was

named for earlier type founder Jacques Sabon.

It was composed by Keystone Typesetting,

Inc., of Orwigsburg, Pennsylvania.